# THE FALL
## OF
# SAXON ENGLAND

# THE FALL
# OF
# SAXON ENGLAND

*Richard Humble*

Arthur Barker Limited London
A subsidiary of Weidenfeld (Publishers) Limited

Printed in Great Britain by
Butler & Tanner Ltd, Frome and London

For Wenny

# Acknowledgments

The author would like to acknowledge the following translations:

Douglas, David C. & Greenaway, George W., *English Historical Documents II*, 1042–1189 (Eyre & Spottiswoode 1953).

Whitelock, Dorothy, *The Anglo-Saxon Chronicle, A Revised Edition* (Eyre & Spottiswoode 1961).

Whitelock, Dorothy, *English Historical Documents I, c. 500–1042* (Eyre & Spottiswoode 1953).

Wright, David, *Beowulf* (Penguin Classics 1957).

# Contents

# Illustrations and Maps

# Preface

This is a book about the birth of England – a subject, especially in these days of specialized enquiry, of almost terrifying complexity. Writing it was not easy, for the simple reason that much of the story is totally unrecorded. In fact Sir Frank Stenton begins his classic study of Anglo-Saxon England with the statement: 'Between the end of Roman government in Britain and the emergence of the earliest English kingdoms there stretches a long period of which the history cannot be written.' Seven hundred and forty-seven pages of text, bibliography, and index follow this candid but by no means encouraging introduction.

I wrote *The Fall of Saxon England* for those who may be tempted to feel, as Sir Winston Churchill put it, that 'This is not much to show after so much toil and learning.' After all, archaeologists reconstruct; anthropologists reconstruct; why should the historian be privileged in surrounding himself with a web of defensive non-statements when he cannot find the hard facts? Dodging the brickbats of the most dyed-in-the-wool academics, I hold that no historian is doing his job if he tells his readers 'we simply do not know', and leaves it at that. Those who want to read about their past are entitled to some interpretation of the unknown, however unorthodox it may be.

And what a story this is – six hundred years of struggle for the mastery of this island. I would be the last to claim that social and cultural advance and the flourishing of learning and the arts do not matter. But as the monks of Lindisfarne discovered – the hard way – there are times when learning and the arts come second: you do not always win over a determined foe by waving a crucifix at him. In *The Fall of Saxon England* I have quoted Leonard Wibberley's *bon mot*: 'Though the pen is mightier than the sword, the sword speaks louder and stronger at any given moment.' And the *dramatis personae* of this book, from Cerdic of Wessex to William of Normandy, would give their hearty and unanimous approval to this.

In a sense, the non-stop struggle of Might versus Right explains the title of *The Fall of Saxon England*. This struggle eventually ground down the stubborn defenders of Roman Britain. Surviving, it became a question of which of the new Saxon kingdoms would be top-dog, and if so for how long. It made Wessex, the only one of those kingdoms to fight off the Danish menace, the hard core of the kingdom of England. And at the last it reached crescendo in the tremendous year of 1066.

For two reasons, I feel that the story told in *The Fall of Saxon England* is of the utmost importance today. It shows that the will to survive can work miracles, but is not always enough. And it shows that the most prosperous-looking society can collapse suddenly and disastrously, given sufficient pressure on one side and apathy on the other. These are both lessons on which we would all do well to ponder.

Finally, I would like to express my deepest thanks for their help and encouragement to my wife Wenny, to my agent Mr Herbert Van Thal, to Richard Natkiel, who drew the maps, and to all at Arthur Barker who have worked with me in producing this book.

# Chapter 1

Where seven sunken Englands
    Lie buried one by one,
Why should one idle spade, I wonder,
Shake up the dust of thanes like thunder
    To smoke and choke the sun?

    G. K. Chesterton, *The Ballad of the White Horse.*

# The victim

Three hundred and fifty years after the collapse of the Roman Empire had been signified by the sack of Rome in AD 410, Western Europe seemed at last to be finding a new security. Rome was still the centre of a world-unifying influence: the Christian Church. The former Roman province of Gaul had emerged as the greatest power on the Continent, and under the persistent efforts of the Carolingian kings a vast new empire was being forged in the west – a Christian empire. And across the English Channel a similar state of affairs was discernible. Britain, the island province of the Roman Empire and the westernmost bastion of the Roman idea, had gone under with the remainder of the Roman West, her frantic pleas to Rome for aid going unanswered. A tangle of barbarian kingdoms overgrew the lost province like ivy. But now, in the latter half of the eighth century, the heyday of the petty raiding chiefs was long gone. In the hands of strongs kings and the leaders of the Christian Church across the Channel, the idea of 'England' was taking shape.

All we know about the final collapse of Roman Britain is that the province went down in a welter of chaos, and that it was an extremely long-drawn-out process. There is certainly no date at which we can say that Rome stopped and England began. It was not recorded by chroniclers at the time, and the first records of the English were drawn up from tradition centuries later. All we can do is to build up the most likely pattern from the jumbled clues we have, like reconstructing an ancient wine-jar from scattered and incomplete fragments.

For example, we know for a fact that Roman Britain began to have serious trouble from across the North Sea in the fourth century AD. In the north, the Picts from Scotland and the Scots from across the Irish Sea had been a standing problem for

3

centuries .The Roman authorities had countered the latter threat by building a military frontier with permanent defences– Hadrian's Wall, and, for a while, the shorter Antonine Wall between Firth and Forth – and stationing troops along it and behind it. By the late fourth century, an official 'minister of defence' was responsible for the safety of northern Britain: the Duke of the Northern Marches. But constant raiding across the North Sea and the Channel had prompted the building of another chain of defences, from the Wash to Southampton Water – mighty fortresses whose ruins still stand, with a fleet of light cruisers, the *Classis Britannica*, patrolling the Narrow Seas. The defences here were co-ordinated by another official with a significant title: the Count of the Saxon Shore.

If these defences had been kept up to strength and reinforced from the Continent when necessary, Roman Britain could have held out. But that was the trouble. Ever since Galba, commanding the armies in Spain, had ousted Nero and become emperor in AD 68, Rome's security had always been threatened by the open secret that any general able to win over enough troops to beat all comers could become emperor himself, no matter what his origins. It is true that this was not always disastrous for the empire – it produced some of the best emperors Rome ever had, men like Vespasian (69–79), Septimius Severus (193–211) and Constantine (312–337). But the civil wars which inevitably raged while these bids for power were being made left the frontiers wide open to barbarian invasions from outside and caused damage which often took decades to repair. This danger, coupled with massive pressure from outside the frontiers of the empire by unheard-of barbarian population-movements in the third and fourth centuries, was the fatal main ingredient in the collapse of the Roman West, and it had particularly disastrous effects on the province of Britain.

The melancholy cycle had begun as early as the year 193, when the governor of Britain, Clodius Albinus, had stripped the province of troops to back his attempt on the imperial throne. It would have been better for Britain if he had won; as it was, the garrison troops from Britain were squandered in defeat and it was some time before the successful contender for the empire, Septimius Severus, could come over to Britain and put matters right. Under the personal hand of Severus, the security of Britain was hammered back to its former strength, and the tough old emperor died at York in

211 while his legions were still trying to finish the job by conquering all Scotland. This was not achieved, but at least the northern frontier was completely re-established. Behind its shield the province settled down to sixty years of general peace and prosperity.

The decline and fall of Roman Britain over the next two hundred years had six major milestones, all of them symptomatic of the weakness of the western Roman Empire, and most of them showing how much of that weakness was self-inflicted. First came the total breakaway of Britain, and the reigns of the sea-emperors Carausius and Allectus (286–293). They held the Channel fleet; from across the Channel they defied the imperial authority; and they struck their own coinage, depicting themselves as the crowned rulers of Britain. The rule of Allectus, who had engineered the murder of Carausius in order to grab supreme power himself, was cut short by the invasion of Constantius Chlorus in 296. Chlorus was a Caesar, one of the deputy-emperors established in the reign of Diocletian (285–305), and he not only eliminated Allectus but buckled down to the job of repairing the ravages which the province's defences had suffered. Chlorus was still in Britain in 306, hammering away at the Picts like Severus before him, when he died at York. His other chief claim to fame is that he was the father of Constantine the Great, who restored peace to the empire. Even so, in the year of Constantine's death (337), the young Caesar Constans was in Britain fighting yet again renewed attacks by the Picts and Scots.

Thirty years of uneasy peace in Britain were then shattered by the most disastrous year the province had ever known: 367, as black a year for Roman Britain as the Indian Mutiny was for British India in 1857. Britain went down under a hail of assaults not only from the Picts and Scots but from Saxons and Franks from across the Channel. The Roman troops in the island never managed to rally for a successful battle, as they had done against Boudicca's Iceni back in the reign of Nero in 61. This time, however, help came virtually at once in the form of a relief expedition led by the Emperor Valentinian's general, Count Theodosius – like Constantius Chlorus, the father of a future emperor of the same name. Theodosius restored the province; once again garrisons patrolled the Wall. But this time Roman Britain enjoyed a much shorter interlude before the next major crisis.

In 383, the commander in Britain, Magnus Maximus, stripped

the province of troops and crossed to France to make a bid for the throne. He was defeated and killed; his troops were squandered, and once again the defences of Britain were overwhelmed. Not until 393 did an imperial commander, Stilicho, once again set about the task of repairing the breaches, and he was a man who typified the straits in which the Western Empire now found itself. He was a Vandal by birth, a member of one of the barbarian nations beyond Rome's frontiers who were now being desperately enrolled by the enfeebled emperors as *foederati*: allies. Stilicho, however, was no mere mercenary: he was the greatest commander of the age, the only man who had a chance of saving the Western Empire by his own efforts. As it was, he came close enough, before palace politics and imperial distrust in Rome pulled him down and killed him in 408 – but Britain was only one of a myriad pressing and desperate problems, and by no means the most urgent. Stilicho had to take the fatal step of pulling troops out of Britain in 399, and the last decade of official contact with Rome began with Britain effectively left to her own defences. In 410 the Emperor Honorius officially notified the British authorities that they would have to look after themselves. Here was dramatic timing with a vengeance, for the message went out from Rome only weeks before the capital fell to the Goths of Alaric, whom Stilicho had held off for so long.

Although travesties of emperors continued to reign in Rome for over another sixty years, the Western Empire never rose again; but in Britain the Roman legacy did not die immediately on severance with the Continent. Baffling flickers of documentary evidence, and the definite proof turned up by the archaeologist's spade, show that the Romano-Britons struggled on until the early years of the sixth century with a fair measure of success. In the end, the invaders who called themselves the English got the upper hand; but before we tell their story it would be well to reconstruct the probable story of the last decades of 'Roman' Britain. However it is interpreted, it emerges as a desperate tale of determination and the will to resist – qualities which the conquering English would in time need even more than had the British before them.

It is now accepted as a fact that, at least in 429, Britain was still effectively in touch with France via the Christian Church. Not only were the Christians of Britain still in contact with their brethren in Christ across the Channel, but they were causing the latter a good deal of alarm by their partiality for a red-hot heresy:

Pelagianism, which would in Communist jargon be described as a 'revisionist' and thoroughly unorthodox rejection of original sin in favour of freedom of will. So it was that Bishop Germanus of Auxerre came to Britain eighteen years after the sack of Rome – not to win pagan souls to Christ but to haul the British Church back into line with the orthodox doctrine of the Church.

The account of Germanus' mission makes it clear that he found late Roman Britain still in existence, but at war. There is an account of a battle against a heathen army of Picts, Scots, and Saxons in which the bishop took command of the British forces and routed the enemy coalition army: with a triple bellow of 'Alleluia!' the British routed the enemy, putting them to flight without striking a blow. That is by the way – but such an alliance of Britain's enemies had been made before, in the disastrous year of 367, and should certainly not be discounted. We are left with the firm impression that, at the time of Germanus' visit to Britain in 429, embattled Britian was still able to take care of itself.

Archaeological evidence backs up this impression of civilization on the defensive, and showing definite and understandable signs of wear. At St Albans – which Germanus visited – digs have revealed the fact that, in about 430, a mosaic floor was taken up to enable a corn-drier to be built, and that the barn which housed the corn-drier was built out of cannibalized materials – new tiles could no longer be found. A wooden pipeline connected with iron collars, dated around 450, proves that, even in the middle of the fifth century, piped water was still regarded as essential by the British. But after this date the clues peter out and we have to turn to the other side – to the records of the invading English – to round out the story.

Three main races were identified by later English chroniclers and historians trying to put the traditions of the conquest into written form: the Angles, the Saxons, and the Jutes. It seems clear enough that all three originated from that part of north-west Europe between the lower Rhine and Schleswig-Holstein – it is no longer fashionable to link the shadowy Jutes with Jutland in Denmark. And the earliest invaders who came to stay seem to have been the Jutes in Kent, who founded a kingdom there and ousted the British from the south-east.

The ninth-century *Anglo-Saxon Chronicle* gives the names of Hengest and Horsa as the leaders of the Jutish invasion of Kent, and states that they drove out the British in a series of battles. Another account to survive is the famous story of how Hengest and Horsa defeated the local British leader, Vortigern. All three names have stuck; there are no others. And so we are left with the interpretation that, twenty years after the visit of Germanus, the British leader in the south-east was called Vortigern. He called in Jutish mercenaries as *foederati* in the time-honoured practice of expediency, as Stilicho had done and others before him, and his mercenaries turned on him.

The *Chronicle* is not a single text: it consists of six main variants on the same theme, designated A, B, C, D, E and F. Hopping from one to the other, the following account emerges. First comes the entry for the year 443:

> (E) In this year the Britons sent across the sea to Rome and begged for help against the Picts, but they got none there, for the Romans were engaged in a campaign against Attila, king of the Huns. And they then sent to the Angles, and made the same request of the chieftains of the English.

Then comes the complex entry for the year 449:

> (C) ... Hengest and Horsa, invited by Vortigern, king of the Britons, came to Britain at the place which is called Ebbsfleet, first to the help of the Britons, but afterwards fought against them. (E) King Vortigern gave them land in the south-east of this land on condition that they should fight against the Picts. They then fought against the Picts and had the victory wherever they came. They then sent to Angeln, bidding them send more help, and had them informed of the cowardice of the Britons and the excellence of the land. They then immediately sent hither a greater force to the help of the others. Those men came from three tribes of Germany; from the Old Saxons, from the Angles, and from the Jutes. From the Jutes came the people of Kent and of the Isle of Wight, namely the tribe which now inhabits the Isle of Wight and that race in Wessex which is still called the race of the Jutes. From the Old Saxons came the East Saxons, the South Saxons, and the West Saxons. From Angeln, which afterwards remained waste, between the Jutes and the Saxons, came the East Angles, the Middle Angles, the Mercians, and all the Northumbrians. Their leaders were

two brothers, Hengest and Horsa, who were sons of Wihtgils. Wihtgils was the son of Witta, the son of Wecta, the son of Woden. From that Woden has descended all our royal family, and that of the Southumbrians also.

The final comment shows that this particular entry was made in the north. As a whole it is a pretty concise blueprint of how the later English interpreted their origins, with Hengest and Horsa cast in the role of the earliest founding fathers.

Four terse entries then record the stages by which the Jutes carved out the new kingdom of Kent:

455   In this year Hengest and Horsa fought against King Vortigern at the place which is called *Ægelesthrep*, and his brother Horsa was killed there; and after that Hengest and his son Æsc succeeded to the kingdom.

456   In this year Hengest and his son Æsc fought against the Britons in the place which is called *Creacanford* and killed 4,000 men; and the Britons then deserted Kent and fled with great fear to London.

465   In this year Hengest and Æsc fought against the Britons near *Wippedesfleot*, and there slew twelve British chiefs, and a thegn of theirs was slain there whose name was Wipped.

473   In this year Hengest and Æsc fought against the Britons and captured countless spoils and the Britons fled from the English as from fire.

Thus the *Chronicle* entries for this thirty-year period, 443–473, show the British once again finding their own resources inadequate to cope with the centuries-old threat from north of the Border, and calling in Teutonic mercenaries who turned against them.

Subsequent *Chronicle* entries turn from the forcible establishment of the kingdom of Kent to other descents on the south coast which led directly to the formation of new English kingdoms at the expense of the British:

477   In this year Ælle and his three sons, Cymen, Wlencing, and Cissa, came into Britain with three ships at the place which is called *Cymenesora*, and there they killed many Britons and drove some into flight into the wood which is called *Andredeslea*.

*Andredeslea* was the forest of the Weald; this was the origin of the kingdom of the South Saxons – Sussex.

As in Kent, however, the invaders clearly had to fight for their new land:

485   In this year Ælle fought against the Britons near the bank of *Mearcredesburna*.

491   In this year Ælle and Cissa besieged *Andredesceaster*, and killed all who were inside, and there was not even a single Briton left alive.

*Andredesceaster* was the English version of the Latin *Anderida*: Pevensey, once a key link in the chain of Saxon Shore forts girdling the eastern coast. Now, with the slaughter and sack of Pevensey, the Saxon Shore had earned its name with a vengeance.

From the South Saxons, the *Chronicle* turns at once to the West Saxons, the founders of the kingdom of Wessex further to the west. The confused entries indicate that there was considerable overlap and clash between the West Saxons under Cerdic and his son Cynric, and the Jutish pioneers from Kent under Stuf and Wihtgar. Certainly both parties were trying their luck on the same sector of the southern coast: the Isle of Wight, Portsmouth, and Southampton Water, as the entries show:

495   In this year two chieftains, Cerdic and his son Cynric, came with five ships to Britain at the place which is called *Cerdicesora*, and they fought against the Britons on the same day.

501   In this year Port and his two sons Bieda and Mægla came to Britain with two ships at the place which is called Portsmouth; and there they killed a [young] Briton of very high rank.

508   In this year Cerdic and Cynric killed a British king, whose name was Natanleod, and 5,000 men with him; and the land right up to Charford was called Netley after him.

514   In this year the West Saxons came into Britain with three ships at the place which is called *Cerdicesora*; and Stuf and Wihtgar fought against the Britons and put them to flight.

519   In this year Cerdic and Cynric succeeded to the kingdom;

and in the same year they fought against the Britons at a
place called Charford.

527 In this year Cerdic and Cynric fought against the British
in the place that is called *Cerdicesleag*.

530 In this year Cerdic and Cynric captured the Isle of Wight
and killed a few men in *Wihtgarabyrig*.

534 In this year Cerdic died; and his son Cynric ruled for
27 years. And they gave the Isle of Wight to their two
kinsmen, Stuf and Wihtgar.

So the *Chronicle* records the establishment of the West Saxons,
the future land of Wessex. We would have a much clearer idea of
their progress if it were possible to identify all the place-names so
earnestly recorded in the original Saxon, but for which it has
proved impossible to find the modern site. Yet so much is missing
that this deficiency is positively trifling. The *Chronicle* records
the birth of Kent, of Sussex, and of Wessex. One further entry for
547 mentions the foundation of the Northumbrian kingdom around
Bamburgh by Ida the son of Eoppa. Of the rest – nothing, not a
clue to the origins of young kingdoms which later went under and
passed into the life of Saxon England as regional place-names:
the land of the East Saxons, the land of the East Angles, the land
of the Middle Angles, or of the Mercians. All this is missing – and
so is one of the most famous controversies in English history, the
facts behind the legend of Arthur, the last great champion of the
British, who won a great victory and halted the English advance for
a generation.

If we rely solely upon the *Chronicle*, the tale is one of un-
interrupted Anglo-Saxon encroachment with the hapless British
losing battle after battle and constantly losing ground. But there
is more than enough other evidence to suggest that it was not as
easy as that. The first piece is provided by a stinging tract on the
woes of the British written by a monk named Gildas in the late
540s. It contains a review of the situation prevailing at the time
of writing – an historical review. Gildas recalls the British 'tyrant'
who called in English mercenaries only to be overwhelmed by
them, but he then says that the rebel mercenaries soon went
home and gave the British the chance to get organized under a
leader called Ambrosius Aurelianus, represented as the 'last of
the Romans' to be found in the island. When the invaders came

again, a long period of up-and-down warfare ensued, with the British decisively winning the upper hand in a great battle at 'Mount Badon'. Where this was, and who the man was who won it, Gildas does not say. It happened, however, around 500, and the result was the precarious peace, threatened only by internal rivalry among the British leaders, which had lasted until his own time.

The next piece of evidence dates from about twenty years after Gildas and is to be found in a history of the Gothic wars fought by the Byzantine Empire. Procopius of Caesarea, who wrote the history, included a chapter on Britain and Germany in which he stated that 'every year' heavy migrations came *out* of Britain: not only refugee Britons fleeing from the invaders, but Teutons as well. This fits with Gildas's story, indicating that there was certainly no room for further expansion in Britain by adventurers from the Continent; not only that, but that the English already in the island were being put under considerable pressure by the revitalized British population.

A collection of Welsh Annals supplies the name of the British victor in the great battle, which is dated 518: 'The battle of Badon, in which Arthur carried the cross of Our Lord Jesus Christ for three days and three nights on his shoulders and the British were victorious.' (The most obvious interpretation of this mystic passage is that Arthur was wearing a surcoat with the emblem of the cross on it, like the Crusaders in later years.) Then there is the ninth-century *History of the British* written by the churchman Nennius, who also identifies Arthur: 'Then Arthur fought against them in those days, with the kings of the Britons, but he himself was leader of battles.' Finally, under the year 539, the Welsh Annals record: 'The strife of *Camlann*, in which Arthur and Medraut perished. . . .' This has a triple significance. First, it tells us when Arthur died; second, it indicates precisely the sort of internecine British civil war which Gildas was lambasting; third, it is the obvious source for the final death-struggle between the ageing King Arthur and the malignant Sir Mordred in the Arthurian legend.

Here, then, was the story which was *not* – for obvious reasons – cherished and preserved in the records of the English: the last great rally of their British foes, which halted the flood-tide of English encroachment from the coast and pressed the invaders so hard that many of them had to return to the Continent. It was the last flicker of the Roman tradition implanted in the province during centuries of Roman rule; but it ended with the British, now ruled by rival kings, falling out with each other and once more leaving the English with the initiative.

Arthur's victory at Mount Badon cannot have won more than fifty years' respite at the outside. Assuming that he managed to halt the British collapse and pen the English uncomfortably tightly into the coastal regions, the British defences collapsed with a crash around the middle of the sixth century and the English flooded inland under their fighting chiefs, never to be halted again. Fifty chaotic years ensued in which the last remnants of a unified Christian Britain were swept away, and at the end of which new and pagan kingdoms held sway amid the ruins. As the sixth century drew to its close, the island was regarded at Rome as a domain of the lost, and the evangelizing mission of St Augustine was sent to reclaim it for the Church. By the time Augustine landed in Kent in 597, the English kingdoms had taken shape. They sprawled across the island from the Channel to the Scottish Lowlands, constantly at war with each other, expanding and contracting, torn by the ups and downs of embryo royal dynasties. It is, however, possible to 'freeze' the process at the year 600 and examine the level of evolution which Saxon England had reached by that date.

The kingdom of Kent, carved out by Hengest and Æsc in the mid fifth century, was now well established as the leading power in the south-east and was ruled by a strong king, Ethelbert. Geography made it inevitable that Kent should be the first English kingdom to absorb current continental influences and the benefits of civilization prevailing across the Channel. Ethelbert had in fact married a Frankish princess, Bertha, who was a Christian and brought her own chaplain with her to England – a fact which made Augustine's job considerably easier, as we shall see. Overlord of the south-east, Ethelbert issued a comprehensive code of laws in the opening years of the seventh century which served as a useful model for later Saxon lawgivers.

The lower Thames served as a natural frontier between Kent and her nearest inland neighbour to the north: Essex, the kingdom of the East Saxons. No English chronicle or written tradition ever recorded the origins of the kingdom, but it was the only kingdom of Saxon England whose royal house did not proudly trace its genealogy back to Woden. The East Saxons claimed instead to be descended from the god Seaxneat, also venerated by the Saxons on the Continent. By 600, the ascendancy of Kent and the convenience of family ties had reduced Essex to the status of a client-kingdom. Under the year 604, the *Chronicle* refers to the Christian mission to Essex: 'where the king was called Sæberht, the son of Ricule, Ethelbert's sister, and Ethelbert had set him as king there.'

While Ethelbert ruled (565–616), Kent and Essex enjoyed friendly relations with the neighbouring kingdom of the East Angles, comprising Suffolk and Norfolk and most of Cambridgeshire. ('Suffolk' and 'Norfolk' are names derived from the 'south folk' and 'north folk' of the East Anglian kingdom.) As with Essex, there are no details for the founding of East Anglia, but the kingdom enjoyed natural land links with the Essex/Kent bloc.

This did not apply to Sussex. The land of the South Saxons, founded in blood by Ælle at the end of the fifth century, was naturally fenced off by the barrier of the forest of the Weald and retained strong individual tendencies for centuries. Small though it was in area, however, Sussex was by no means a united kingdom and in fact it represented, in miniature, the whole complex patchwork of Saxon England. In the east of the country, the land of the *Hæstingas* was regarded for centuries as separate from that of the South Saxons themselves; and their separatist traditions have their memorial in the name of Hastings which has survived them.

Looking westwards along the axis of the Thames valley, we can discern a jumble of small peoples, later destined for absorption by the larger kingdoms, but which still preserved some semblance of independence in 600. First came the Middle Saxons, centred on modern Middlesex, and then the Middle Angles, further inland. The core of Middle Anglia may be described as a triangle connecting the modern towns of Leicester, Stamford, and Northampton. South of the Wash, the *Gyrwe*, between the Welland and the Ouse, separated Middle Anglia from East Anglia. West of Middle Anglia lay the lands of the Mercians, centred on Lichfield, Tamworth, and Repton – the central power of Saxon England, destined for temporary overlordship of all England south of the Humber. 'Buffer states' between the western Saxon kingdoms and the British kingdoms now confined to the Welsh mountains included the *Wreocensæte*, the 'Wrekin-dwellers', around Shrewsbury, and the *Magonsæte* on the Wye, further to the South, in the Hereford area. Another individual people were the *Hwicce*, in the lower Severn valley.

The last major Saxon power south of the Humber was Wessex, kingdom of the West Saxons. The history of Wessex for over two centuries was one of expansion on two fronts: westward at the expense of the 'West Welsh', the British who had retreated into the Devon/Cornwall peninsula, and northward towards the line of the Thames, resulting in repeated head-on clashes with Mercian expansion. Between modern Southampton and Portsmouth the lands of the *Meonware* provided a convenient buffer between Wessex and Sussex.

North of the Humber, the over-all picture was no less complex than in the south. In 600, the small British kingdom of Elmet was still holding out around the sites of modern Leeds, Bradford, and Huddersfield, blocking the expansion of the Saxons towards the Irish Sea. To the north, the basic elements of 'North Humbria' consisted of two kingdoms almost constantly at war with each other, with temporary union resulting when one of them managed to get the better of the other. The southern kingdom, Deira, stretched from the Humber estuary to the Tees. Its first recorded king was Ælle, whom the *Chronicle* records as beginning his reign in 560 and ruling for thirty years. Ælle's accession to power followed on the death of Ida, who had founded the northern kingdom of Bernicia in 547. The descendants of Ida and Ælle kept Bernicia and Deira at odds for years, but this did not prevent Northumbria from becoming the most powerful kingdom in Saxon England during the seventh century.

In Cumberland, as in Wales and Cornwall, the British continued to hold on; while to the north, the legacy of the centuries-old Pictish menace had crystallized into the kingdom of Strathclyde, uneasy neighbour of Bernicia.

Significant entries in the *Chronicle* make it pretty clear that British resistance in central and southern England had died hard and had not been decisively broken until as recently as the 570s. For 571, the *Chronicle* records a decisive British defeat by Cuthwulf of Wessex at *Biedcanford* and Cuthwulf's subsequent capture of Aylesbury, Limbury, Bensington, and Eynsham – which means that before this battle the British had still been holding ground within forty miles of London. Another key battle against the

British is recorded in the annal for 577, six years later: 'In this year Cuthwine and Ceawlin* fought against the Britons and killed three kings, Conmail, Condidan, and Farinmail, at the place which is called Dyrham; and they captured three of their cities, Gloucester, Cirencester, and Bath.' These two defeats shattered the last bastion of resistance held by the British in the south, and left Elmet as the only recorded British kingdom inland. Wessex's follow-up and continued expansion drove the British further apart and forced them into the 'Celtic fringe' – Cornwall and Wales.

It is hardly surprising that historians, for the sake of convenience, have respected the word 'Heptarchy' – the Seven Kingdoms – to describe Saxon England. The seven are Wessex, Mercia, Northumbria, East Anglia, Essex, Kent, and Sussex. But in the year 600, Saxon England was far more splintered than that. As the seventh century proceeded, three phenomena imposed much more unity on the island; and those three phenomena were the re-imposition of the Christian Church, the supremacy of Northumbria, and the rise of a powerful new Mercia to the domination of central and southern England.

The Roman mission to Saxon England in 597 was not, in fact, quite the heroic achievement which it was hailed to be in later years, although there can be no doubt that it was a momentous event in the history of the island. The mission's leader, Augustine, found an ideal situation when he and his monks finally arrived in Kent: a seed-bed ready for the sowing of the Christian message, thanks to royal patronage. But it is no disparagement of Augustine to say that he was certainly not cast in the mould of the heroic missionary. All the energy and determination which kept the English mission in being came from Augustine's master, the pope: Gregory I, afterwards canonized, and still remembered as 'the Great'.

Anglo-Saxon scholars and churchmen always remembered Gregory with affection for having sent the word of God back to their land. The Northumbrian historian Bede went so far as to credit Gregory with the famous story of having seen little blond boys on sale in the slave market in Rome – itself a telling commentary on the values of the Church at the time – and asking what manner of folk they were. The result was a series of scholarly, but to modern ears ghastly, puns. 'Angles.' 'Not Angles, but angels.'

* Of Wessex.

'What is their land?' 'Deira.' '*De ira*'* of God shall they be saved. 'Who is their king?' 'Ælle.' 'And Alleluias shall be sung in his land.' Bede says that this happened before Gregory became pope, and he certainly became obsessed with reclaiming a former province of the Church before his accession. Under the Roman occupation, the Christian administration of Britain had echoed the civilian, with archbishoprics at York and London. And the man Gregory chose to go to England and restore this state of affairs was one of 'his men' – Augustine, prior of the monastery of St Andrew which Gregory had founded in Rome.

The story of Augustine's mission is untidy and precarious, to say the least. It would never even have got across the Channel had not Gregory put his foot down and sent Augustine back to the job after the missionaries had lost heart and packed him off to Rome to intercede with the pope. When they arrived in Kent, they became the first religious missionaries on record to find their faith already being practised in the household of the king to whom they bore their message. Christianity was not totally new to Ethelbert, thanks to Queen Bertha and her Frankish chaplain, Liudhard; but the king was definitely uneasy when he first met Augustine and his followers. Bede says that they came 'carrying before them a silver crucifix instead of a banner, and an image of the Lord Saviour painted on a board, singing the litanies', and that Ethelbert, smelling witchcraft, insisted on the encounter taking place out in the open air so that no evil spirits could be turned against him. But all went well. Ethelbert gave the missionaries a ruinous old Roman church building – St Martin's in Canterbury, which Queen Bertha had been using for her devotions – and permitted Augustine's band to preach and convert. When the king himself was baptized, the initial success of the mission was assured, and was marked in due course by the establishment of the see of Canterbury.

That this was only envisaged at the time as a temporary measure was soon made perfectly clear. In 601, a second mission arrived in England from Rome. Augustine received not only his official *pallium* but a sheaf of detailed instructions from Gregory. As soon as possible, Augustine was to transfer his seat from Canterbury to London and proceed with the conversion of the interior. But despite the favourable circumstances due to Ethelbert's overlordship

---

* 'From the wrath'.

of the south-east, Augustine's mission proceeded at a snail's pace with its work. By 605, two more sees had been founded: Rochester, with Mellitus as its first bishop, and London, in East Saxon territory, under Justus. These extremely limited gains for an over-all period of seven years were more than offset by Augustine's disastrous failure to seal an alliance with the native British Church. With the aid of Ethelbert, a full-dress synod was held at which Augustine proved a total failure as a diplomat. He offended the British bishops by castigating them for their failure to convert the English and by their unorthodox customs, especially that angular bone of religious contention, the observance of the Easter feast. His giving them the alternative of 'war from their enemies, if they would not have peace from their friends' deepened the umbrage of the British contingent still further and brought the negotiations to an abrupt halt. And it certainly helped drive the British into a series of military alliances with pagan English forces against the English kingdoms which had been recently converted, a choice which the British clearly made as the lesser of two evils.

We do not know when Augustine died, but it was some time between 604 and 609. Lawrence replaced him as archbishop of the Church in England, and under Lawrence the Roman mission continued its limping and uncertain advance. Ethelbert's powerful neighbour, Rædwald of the East Angles, was nominally converted to the faith, but Rædwald was a canny ruler who believed in covering himself against all eventualities. He permitted a Christian altar to be set up in a pagan temple – just in case. To be fair, it must be admitted that the Christian mission in England was more than somewhat hampered by the instructions of Pope Gregory, which advocated a cautious approach, using, rather than extirpating, native pagan customs:

> It is doubtless impossible to remove all abuses from rough hearts at a stroke, as one who strives to scale the heights goes upward by steady paces and not by leaps and bounds ... that, by a change of heart, they should lose one thing in their sacrifices but preserve another; in other words, that the beasts they sacrificed before should still be offered, but that in offering them to the true God and not to idols they should not be the same sacrifices as they were before.

It sounds an intelligent and enlightened approach but it caused much confusion among the English, and in the short term made the first roots put down by the Roman missions of 597 and 601 dangerously shallow, as events were soon to prove.

Ethelbert, first royal patron of the Roman Church in England, died in 616, and the result was immediate and near permanent collapse. There was a pagan reaction in Kent, Ethelbert's successor, Eadbald, reviving the good old customs by marrying his father's widow. Mellitus fled from London; Justus abandoned Rochester. Lawrence himself was only prevented from abandoning Canterbury by a dream in which St Peter appeared to him and flogged him violently for his weakness of heart. Lawrence died soon after and was replaced by Mellitus, who lived until 624; his successor was Justus, under whose primacy the see of Rochester was re-established. But London remained in pagan hands; and the last flicker of evangelical zeal from Canterbury, the attempt to carry out Gregory's programme and re-create the ancient see of York, was wrecked by the hostile fortunes of embattled Northumbria.

Four years before Augustine had landed in Kent, Æthelfrith of Bernicia had established himself as overlord of Northumbria and the house of Deira went into another of its regular eclipses. Æthelfrith cemented his power by a decisive victory over the Scots at *Degsastan* in 603, after which 'no king of the Scots dared to lead an army against this nation', according to the *Chronicle*. In about 605, Æthelfrith smashed a strong British host at Chester, 'and there killed a countless number of Britons ... There were also killed 200 priests who had come there to pray for the army of the Britons.' The *Chronicle* did not fail to point the moral: 'And thus was fulfilled Augustine's prophecy, by which he said: "If the Britons do not wish to have peace with us, they shall perish at the hands of the Saxons." ' But Æthelfrith's career was halted by his death at the hands of the East Anglian king, Rædwald, in 617. Rædwald had given asylum to Edwin, the head of the house of Deira, and after the defeat of Æthelfrith Edwin became the new overlord of Northumbria. After the death of his former patron Rædwald – one candidate for the missing body in the magnificent commemorative ship-burial at Sutton Hoo in Suffolk – Edwin became the most powerful ruler in England.

The English coined a word of their own to describe such overlords, however temporary they turned out to be: Bretwaldas.

Bede lists the first Bretwaldas as follows: Ælle of the South Saxons (back in the late fifth century), Ceawlin of Wessex, Ethelbert of Kent, Rædwald of East Anglia, and Edwin of Northumbria. It was more an honorific title than anything else: a recognition of ascendancy. Edwin, however, certainly deserved the title. And it was in Edwin's reign (617–633) that the archbishopric of York was shakily re-established.

As in the days of Augustine, the advance of the faith was helped by the effects of a royal marriage, for Edwin married Ethelbert's daughter Æthelberg, who was a Christian, and promised to respect her religion. Archbishop Justus consecrated Paulinus, who had been a member of the 601 mission, as the new archbishop of York, and sent him north with Edwin's new bride. The *Chronicle* tells a dramatic story about how Edwin was induced to embrace Christianity. The Northumbrian king was at war with Wessex, whose king, Cwichelm, sent an assassin to kill Edwin. It was a close failure: Edwin was wounded and two of his thanes killed. Edwin vowed to favour the Church still more if he was granted vengeance over his would-be murderer, and a smashing Northumbrian victory over the West Saxons in 626 brought the see of York into existence. Edwin himself was baptized at Easter in 627. Under his grateful patronage, the new province of the Church flourished, with mass conversions being made by the energetic Paulinus. But all these hopeful beginnings wilted with the overthrow and death of Edwin in the year 633.

A new power was growing in central England: Mercia. Under the fierce leadership of a tough and unshakably pagan fighting king, Penda, the Mercians had started at last to exploit their central position in the island. Penda became king of the Mercians in 626, and forced the West Saxons, under Cwichelm and Cynegils, to come to terms at Cirencester. And in 633, fighting in alliance with the British king, Cadwallon of Gwynnedd, he tackled Edwin himself and brought him down. British and Mercian raids harried leaderless Northumbria; Paulinus fled from York with Edwin's widow and found asylum in Kent. Only one courageous churchman, James the Deacon, held on at York; but the Roman faith had been uprooted from the north. When Christianity was re-established there, it did not come from Canterbury but from the wandering missionaries of the hybrid Celtic Church originally founded in Ireland.

As Roman Britain was splintering and cracking in the fifth

century, a Romano-British nobleman, Patrick, heard the call and
crossed the sea to Ireland with the faith. There he founded a
branch of the Church which was necessarily totally cut off from
Rome. In time, great monasteries arose in Ireland, observing
customs which were very different from those of the Roman
Church. But it was from Ireland that the great Celtic missionary,
St Columba, crossed to Scotland to found the monastery of Iona
and bring the faith to the heathen Picts. By the time of Columba's
death in 597 – just as Augustine was starting his work in Kent –
the influence of the Celtic Church had been firmly established in the
north. And the renascent fortunes of Northumbria proved the instrument by which it achieved the temporary eclipse of Canterbury.

Hopes for an era of unity and peace in the north were shattered
by Edwin's death in battle. His eldest son, Osfrith, died with
him. Edwin's cousin, Osric, hung on as king of Deira until the
summer of 633, when he, too, was killed in battle by Cadwallon.
Eanfrith of Bernicia, Æthelfrith's son, became ruler of Bernicia
for a spell but he also fell to Cadwallon in the fateful year of
633. Yet the career of Cadwallon – the last great fighting leader,
in the tradition of Arthur, of the dispossessed British – ended at
the close of 633, with his own defeat and death at the hands of
Oswald of Bernicia, another of Æthelfrith's heirs.

While in exile during Edwin's reign, Oswald and Eanfrith had
found asylum among the monks of Columba's foundation on
Iona. Once Oswald had established himself as king of Northumbria, it was to Iona that he looked for spiritual sustenance. He had
won his fight against Cadwallon, like the Roman emperor Constantine, under the sign of the Cross; and in addition to being
naturally grateful for his victory, he was a genuinely devout
convert. In 634, Bishop Aidan came from Iona to Northumbria
with a mission of monks, establishing himself on the offshore island
of Lindisfarne. The Celtic Church of Columba had come to the
northern English, and within a few years it was to spread south as far
as the Thames – a powerful contrast to the feeble efforts of Augustine and his successors down at Canterbury.

The Celtic missionaries went about their work amid all the
turbulence and incessant warfare which bedevilled Saxon England
in the seventh century – the century of Northumbrian supremacy.
Oswald's reign only lasted nine years before he was killed in battle
by Penda of Mercia in 645, but his brother Oswiu took over and

B

reigned until 670 – one of the very few Northumbrian kings to die in bed. It was a momentous reign for two reasons. The first was the defeat of pagan Mercia, with a crushing victory over Penda at *Winwædfeld* in 655, which brought Mercia under Northumbrian domination for a while and opened up the whole kingdom to the Celtic missionaries. The second was the great synod held at Whitby in 663, under Oswiu's chairmanship, at which the Roman Church was accepted as the official branch of the faith in England. This was the result of a surprising come-back on the part of Canterbury, but the real significance was the way in which both clerical parties in the debate turned to the king of Northumbria, without whose backing neither would have any real chance of getting the casting vote.

By the time of the Synod of Whitby, the pattern of the Church's development in England was as chaotic as that of the political kingdoms themselves.

Northumbria and Mercia remained subject to the Celtic 'mother church' of the northern English, and a Celtic missionary, Cedd, had re-converted the East Saxons and was accepted as their bishop. Kent remained subject to the spiritual authority of Canterbury, which had appointed a bishop for East Anglia. Meanwhile, the faith had been implanted in Wessex by two freelance bishops from Gaul, Birinus and Agilbert, the latter of whom attended the Whitby synod. Both of the latter had been consecrated on the Continent. Yet although Oswiu's verdict at Whitby made it clear that the Roman faith of Canterbury would be the one to receive official secular backing, at least in northern England, the various shoots of the Church in England had still to be organized and pruned into a cohesive whole. This was effectively begun by Theodore of Tarsus, consecrated archbishop of Canterbury by Pope Vitalian in 668, who took up his duties in England in May 669. In another great synod, at Hertford in 673, Theodore began the task of hammering unity into the English Church. When, in 735, the see of York became an archbishopric, the definitive framework of the English Church had taken shape.

In practical terms, however, Theodore's framework for the English Church took centuries before it was strong enough to stand on its own, and in seventh- and eighth-century England the patronage of the local king was still very much needed by the bishops. This period of the Church's growth is important, for it developed side by side with the evolution of the secular king-doms.

By the year 700, the Church had put an indelible stamp on the life of Saxon England. Rich patrons were bringing in architects from the Continent to build *mynstres* – minsters, churches – and monasteries. The wealth of the Church was beginning to put out the first shoots of a superb English-based style of religious art. And now the king's laws were issued with the blessing and guidance of the Church, which was taking over some of the old fines and compensation-payments which had always been an integral part of Teutonic justice. Pope Gregory's advice that the English should be led 'to lose one thing in their sacrifices but preserve another' had been wisely kept, and it showed clearly in the laws of the time. A good example of how Saxon society was developing in Theodore's time is provided by the law code issued by King Ine of Wessex (688–726), and a few extracts are quoted here. They reflect the rigid grading of Saxon society, from the king down to the slave; minimum and maximum penalties are violent extremes and reflect on a violent and strife-torn age. But for all that, they record the steady advancement of order, stability, and wealth:

A child is to be baptized within 30 days; if it is not, 30 shillings compensation is to be paid.

If it then die without being baptized, he is to compensate for it with all that he possesses.

If a slave works on Sunday at his master's command, he is to be free, and the master is to pay 30 shillings as a fine.

If, however, the slave works without his knowledge, he is to be flogged.

If then a freeman works on that day without his lord's command, he is to forfeit his freedom.

Church-scot* is to be given by Martinmas; if anyone does not discharge it, he is to be liable to 60 shillings and to render the church-scot twelvefold.

Crimes of violence come *after* offences against the Church:

If anyone steals without his wife and his children knowing, he is to pay 60 shillings as a fine.

* A payment to the Church in kind, distinct from the tithe.

If, however, he steals with the knowledge of all his household, they are all to go into slavery.

A ten-year-old boy can be [considered] privy to a theft.

If anyone within the boundaries of our kingdom commit robbery and rapine, he is to give back the plunder and give 60 shillings as a fine.

If a man from a distance or a foreigner goes through the wood off the track, and does not shout nor blow a horn, he is to be assumed to be a thief, to be either killed or redeemed.

He who slays a thief may declare with an oath that he slew him fleeing as a thief, and the kinsmen of the dead man are to swear to him an oath not to carry on a feud. If, however, he conceals it and it is revealed later, he is then to pay for him.

Against these and similar attempts to create an ordered and law-abiding way of life, the power-struggles of the Saxon kingdoms continued as before. Oswiu of Northumbria, the arbitrator at Whitby, died in 670. Before he quitted the scene, Northumbrian power south of the Humber had been broken by Wulfhere, king of Mercia, who reduced Essex to dependency and finally invaded Northumbria itself. Ecgfrith, Oswiu's son, shattered Wulfhere's ascendancy but was himself defeated by Wulfhere's brother Ethelred in 678. Ecgfrith was the last of the great Northumbrian kings. He fell in 685 while leading a raiding party far to the north, deep inside the territory of the Picts of southern Scotland. The next Northumbrian king, Aldfrith, cherished no territorial ambitions to the north or south. His great claim to fame, as Bede testified, was his enthusiastic patronage of the arts, which elevated Northumbrian learning and literature to a level unique in Western Europe in the eighth century.

In the south, constant warring with Mercia had developed the resilience of Wessex, which in the late seventh century produced two remarkable kings. The first of these, Ceadwalla (685–688), was noted for his wars against Kent and his conquest of Sussex. The second was Ine the lawgiver, who remained the most powerful ruler in southern England for thirty years. Nothing, however, availed against the great expansionist policy of the two dominant kings of the eighth century, both of Mercia: Æthelbald (716–757) and Offa (757–796).

Offa of Mercia was the most important Saxon king before Alfred the Great. The extent of his power and the height of his personal state made him the first prototype king of England. There was not a kingdom in the island that did not acknowledge his supremacy while he was in his prime. Alfred later paid tribute to Offa's stature as a lawgiver, although no copies of Offa's laws have survived. He struck his own distinctive coinage. He was the first English ruler to draw a definite frontier with Wales, by means of the great dyke which still bears his name. In addition, Offa was a respected peer of the monarchs of Western Europe; and it was in his reign that the riches of the English Church were raised to un-precedented heights. In short, the reign of Offa brought a glorious end to the first chapter of the history of the English. The jarring wars of the Heptarchy were stilled for over thirty years. Learning and the arts flourished, and the end of the eighth century ap-proached with Saxon England at a peak of development which would not be regained for two hundred years.

Yet there was a fatal flaw in the picture. The English had never had to worry about any threat to their existence from over-seas, any danger from a foe strong enough to make the English kings concentrate on fortifying their coasts, as the Romans had done before them, instead of overcoming or fighting off their inland neighbours. From across the North Sea a terrible reckoning was about to be presented for this negligence. 'Saxon England,' in Winston Churchill's vivid phrase, 'was ripe for the sickle.'

## Chapter 2

The Northmen came about our land
    A Christless chivalry:
Who knew not of the arch or pen,
Great, beautiful half-witted men
    From the sunrise and the sea.

Misshapen ships stood on the deep
    Full of strange gold and fire,
And hairy men, as huge as sin,
With hornèd heads, came wading in
    Through the long, low sea-mire.

G. K. Chesterton, *The Ballad of the White Horse.*

# Hit and run

It is important to remember that it was in the reign of Offa of Mercia, the undisputed overlord of Saxon England, that the vikings first came to Britain. Their first raid revealed the Achilles' heel of the English. Never had such a powerful ruler prevailed in the island since the collapse of the western Roman Empire; yet the coastal provinces under his control were powerless against these new sea-borne raiders.

They came in 789, three years after Pope Hadrian had honoured Offa by sending a special mission from Rome to England, and while Offa was chaffering with Charlemagne himself over the terms of the marriage of his daughter to Charlemagne's son. The *Chronicle* tells us that 'three ships of the Northmen' were involved. Certainly they were not recognized for the menace they were. When they landed near Dorchester on the south coast, the king's reeve, Beaduheard, rode down to the coast to meet them.

This challenge of the stranger's identity and his business in the land was established routine by the late eighth century. The writer of the epic poem *Beowulf*, which was composed during this century, had inserted such an episode to show what a well-ordered kingdom Hrothgar of the Danes was ruling. When Beowulf and his Geat warriors arrived:

... Hrothgar's officer ... rode down to the beach, vehemently brandishing the great spear which he held, and challenged:

'What sort of people may you be who have come in arms across the ocean in that great ship? For years I have been coast-guard, and kept watch over the sea so that no pirate fleet might raid the Danish coast. No armed men have ever ventured to land here so openly! Nor did you make certain of either the permission or consent of our leaders. But I have never seen anywhere a more formidable champion than that armed man in your midst, who is certainly no mere retainer carrying weapons, unless his heroic bearing and appearance belie him. Yet in case you are spies I must know all about you before you go further into Danish territory. Now listen to plain speaking, you foreign seamen. You had better tell me why you have come, and at once.'

It is possible that Beaduheard had actually listened to a recitation of *Beowulf* in his lord's hall, and that a memory of these words flickered in his mind as he rode up to the unknown leader of this band of armed aliens. He certainly cannot have had much time to reflect on it, for what happened next stilled his thoughts for ever. There was no exchange of formal courtesies. Beaduheard and his small retinue – perhaps no more than half a dozen at most – were set upon and killed in a brief, hacking flurry which remains the first recorded episode in the long struggle between Saxon and Northman.

'Three ships of the Northmen' would mean a raiding force of about a hundred fighting men if we take the Gokstad ship, accepted as a classic viking vessel, as the basic unit. This vessel had rowing-positions for thirty-two men. Such a force, landing at an un-defended sector of English coast, could have done considerable damage in a hit-and-run strike, but this does not seem to have happened with the Dorchester raid of 789. Certainly no abbeys or churches near the coast were plundered; if they had been, the English chroniclers would have lamented the atrocity in copious terms. Perhaps the viking leader was disconcerted to find official-dom making its presence felt so soon after the landing, and feared that stronger forces were at hand to trap him. This would explain a hasty re-embarkation.

Where did the Dorchester raiders come from? This is another mystery, one which we owe partly to the ignorance of the English at the time. Contemporary accounts tend to lump all Scandinavian raiders together as 'Danes', and add to the confusion with refer-ences which make it equally likely that they came from Norway. But it is a fair guess that the next viking raiders did come from Norway, for they struck at the opposite end of the island: at Lindisfarne off the coast of Northumbria.

The days were long gone when Northumbria had held sway

as the dominant kingdom of Saxon England, with its power radiating south across the Humber. But the legacy of those days was a rich one, with lavishly endowed monasteries and churches ripe for the plucking. And it was to Lindisfarne that they came – Lindisfarne, the Holy of Holies of the Church in northern England.

Details of the Lindisfarne raid of 793 are even vaguer than those of the landing near Dorchester four years before. The English sources give no hint of the strength of the viking force, let alone of who led it. To the historians of the age it was a horrifying event, only to be explained as God's punishment of a sinful people. (Northumbria had lapsed back into deep civil turmoil over the last four years, with a brisk turnover of usurpers and legitimate kings either murdered or expelled.) The *Chronicle*'s entry for 793 opens in appropriate style:

> In this year dire portents appeared over Northumbria and sorely frightened the people. They consisted of immense whirlwinds and flashes of lightning, and fiery dragons were seen flying in the air. A great famine immediately followed those signs, and a little after that in the same year, on 8 June, the ravages of heathen men miserably destroyed God's church on Lindisfarne, with plunder and slaughter.

The famous community of Lindisfarne, totally defenceless, was scattered and sacked. The monastery itself was plundered of its gold, its gems, and its sacred emblems, and a thrill of horror ran through the English Church. The Northumbrian scholar Alcuin, in attendance far away at the court of Charlemagne, summed it all up when he wrote:

> Lo, it is nearly 350 years that we and our fathers have inhabited this most lovely land, and never before has such terror appeared in Britain as we have now suffered from a pagan race, nor was it thought that such an inroad from the sea could be made. Behold, the church of St Cuthbert spattered with the blood of the priests of God, despoiled of all its ornaments; a place more venerable than all in Britain is given as a prey to pagan peoples. And where first, after the departure of St Paulinus from York, the Christian religion in our race took its rise, there misery and calamity have begun. Who does not fear this? Who does not lament this as if his country were captured?

This famous passage is an extract from a letter to King Ethelred of Northumbria, written by Alcuin when he heard the news. The letter is too long to quote in full here; Alcuin extends his condolences into a red-hot homily aimed squarely at the ruler of a sinful people. After his prim admission, 'I do not say that formerly there were no sins of fornication among the people', Alcuin gives a warning catalogue of 'fornications', 'adulteries', 'incest', 'avarice', 'robbery', 'violent judgments', and even decadent modern fashion – 'Look at your trimming of beard and hair, in which you have wished to resemble the pagans.' Homilies like this, written by churchmen to crowned heads, were fairly commonplace in Saxon England. But this one is much more comprehensive than most, and it was inspired by the shock of the Lindisfarne raid.

Alcuin followed up his letter to King Ethelred by writing another, which is equally interesting. The recipient was Bishop Higbald, head of the refugee monks who survived the raid, and Alcuin's letter clearly shows that the raiders were after slaves as well as portable loot. It ends: 'When our lord King Charles returns home, having by the mercy of God subdued his enemies, we plan, God helping us, to go to him; and if we can then be of any profit to your Holiness, regarding either the youths who have been led into captivity by the pagans or any other of your needs, we will take diligent care to bring it about.'

The following year, 794, the vikings hit Northumbria again, and this time the target was Jarrow on the lower Tyne. Jarrow represented the finest flower of eighth-century Northumbrian civilization – the Jarrow of Bede, whose *Ecclesiastical History* is still a classic source of information on the great days of Northumbria.

The fact that two famous religious foundations sixty miles from each other should have been selected as viking objectives in two consecutive years calls for comment. First, it is more than likely that when the Lindisfarne raiders returned home with their loot in 793 the word got round that rich pickings were to be had for the taking on the north-east coast of England. We know that viking commanders were able to pass on navigational details of formerly unknown waters to others, who could then set off and make confident landfalls of their own. This happened during the viking voyages from Greenland to North America at the turn of the tenth century; the first accidental landfall was plotted with sufficient accuracy for the next voyage – one of deliberate exploration – to reach its destination with little or no trouble worth recording. Even if the viking leader of the raid on Jarrow was not the same man who had savaged Lindisfarne the year before – and this possibility cannot be ruled out – he could certainly have obtained sufficient information to prevent him from heading blindly into trouble at an unknown destination.

Assuming that he did, it did him little good. The Jarrow raid ended in fiasco. The monastery was duly plundered but this time the raiders had to fight for it, and one of their leaders was killed. Nor was this all. Despite their seamanship, the raiders were caught unawares by a sudden storm and lost some ships. We are not told how many, but the *Chronicle* records with relish that those who did not drown were all killed as soon as they reached the shore. It was a battered viking fleet that headed home across the North Sea. Tynesiders can still recall with pride that it was their forbears who drew first blood in Saxon England's long fight for survival against the viking menace.

Dorchester, 789. Lindisfarne, 793. Jarrow, 794. And then, for the space of forty years, there is not a mention of any further viking raids on Saxon England. Yet those four decades were crammed with dramatic and far-reaching events. They saw the tide of Scandinavian expansion well northward around the British Isles, with viking settlements being made on the Shetlands, the Orkneys, the Hebrides, the Isle of Man, and the Irish coast. And in England repeated outbreaks of war between the major kingdoms overturned the balance of power created by Offa of Mercia, resulting in the final ascendancy of the kingdom destined to champion Saxon England's fight against the Northmen: Wessex.

Offa died in 796. The power he had amassed and hoarded like a miser had seemed indestructible. He was the first English king ever to treat on equal terms with pope and emperor. (Although it is true that Charlemagne was not actually crowned emperor until after Offa's death, he had been the master of Western Europe for years.) Offa had been sure enough of his own power to style himself *Rex Anglorum* and *Rex Totius Anglorum Patriae* – 'King of the English' and 'King of the whole country of the English'. While he still lived, he had had his son Ecgfrith crowned king of Mercia (the first official coronation of an English king, be it noted). Offa had married off his daughters to King Ethelred of Northumbria and King Beorhtric of Wessex and had reduced the

kingdom of Kent to a Mercian province. But all these achievements had been the work of his own hands; they had no tap-roots
and they withered on his death.

Ecgfrith did not survive his father by as much as six months.
The Mercian throne passed to a distant member of the royal line,
Cenwulf. His immediate problem was Kent, which had broken
out in revolt in the last weeks of Offa's life. Cenwulf smashed the
Kentishmen in battle and earned a temporary respite by putting
in his own brother, Cuthred, as king. No sooner had the Kentish
front been stabilized than Northumbria broke away, with King
Ethelred being murdered by his own subjects. The new king,
Eardwulf, took pains to have his new power endorsed by the
Church: he was consecrated and enthroned at York by the archbishop of York and the bishops of Hexham, Lindisfarne, and
Whithorn. But the most far-reaching blow at the Mercian ascendancy came in 802, when King Beorhtric of Wessex died. The
new king of Wessex was a man whom Offa and Ethelred had driven
into exile in his youth: Egbert, who was to crown his career by
conquering Mercia itself.

The inevitable showdown between Mercia and Wessex was
nevertheless postponed for twenty years. Both Cenwulf and
Egbert had problems of their own. In 802, Cenwulf had to cope
with an attack by Eardwulf of Northumbria, who had been
swift to reopen the friendly channels between his country and the
court of Charlemagne. Cenwulf also re-established direct control
over Kent when his brother Cuthred died in 807. But his main
concern was to resume the programme of westerly expansion at
the expense of the Welsh – the programme which Offa had so
clearly delineated by his building of Offa's Dyke. Between 816 and
818 Cenwulf's army overran the old Welsh kingdoms of Dyfed
(Pembrokeshire) and Powys (Snowdonia). Cenwulf died in 821 and
the place of his death – at Basingwerk in Flintshire – suggests that
he was preparing yet another campaign against the Welsh. His
brother Ceolwulf, who inherited the Mercian throne, carried on
Cenwulf's work, taking Deganwy on the Conway estuary and
driving out the king of Powys in 822.

Signal triumphs. But for Mercia a mere three years of independence as a sovereign state remained.

Egbert of Wessex adopted a policy strikingly similar to that of
Cenwulf of Mercia. In Egbert's case, however, the new enemies

were the descendants of the British still holding out against Saxon domination in Cornwall. They had long ago been separated from their kinsfolk in Wales by the expansion of the West Saxons, but were still called the 'West Welsh' by the Saxon English. The Cornishmen were tough and vicious fighters with centuries of experience in survival behind them. They fought and were defeated in battle after battle; Egbert's forces marched right through Cornwall on punitive expeditions – but the Cornishmen still fought back. Like the Roman legions in Caledonia, Egbert found out by bitter experience that to a determined people there is all the difference in the world between defeat and subjugation. But quite suddenly, in 823, Egbert was presented with entirely new possibilities.

In that year Ceolwulf of Mercia was deposed and the kingdom passed to a thane, a king's lord (presumably the leader of the deposing faction) named Beornwulf. The new king managed to get his authority recognized in Kent, Middlesex, and Essex – a good enough start for a dubious candidate for the throne, offering the usurper a wide enough foundation from which to extend his power by degrees over the entire fringe of former Mercian dependencies. But Beornwulf never got the chance. In 825, Egbert broke off his current war with Cornwall and turned against Mercia.

It was a campaign which can only really be described by the twentieth-century word *Blitzkrieg* – a decisive 'battle without a morrow' followed by the enemy's capitulation. The West Saxon and Mercian hosts met at *Ellendun* (later Wroughton) and Egbert won. Next came the thorough exploitation of the victory. Egbert made up a separate task force which he entrusted to his son Æthelwulf, added Ealhstan, Bishop of Sherborne, and Ealdorman Wulfheard, to make it into a full-blooded military and diplomatic mission, and sent it east into Kent. When he received the submission of the dwindling Kentish forces loyal to Mercia, Egbert became master not only of Kent, but of Surrey, Sussex, and Essex as well. The wretched Beornwulf fled east and sought asylum in East Anglia. It was a fatal move. 'Because of their fear of the Mercians', the king of East Anglia appealed to Egbert for peace and protection, and had Beornwulf killed as a gesture of his good faith. By the end of the year 825, Egbert of Wessex was master of all England from the Bristol Channel to the Wash.

The Mercian hinterland still held out; its people even found a new king, a thegn named Ludeca. This worthy lasted until 827, when he was killed and replaced by a similar adventurer, Wiglaf. But after the conquest of the south it was obvious what Egbert's next move was going to be; and in 829, with the whole of southern England behind him, Egbert fell on Mercia. The kingdom which twenty-five years earlier had been paramount in England was totally defeated; Wiglaf fled, and Egbert did not replace him. The West Saxon king now took the title of *Rex Merciorum* – 'King of the Mercians'. The great campaign of 829 was crowned by the submission of the Northumbrians to Egbert in northern Derbyshire: 'and they offered him submission and peace there, and on that they separated'.

Quite apart from the sheer speed of Egbert's conquests, the reduction of mighty Mercia in the space of five years gave him a new status. The *Chronicle*'s entry for 829 hails Egbert as the latest of England's official overlords, the Bretwaldas:

> And that year King Egbert conquered the kingdom of the Mercians, and everything south of the Humber; and he was the eighth king who was 'Bretwalda'. The first who had so great authority was Ælle, king of the South Saxons, the second was Ceawlin, king of the West Saxons, the third was Ethelbert, king of the people of Kent, the fourth was Rædwald, king of the East Angles, the fifth was Edwin, king of the Northumbrians, the sixth was Oswald who reigned after him, the seventh was Oswiu, Oswald's brother, the eighth was Egbert, king of the West Saxons.

This entry is a blatant piece of West Saxon propaganda, for the three great kings of the Mercian supremacy – Æthelbald, Offa, and Cenwulf – are conspicuous by their absence. If they are added to this list of the Bretwaldas, the result is a revealing score-sheet of the ups and downs of the Heptarchy – Kent, Sussex, Essex, East Anglia, Mercia, Northumbria, and Wessex – between the end of the fifth century and the year 830. It reads as follows:

Northumbria: 3
Mercia: 3
Wessex: 2
East Anglia, Kent, Sussex (each): 1.

Thus the overthrow of Mercia was just the latest of swings in a balance of power which had been tilting to and fro, virtually non-stop, for over three hundred years. Egbert's triumph reflected this pattern; it did not end it. Within a year of her defeat by Wessex, Mercia had broken away again and King Wiglaf was back on his throne. London, a Mercian town, was Mercian once more, and it stayed Mercian until Alfred won it back from the Danes later in the century. Moreover, the traditional no-man's-land between Wessex and Mercia – Berkshire – remained predominantly Mercian. Set apart from this recovery on the part of Mercia, Egbert's conquests in the south remained: he had welded Kent, Surrey, Sussex, and Essex to the original lands of the West Saxons.

Egbert, however, never attained Offa's status. He gave his heir, Æthelwulf, vice-regal powers in Kent, Surrey, Sussex, and Essex, keeping control of the Wessex heartland himself. And it was at Æthelwulf's lands that the vikings suddenly struck in 835 – out of the blue, forty-one years after the last raid on Jarrow. Information on this new attack is curt and probably no fuller than any report that came to the ears of Egbert himself: 'In this year heathen men ravaged Sheppey.'

The attack on the Isle of Sheppey at the mouth of the Medway river in the lower Thames estuary seems to have been an enlarged version of the original raid on Lindisfarne: the plundering of a small offshore island, followed by a retreat. But the attack of the following year, 836, was totally different.

It happened in the west of Egbert's kingdom, at Carhampton in Devon. The biggest viking fleet yet to land in England disgorged an army eager for battle. The figures in the various manuscripts of the *Chronicle* vary between twenty-five and thirty-five ships, but the record is unequivocal: 'King Egbert fought against the crews ... at Carhampton, and a great slaughter was made there, and the Danes had possession of the battle-field.' This was something completely new to the English. The alien raiders had got the upper hand in a set-piece battle against the most renowned fighting king of the age – although 'possession of the battlefield' was clearly the prelude to the eventual withdrawal of the viking force.

Worse was to come two years later. In 838, 'a great naval force' came out of the West and made common cause with Egbert's most hardy foes: the Cornishmen. This was two years after the first viking colony was established at Dublin, and it is possible that the first viking contacts with the Cornishmen had been made by viking traders. But there was nothing mercantile about the expedition of 838. Egbert reacted promptly in the face of this new threat. Undeterred by his defeat at Carhampton in 836, he advanced to meet the coalition host and smashed it at Hingston Down. It was the last recorded achievement of his momentous reign. Egbert died in 839, and was succeeded by Æthelwulf.

It proved a perilous legacy. Throughout the first decade after Egbert's death, the tempo of viking attacks mounted steadily. In 840, the raiders struck at the very cradle of West Saxon tradition: Southampton Water, where Cerdic and Cynric reputedly landed to found the West Saxon dynasty at the end of the fifth century. A fleet of thirty-three to thirty-four ships landed at Southampton but was defeated in battle by Ealdorman Wulfheard's host. At Portland, Wulfheard's colleague Æthelhelm was not so lucky. A hard-fought battle finally tilted against the Wessex men, and although 'for a long time he put the enemy to flight', Æthelhelm was killed and victory went to the Danes.

In the early 840s, the viking attacks on Saxon England became general. Within twelve months they were stabbing northwards along the east coast. Raids in 841 started with the slaughter of Ealdorman Hereberht's forces on Romney Marsh, followed by subsequent raids on Kent, East Anglia, and Lindsey in Lincolnshire. The *Chronicle* records the first attacks on Rochester and London in 842, but other sources are required to get a more general idea of the widening scope of the viking forays. Nithard, a French chronicler, provides the first recorded instance of what became a popular viking programme: a sweep along the French coast followed by a pounce across the Channel to attack a target in England. In Nithard's *History of the Sons of King Louis the Pious* for 842, we find: 'About the same time the Northmen ravaged Quentavic,* and then crossed the sea and likewise plundered *Hamwig* (Southampton) and *Nordhunnwig* (Northam).' Shortly after this, the western vikings landed at Carhampton again, and King Æthelwulf lost to them as his father had done. This defeat, however, was soon revenged by 'Ealdorman Eanwulf with the people of Somerset and Bishop Ealhstan and Ealdorman Osric with the people of Dorset'. The two ealdorman and the good bishop concentrated their forces against a viking army which had taken a stand at the mouth of the River Parret, 'and there made a great slaughter and had the victory'.

* Near Étaples.

Roger of Wendover's *Flowers of the Histories* offers proof that Alcuin's Jeremiah-like prophecy of 793 had been fulfilled. Northumbria was still racked with civil war – and further viking attacks. In 844, '. . . Ethelred, king of the Northumbrians, was expelled from the kingdom, and Rædwulf succeeded to the kingdom; and when, hastily invested with the crown, he fought a battle with the pagans at Elvet, he and Ealdorman Alfred fell with a large part of their subjects, and then Ethelred reigned again.' This slightly breathless entry is particularly significant. It shows clearly that the vikings were swift to profit from the internal divisions of the English, and 'Elvet' was part of the city of Durham itself, which is well inland from the coast. From this fragment of evidence it is fair to deduce that, although the *Chronicle* refers mainly to Wessex and the south, Northumbria and Mercia were also the victims of viking attacks in the 840s – attacks concentrating first on coastal targets, and then probing deeper and deeper inland.

The year 851 opened promisingly for the Wessex men, with another victory won in Devon. '. . . Ealdorman Ceorl with the contingent of the men of Devon fought against the heathen army at *Wicganbeorg*, and the English made a great slaughter there and had the victory.' But the most crucial action took place in the east. For the first time, a viking force ventured to winter on English soil, digging in on the Isle of Thanet. They were the harbingers of the huge fleet – set as high as 350 ships – which swept into the Thames estuary in 851. Canterbury fell, and London. Brihtwulf, king of Mercia, was driven south across the Thames to take refuge in West Saxon territory. But the situation was restored in short order by Æthelwulf and his son Æthelbald, who raised the full muster of Wessex men and smashed the raiding army – 'the greatest slaughter . . . that we ever heard of', as the *Chronicle* puts it. Nor was this all. Æthelwulf had followed his father's example and installed his son Athelstan as king of Kent, and Athelstan was clearly a leader of energy and vision. He built up a coastal defence force, and in the same year as his father's victory inland he won the first recorded sea-fight between the English and a viking fleet, at Sandwich. Nine ships were captured from the raiders and the others fled.

Although the English were basically reliant upon the forces that could be raised by the ealdorman of each shire – an essentially local framework of defence – it is clear that down to 851 they were giving as good as they got. The viking raids were getting bigger and would continue to do so. They were staying for longer, and they were ranging much deeper inland. But the Wessex men at least had proved that they could be 'seen off' in battle. The red devils from the sea were not invincible. And after Æthelwulf's great victory of 851 there was another brief lull, which saw the development of an *entente* between Mercia and Wessex.

Burgred, king of Mercia, appealed to Æthelwulf for aid in defeating the Welsh; this was granted, and Burgred was subsequently given Æthelwulf's daughter in marriage. Yet in the same year as the joint expedition against the Welsh – 853 – there was more trouble in Thanet, with the ealdormen of Kent and Surrey falling in battle against a viking force. Two years later another viking host wintered on the Isle of Sheppey for the first time.

We have one extremely important clue as to the range of viking operations at this period, and it does not come from the *Chronicle*. It is in fact to be found in a charter of King Burgred, granting land privileges to Ealhun, bishop of Worcester, in 855. Saxon charters had a simple form; they opened with a pious invocation of the name of God, got straight down to business (often in surprising detail), and the provisions of the charter were then witnessed by the king, together with a formidable selection of archbishops, bishops, ealdormen, and thanes in attendance. The concluding paragraph normally confirmed the date of issue; and in the case of Burgred's charter of 855 there was particularly good reason to remember the year. 'And the donation of this privilege', runs the wording, 'was done in the year of our Lord's incarnation 855, the third indiction, in the place which is called *Oswaldesdun*, when the pagans were in the province of the Wrekin-dwellers.'

How a viking force was operating in the Shrewsbury region in 855 we can only guess. The invaders had several possible lines of approach: up the Severn from the Bristol Channel, south from the Dee estuary, or westward from the upper Trent. It is more than likely that the vikings had made an alliance with the Welsh, which would explain Burgred's concern to keep the Welsh firmly subdued – but as Wessex forces were involved in the campaign of 853 it is odd that the decidedly pro-Wessex *Chronicle* does not mention that Burgred and Æthelwulf were fighting vikings as well as Welshmen.

Meanwhile the solidarity of the West Saxon kingdom was

jeopardized by the religious convictions of King Æthelwulf. In 855 he took himself off to Rome on a pilgrimage, entrusting his kingdom to Æthelbald, his eldest surviving son. (We are not told what had happened to Athelstan, the victor of Sandwich.) Æthelwulf returned in 857; he had a delicate job ahead of him, for he had been told that his son had attempted to prevent his reassumption of the reins of power. From the pages of Asser, King Alfred's biographer, it seems that Æthelbald's plotting was foiled by the leading ealdormen, and Æthelwulf's return was a popular one. He bore no apparent grudge, but partitioned the kingdom on lines that King Lear would have done well to emulate. Æthelbald ruled in Wessex proper and Æthelwulf in Kent and the southeast. Æthelwulf died in 858, leaving his part of the kingdom to his second son, Ethelbert. Two years later Æthelbald died and Ethelbert reunited Wessex, dying childless in 866 and being succeeded by Ethelred, the last of Æthelwulf's sons bar one: Alfred.

This tangled passage of West Saxon dynastic history was only just resolved in time. In 865, yet another viking army established itself on Thanet, 'and made peace with the people of Kent. And the people of Kent promised them money for that peace' – the first record of Danegeld protection-money in English history. With a puff of moral indignation, the *Chronicle* adds that 'under cover of that peace and promise of money the army stole away inland by night and ravaged all eastern Kent'.

This raid was a turning-point. It was the last of the hit-and-run plunder-raids on Saxon England which had begun at the end of the eighth century. For in the year of the accession of Ethelred of Wessex, 866, the English were faced with an entirely new peril. The Great Army of the Danes landed in England, 'and took up winter quarters in East Anglia; and there they were supplied with horses, and the East Angles made peace with them'.

Conquest had succeeded plunder as the motive of the 'heathen men' from across the sea. From the moment the Great Army landed in 866, the English must fight for their very survival.

# Chapter 3

Until he came to the White Horse Vale
    And saw across the plains,
In twilight high and far and fell,
Like the fiery terraces of hell,
    The camp-fires of the Danes –

The fires of the Great Army
    That was made of iron men,
Whose lights of sacrilege and scorn
Ran round England red as morn,
Fires over Glastonbury Thorn –
    Fires out on Ely Fen.

    G. K. Chesterton, *The Ballad of the White Horse.*

# The Great Army

The entire sweep of England's history contains no parallel to the story of the Great Army of the Danes. For fifteen years it terrorized England like a Frankenstein monster. The Army roamed and struck as it pleased, and the living history of the island was dictated by its movements and by the fate of its victims. The hammer-blows it dealt out completely destroyed the traditional pattern and life-style of the original Saxon kingdoms and forged a new England. Ravaged and exhausted by the seemingly endless nightmare of the Danes, the English could not see what was happening to them at the time. While the Great Army marched as an alien host, it was the paramount foe. But it did not eventually quit England, glutted with its spoils; it did not even remain as a conquering, occupying force. Like a mutating poison virus, the Great Army sank deep into the body of its host and put an enduring mark upon it.

In later years, Scandinavian and English tradition spun a web of drama and romance around the leaders of the Great Army. Revenge, the story went, was their motive for coming to England: revenge for the dastardly slaying of Ragnar Lothbrok, 'Hairy-Breeches', the most celebrated viking of the age. (He may or may not have been the same person as the historical viking called Ragnar, who led a fleet up the River Seine and sacked Paris in 845.) Legend has it that Ragnar Lothbrok fell alive into the hands of King Ælle of Northumbria during a raid on England. Ælle flung the captive Ragnar into a pit of adders where he met his death with grim relish, thinking of the revenge his sons would deal out. The Great Army, then, was led by the sons of Ragnar Loth-brok: Halfdan, Ubbi, and the terrifying Ivar the Boneless, begotten in defiance of a solemn vow and in consequence of that born with gristle instead of bones. And it was their intention to make the whole race of the English pay in blood and treasure for their father's death.

So much for the stories; their subsequent embroidery for the enjoyment of posterity when the time came for the skalds to recite in hall can be imagined. The fact remains that the leaders of the Great Army set about Saxon England with all the method of a gang of lumberjacks clearing a virgin forest. Their first need was a secure base of operations, and for this they selected East Anglia.

The kingdom of the East Angles had managed to ride the turbulent centuries of the Heptarchy like a cork. It had been helped by geography; out on the eastern periphery of the island, East Anglia had tended to hold the balance between Wessex, Mercia, Northumbria, and the south-eastern kingdoms. Once, profiting from a neighbouring power-vacuum, it had even produced a Bretwalda, Rædwald. Since the days of Rædwald, in the early seventh century, East Anglia had survived as an independent kingdom, coming to terms with Northumbria, Mercia, and Wessex as their respective stars waxed and waned, and avoiding wholesale absorption by any of them. But the arrival of the Great Army in 866 was a totally different matter. There was no chance of raising an army to tackle such an organized host; no time to summon help from the neighbouring kingdoms. To avoid total catastrophe there was nothing to do but to come to instant terms, and this East Anglia did. There was almost certainly a paid tribute, but far more significant (as even the chroniclers of later years recognized) was the mass round-up of horses which were handed over to the Danes. Viking forces had wintered on English soil before. But this was the first time that a viking army had acquired instant mobility. It was this mobility which was to bring Saxon England to the brink of total extinction.

The Great Army passed the winter of 866–7 in East Anglia and with the coming of spring set out on its first great campaign in England.

It seems obvious that the leaders of the Great Army had spent the winter months in gathering information from their unwilling hosts, for the Army made straight for Northumbria. Setting aside the story of Ragnar's death and the motive of revenge on the Northumbrians, it must be pointed out that Northumbria was in the throes of yet another of her civil wars, and was therefore eminently vulnerable. The Great Army was clearly led by shrewd and practical commanders who were not going to be trapped into any wasteful ventures in a hostile land. Northumbria, then, was on all counts the obvious target for the first campaign of the Great Army.

Speed was the keynote of this, as of later campaigns, which followed the same basic pattern: a swift drive deep into enemy territory and the seizure of a base from which to defy all comers. The army drove straight through Lincolnshire for the Humber estuary, wasting no time in general mayhem *en route*. It crossed the Humber and pushed on to York, took the city, and dug in. York had been one of the legionary fortresses in the days of Roman Britain and it remained a natural strong-point for centuries – the city's last ordeal against a besieging army was holding out for King Charles I during the Civil War. Once ensconced inside the old walls of York, the Great Army could await the reactions of the Northumbrians with equanimity.

The Wessex-orientated *Chronicle* is sniffish about the performance of the Northumbrians in this major crisis:

> And there was great civil strife going on in that people, and they had deposed their king Osbert and taken a king with no heredi-tary right, Ælla. And not until late in the year did they unite sufficiently to fight the raiding army; and nevertheless they collected a large army and attacked the enemy in York, and broke into the city; and some of them got inside, and an im-mense slaughter was made of the Northumbrians, some inside and some outside, and both kings were killed, and the survivors made peace with the enemy.

Here is a typically breathless and confused account of what was obviously a knock-down killing-match from which the North-umbrians emerged badly mauled. There is no way of knowing whether or not the 'Ælla' mentioned was the man who had reputedly thrown Ragnar Lothbrok into the snake-pit; if he had been, he would have been ten times luckier to have been killed in action than to have fallen alive into the hands of the Danes. Although there can be no doubt that the factious Northumbrians had themselves to blame for letting the Great Army march into York, the northern English certainly buried the hatchet and tried to set matters to rights. But their failure gave the Great Army its first victory over the English in a set-piece battle – and another secure base in which to winter.

The punishment dealt out to the Northumbrians in the battle of York was heavy enough for the Great Army to fear no more trouble from that quarter for the time being. In the following year, 868, it turned south to try accounts with Mercia. Again, the first objective of the Danes was a base, and they chose Nottingham. Unlike Northumbria, however, Mercia was a comparatively well-ordered kingdom, and King Burgred took full advantage of the current *entente* with Wessex to ask King Ethelred for help. Ethelred came himself at the head of an expeditionary force, together with his brother Alfred; and this was almost certainly the young Alfred's first taste of campaigning. After joining up with the Mercian host, the Wessex men marched against Nottingham and besieged the Danes there. This may have been a deliberate and eminently sensible attempt to starve the Great Army into submission, but it failed. Considering the later difficulties encountered by Alfred in keeping a strong army in the field, it may be that the Wessex men refused to stay on indefinite campaign in a foreign country and insisted on going home. Certainly the West Saxon force did not sit it out to the end; the siege was lifted. As the *Chronicle* has it: 'There occurred no serious battle there, and the Mercians made peace with the enemy.'

Just under eleven centuries later, Adolf Hitler was to sum up Nazi policy in German-occupied Russia with the words 'conquer – rule – exploit'; and this was a good enough summary of the programme of the Great Army when Ivar and Halfdan pulled back from their first foray into Mercia. After conquering the Northumbrian capital the year before, the Danish leaders had initiated their plan to keep southern Northumbria at least firmly under their thumb by setting up a puppet king of their own nomination: 'a certain Egbert, of English race', who, in the words of Roger of Wendover, 'acquired the kingdom under the Danish power and ruled it for six years'. It was natural for the Great Army to return to York from Nottingham and make certain that Egbert was doing as he had been told. There the Danish host remained for the whole of 869, the undisputed masters of the region.

The *Chronicle*'s entry for 870 suggests that Ivar and Halfdan had reason to regret the inactivity of the previous year. The entry is worth quoting in full: 'In this year the raiding army rode across Mercia into East Anglia, and took up winter quarters at Thetford.

And that winter King Edmund fought against them, and the Danes had the victory, and killed the king and conquered all the land.' Behind this bald recital it is possible to deduce what happened: that Egbert of Northumbria had been ordered to maintain normal relations with the neighbouring English powers, and that the Danish leaders had thus learned that Edmund of the East Angles was raising an army either for the defence of his own kingdom or to march against the Danes in York. Such news would explain another rapid march by the Army, retracing the path of the first campaign, across Lincolnshire, the establishment of the base at Thetford, and a decisive battle with Edmund's forces. Whether or not this was what actually happened, the 870 campaign gave the English a martyr whose name still lives today in the Suffolk town of Bury St Edmunds. The saint's day of the slain king was celebrated by the English on 20 November.

If the Great Army paused to set up another puppet government in East Anglia there is no record of it. Instead, the chronicles proceed pell-mell to the epic campaign of 871, when the Army swept south-west to the Thames, the Wessex–Mercia frontier. There they dug in at Reading, a royal residence at the time, and two Danish earls took a column across the river on the first invasion of the Wessex heartland. This proved costly, for once again the local defence system of Wessex proved its worth. Ealdorman Æthelwulf massed his forces and tackled the Danes at Englefield. He won a total victory, and one of the Danish earls was killed in the fight. Meanwhile Ethelred and Alfred were raising the full muster of Wessex and preparing to move against the main body of the Great Army. Æthelwulf joined the king's army with the victors of Englefield and the men of Wessex advanced to tackle the Great Army head-on.

Asser tells us that the Danes had fortified their position at Reading with a rampart, and one's mind immediately leaps to the massive walls of the circular viking fortress at Trelleborg in Denmark. It is more likely, however, that the Great Army prepared for battle in the open field; the phraseology of the *Chronicle* suggests another day-long pounding-match between the two armies, with the Danes getting the better of it. Heartened by their victory, the Great Army pushed into Berkshire, along the chalk ridge of Ashdown. But it soon found that Ethelred's army was still in the field and on its heels. Battle was inevitable, and after four days of manœuvre the Great Army formed up and prepared to wrestle a second fall with the West Saxon host.

If Shakespeare had ever produced one of his historical 'epics' on Alfred, he would certainly have plundered with gusto from Asser's famous account of the battle of Ashdown. According to the latter, both sides were drawn up in battle array and the first clash of arms was imminent. Ethelred, however, was hearing Mass in his tent and refused to be hurried or to abbreviate his devotions, whereupon Alfred led his division 'like a wild boar' against the Danish line and precipitated the battle, with Ethelred's men pitching in as soon as the king had completed his duty to God. It was literally an uphill fight all the way for the West Saxons, for the Danes had been canny in holding the high ground; the fighting raged around a thorn tree in the heart of the Danish line. The battle went on until night, by which time the two Danish divisions had been driven from their positions. Ashdown was one of the most celebrated battles of the Danish wars, and it was a total victory for Ethelred and Alfred.

Englefield, Reading, and Ashdown were the three hardest fights which the Great Army had had since its landing in East Anglia five years before – but they were only the beginning of the 871 campaign. As the Great Army pulled slowly back to the east, Ethelred and Alfred followed it up; and two weeks after Ashdown another head-on battle was fought at Basing, the victory going to the Great Army. Ethelred and Alfred, however, had by no means given up the struggle and two months later yet another battle was fought at a place which the *Chronicle* calls *Meretun*. It was another inconclusive killing-match with the Danes still holding their ground at the end of the day; losses on both sides were heavy, and the *Chronicle* records the death of another fighting English bishop, Heahmund of Sherborne.

Anyone tracing the line of march of the Great Army comes back to the tantalizing enigma of its original strength and how the Danes coped with their running tally of losses. By the time of the fight at *Meretun*, these losses must have been becoming alarming; and the *Chronicle* provides the maddeningly vague statement that 'after this battle a great summer army came to Reading'. Where from? The Great Army can hardly have left sufficient garrisons in its wake to make up such an imposing relief force. This 'great summer army' was more likely made up of fresh reinforcements from home – but once again there is no definite proof or naming of numbers or leaders. One conclusion seems safe enough: it gave the Great Army a much-needed blood transfusion.

On the West Saxon 'side of the hill', Alfred's hour had come. Ethelred died shortly after Easter and the obvious successor was the tough fighting prince who had made his name at Ashdown. A month after assuming the kingship, he was in action again 'with a small force' at Wilton, a battle which went the same way as the one at *Meretun*. Despite initial successes, the West Saxon forces could not break the Great Army's shield-wall and were forced to withdraw. It was the last large-scale fight of the 871 campaign, although sporadic fighting continued until the end of the year. According to the *Chronicle*, 'during that year nine general engagements were fought against the Danish army in the kingdom south of the Thames, besides the expeditions which the king's brother Alfred and [single] ealdormen and king's thegns often rode on, which were not counted. And that year nine (Danish) earls were killed and one king. And the West Saxons made peace with the enemy that year.'

Alfred's decision to buy time was certainly good news for his kingdom, which had won encouraging battle honours in the first round of its fight for survival but had had to pay heavily for them. But it was another definite reflection on the disunity of Saxon England. Only a large-scale coalition army could have had a hope of defeating the Great Army so heavily that it could be induced to quit England. Conversely, the Great Army thrived on the piecemeal opposition which the English put up. When the East Anglians had come to terms with the Danes in 866, they left the enemy free to attack Northumbria. And in precisely the same fashion, Alfred's truce with the Danes at the end of 871 left them free to turn on Mercia.

The Great Army seems to have spent the winter of 871–2 in its lair at Reading. In the following year it moved down the Thames to the Mercian town of London and took up new quarters there. The Danes had no trouble in getting the local Mercians to come to terms with them – but almost at once they had to set off on another of their epic marches. Ominous news had come from Northumbria.

After long decades of civil war the Northumbrians had become well acquainted with the making and unmaking of kings; and after the Great Army headed south in 870 it was hardly surprising that they should turn against the puppet Egbert whom the Danes had foisted upon them. And in 872, when the Great Army was in London, it happened. An insurrection drove out 'King' Egbert from York. He was not alone, and his companion in exile shows how shrewd the Danish leaders really were. They had recognized the hand-in-glove relationship between Church and king in the government of Saxon England, and had accordingly maintained Archbishop Wulfhere of York in his see to help Egbert in governing the Northumbrians as the Danes wished. Clearly Wulfhere was tarred with the same brush as Egbert – a quisling – in the eyes of the insurgents, and was driven out of York as well. Wulfhere and Egbert headed south as refugees. They arrived at the court of Burgred of Mercia 'and were honourably received by him'.

Clearly Burgred, to use another twentieth-century term, was an 'appeaser' as far as the Great Army was concerned. Twenty years before, he had been willing enough to ask Æthelwulf of Wessex for help in conquering the Welsh. But the menace of the Great Army was a very different matter, and too much for him. He agreed to terms which gave the Army free passage across Mercian territory to Northumbria, where the Danes spent what was clearly an unsuccessful year in trying to smash the rebellion. The Northumbrian leader was called Ricsige; he was accepted as king by the Northumbrians in 873, in which year the ex-king Egbert died. It is faintly possible that Egbert's death was engineered by Burgred in a feeble attempt to assert himself, and that the Danish leaders thereupon decided to make an end of Mercia as an independent power. This makes sense, for they had seen two formerly acquiescent Saxon kingdoms – East Anglia and Northumbria – resume hostilities as soon as the Great Army was engaged elsewhere. And it certainly explains what followed.

After its campaign in Northumbria in 873, the Great Army swung south before the northern rebels were subdued, and took up winter quarters at Torksey, in Lincolnshire – Mercian territory. This was done, we are told, with Burgred's formal agreement. But the 874 campaign ended Burgred's hopes of temporizing with the Danes once and for all:

In this year the army went from Lindsey to Repton and took up winter quarters there, and drove King Burgred across the sea,

after he had held the kingdom for 22 years. And they conquered
all that land. And he went to Rome and settled there; and his
body is buried in the church of St Mary in the English
quarter. And the same year they gave the kingdom of the
Mercians to be held by Ceolwulf, a foolish king's thegn; and he
swore oaths to them and gave hostages, that it should be ready
for them on whatever day they wished to have it, and he would
be ready, himself and all who would follow him, at the enemy's
service.

Thus did the *Chronicle* write the terse epitaph of Saxon Mercia,
once the leading power in the island.

Despite the contemptuous phraseology of the *Chronicle* with
regard to the 'foolish king's thegn' who sold himself to the Danes
for a crown, it is a fact that the Danish leaders were still intending
to rule their English conquests via the existing social machinery,
Church and king – although this had already proved a failure as far
as Northumbria was concerned. Whatever looting may have gone
on during the conquest of Mercia, the ecclesiastical framework
of the kingdom, far from being destroyed, was accepted as
indispensable. We have a charter issued by Ceolwulf in the year
875, a completely typical Saxon charter, which certainly does not
suggest that the Mercians under Ceolwulf were dancing as the
Danes piped. The transaction – an agreement to free the diocese
of Worcester from the expense of feeding the king's horses – was
witnessed by Ceolwulf, the bishops of Lichfield, Worcester, and
Hereford, and two ealdormen. It could be argued that this was a
trivial affair, the only sort of thing which the Danes permitted
their new puppet to handle; but somehow it does not ring true, if
one is only thinking of a rubber-stamp government which was
only tolerated so long as it extracted the last drop of military potential from the conquered kingdom for the benefit of its new
masters. Rather than condemning Ceolwulf and his bishops as a
crew of self-interested traitors, we can even regard them as
accepting office to save their people from worse miseries – much
as Marshal Pétain did in the defeated France of 1940.

With the subjugation of Mercia, the Great Army was master
of Saxon England from the Thames to the Humber, from the
East Anglian coast to the Bristol Channel. Wessex and Northumbria were hopelessly separated from each other, and the Danes

c

had clearly received more reinforcements from home – although there is no concrete proof of this – for now they felt confident enough to take the momentous step of dividing the Great Army in order to finish off the two surviving Saxon kingdoms. Halfdan and his division marched north to crush Northumbria; Guthrum, Oscetel, and Anwend headed east into East Anglia, where their division based itself on Cambridge for the whole of 875.

That year saw the elimination of Northumbria by Halfdan in a campaign which was as decisive as that against Mercia had been the year before. The Danes made a clean sweep of the wide territories between Humber and Tyne, and made their winter quarters for 875–6 on the latter river. King Ricsige and his loyalist adherents obviously fought with as much determination as had Ethelred and Alfred, but were pushed back north of the Tyne into the ancient sub-kingdom of Bernicia, independent of old, the northernmost province of Saxon Northumbria. Halfdan's men, we are told, 'often ravaged among the Picts and Strathclyde Britons' in 875, which means that they were ranging far north of the Tweed. But in the main the Danes were content with the Tyne as the northernmost 'frontier' of conquered Northumbria. Between Tyne and Tweed the dispossessed heirs of Northumbria's proud traditions survived in what became known as 'English' Northumbria – a ragged fragment, a lost province. Although he was using the words to describe the later misfortunes of Wessex, Winston Churchill's comment is no less applicable to the fate of Saxon Northumbria: 'Low were the fortunes of the once ruthless English. Pent in their mountains, the lineal descendants of the Ancient Britons, slatternly, forlorn, but unconquered, may well have grinned.'

The seal of triumph was set on the Danish conquest of Northumbria in the following year. The *Chronicle* describes it in a laconic sentence which marks one of the most important landmarks in English history: 'And that year Healfdene* shared out the land of the Northumbrians, and they proceeded to plough and support themselves.' It was not, after all, to be a cut-and-dried case of 'conquer – rule – exploit'. The patient process of assimilation had already set to work on the northern wing of the Great Army; while in the south, the supreme ordeal of Wessex was at hand.

* Halfdan.

*Chapter 4*

'I am that oft-defeated King
    Whose failure fills the land.
Who fled before the Danes of old,
Who chaffered with the Danes for gold,
Who now upon the Wessex wold
    Hardly has feet to stand.

'But out of the mouth of the Mother of God
    I have seen the truth like fire.
This – that the sky grows darker yet
    And the sea rises higher.'


In Wessex in the forest,
    In the breaking of the spears,
We set a sign on Guthrum
    To blaze a thousand years. . . .

Far out to the winding river
    The blood ran down for days,
When we put the cross on Guthrum
    In the parting of the ways.

    G. K. Chesterton, *The Ballad of the White Horse.*

# Wessex survives

In the summer of 875, while Danish war-parties were roaming far beyond the northern boundaries of Northumbria at the expense of the 'Picts and the Strathclyde Britons', a sea-borne viking force sailed on a harrying expedition against the coast of Wessex. It was not an invasion fleet – it was more of a naval fighting patrol, sent to sound out the sea-borne defences of the last English kingdom which dared to hold out against the might and terror of the Great Army. And it got the information it wanted the hard way. 'And that summer,' says the *Chronicle*, 'King Alfred went out to sea with a naval force, and fought against the crews of seven ships, and captured one ship and put the rest to flight.'

Being able to beat the Danes on land was only one of Alfred's subsequent claims to fame, and one of the others has gained him the title of 'the father of the English navy'. But Alfred was clearly not the first English ruler to grasp the fact that England's true outer line of defence was the ability to destroy enemies before they so much as touched English soil. Such an argument does less than justice to Alfred's predecessors. As we know, Alfred's eldest brother, Athelstan, had won the first sea-fight against the vikings back in 851, and he could hardly have done that by taking out his soldiers in a hastily requisitioned fleet of fishing-smacks. We can only deduce the obvious fact: that Wessex, whose southern frontier was all coastline, had always had some form of coastal defence force, and that this was gradually built up in the ninth century, first under Egbert, then under Æthelwulf and Athelstan, and finally under Alfred.

The fact remains, however, that taken as a whole the defensive capacity of Wessex was in theory hopelessly inadequate to cope with the disciplined menace of the Great Army, and that properly speaking Alfred should not have stood a chance of saving his kingdom. He not only did this, and left it with a powerful fleet and a rota-based army capable of waging protracted campaigns, but he had actually taken the initiative from the Danes by the time he died in 900. Nearly all of Alfred's military strengthening of Wessex, however, took place in the last ten years of his great reign, and little or none of it had even been started in the terrible years of 876–8, when Wessex, the last hope of the English, tottered on the verge of defeat and extinction.

Before telling this story, therefore, we must examine the structure of the West Saxon kingdom at the time of Alfred's accession, the strengths on which he could rely, and the weaknesses which formed the biggest dangers.

At the top of the social pyramid stood the king, the reigning representative of the ruling line which the West Saxons were proud to trace back to Cerdic, the Saxon adventurer who had founded the kingdom. Next to the king himself were all those who claimed a similar ancestry and enjoyed a unique status: the athelings, princes of the blood, as we would say. There was always a sufficiently plentiful number of athelings to guarantee the continuity of the ruling line – but conversely this meant that there was always the threat of an atheling making a bid for the throne and getting away with it. In kingdoms like Northumbria, an undisputed succession had become the exception rather than the rule, as we have seen. Alfred was luckier: as long as the Great Army remained the paramount threat to Wessex, the fear of the Danes cancelled out the possibility of civil strife in Wessex. The leading aristocracy of the realm, the athelings, had special privileges and responsibilities which included military service and command in the field.

Next in precedence to the athelings came the ealdormen, the dignitaries through which the king put his decrees into practice in the shires. The word 'shires' is something of an anachronism when speaking of Alfred's Wessex, for the modern county boundaries lay far in the future. This the *Chronicle* makes quite clear by its many references to 'Ealdorman X with the people of so-and-so', in which the regional identification varies considerably. In some cases a recognizable county-name is used; in others, a neighbourhood – as in the reference to 'Ealdorman Æthelmund' from 'the province of the *Hwicce*' in the annal for 802. Later, when Alfred was centring the defence of Wessex on fortified towns or *burhs*, town names begin to appear as key responsibilities for the ealdormen – as in 886, when Alfred entrusted the defence of London to Ealdorman Ethelred of Mercia. The ealdormen were royal viceroys. Their office was hereditary as likely as not. Their signatures were required, along with those of the local bishops, to witness royal charters. And it was the ealdorman who called out the *fyrd*, the local shire levy, for military service, and commanded the resulting turn-out on campaign. The ealdormen, in short, were vital cogs in the day-to-day running of the realm, and enjoyed high social status. The Danes had a word of their own for their equivalent of the Saxon ealdormen: *jarls*, or earls. They were the ruling nobility of Saxon England and vital to its life in peace or war. Athelings, ealdormen, archbishops, and bishops, together formed the king's council, *witanagemot* or *witan*, which convened to approve and witness new laws and charters and, perhaps most important of all, to elect a new king on the death of the reigning monarch. The royal line and its heirs formed the candidates but the crown was not passed down by primogeniture. Alfred succeeded his elder brother Ethelred in 871, not Ethelred's son Æthelwold. The approval of the Witan guaranteed the formal accession of the new king.

Further down the social ladder came the dividing-line between *eorlas* – men entitled to noble rank – and *ceorlas*, men who were not. This was a porous barrier, and the keys to rapid preferment were individual prosperity and military service. The *thegn* or thane was originally a companion in arms – king's thane or ealdorman's thane – and was the true ancestor of the medieval landed knight. He might by good service become an *eorl*, 'then was he afterwards entitled to an earl's rights'. The same applied to the *ceorl*, the independent landed householder. Yeoman farmers, *ceorls* had to turn out and serve in the *fyrd* when required by their lords; in return they had their rights of property guaranteed by law. 'And if a *ceorl* prospered, that he possessed fully five hides of land of his own, a bell and a castle-gate, a seat and special office in the king's hall, then was he thenceforth entitled to the rights of a thegn.' Similar social preferment was open to traders: 'And if a trader prospered, that he crossed thrice the open sea at his own expense, he was then afterwards entitled to the rights of a thegn.'

Below the *ceorl*, the degrees of dependence on a lord led down through a welter of fine distinctions to the totally dependent *gebur*, whose life was completely dominated by labour-services to his superiors. As the thane was the forbear of the later medieval landed knight, so the *gebur* became the later medieval villein: a bondman. In practical terms there was little to set the *gebur* apart from the slave, but the legal distinction from slavery was sharp and clear. An emancipated slave could start in at the bottom of the social ladder, but he, too, could only work his way up it by an official remission of bondage by his lord.

The defence of the realm was, as we have seen, basically a local affair. If enemies attacked Devon, for example, the ealdorman of Devon would call out the *fyrd* and march out to battle. If the king happened to be in that part of the country, he would take the field with the host, perhaps calling in the *fyrd* of the neighbouring shires if there were time. Before Alfred, the results of battles with the viking raiders showed that the fighting value of these motley 'instant armies' was surprisingly high, with the chances of victory or defeat being at least half and half. The lowliest troops turned out by the *fyrd* naturally had the lowest fighting value. They would be spearmen, with billhooks and axes as side-arms for close-quarter work. The king's and ealdorman's thanes were the best-armed, hard core of the host, with the richest boasting armour and finely built swords and battle-axes. The quality of such arms depended on the owner's wealth. One of the oldest attributes of the king was his munificence as 'ying-giver' and rewarder of good service by his thanes with gifts of weapons or armour.

But although the *fyrd* was no mere Home Guard, and could certainly put up a good performance even when matched with the Great Army of the Danes, its fundamental trouble was that it was nothing more than an emergency expedient. Neither ealdorman nor king could keep it in the field indefinitely, nor lead it far beyond the boundary of the shire of its origin, without its numbers melting away as men simply decided that they had done their share and went home to get on with the farming. As suggested in the previous chapter, this was probably why the coalition host of Wessex and Mercia let the Great Army off the hook while the Danes were besieged in Nottingham in 868. And this inability to have a battle-worthy army constantly at hand resulted in the near-destruction of Wessex when the Great Army invaded in 876.

This was the southern division of the Army, commanded by the three kings, Guthrum, Oscetel, and Anwend, which had spent the previous year in Cambridge while Halfdan and the northern division smashed Northumbria. Guthrum was the dominant member of this royal triumvirate, which now marched south bent on the destruction of Wessex. However, this was a new chapter in the story of the Great Army, for Guthrum and his colleagues were resolved to augment their prowess on the battlefield with diplomatic treachery.

A cynic, savouring the boundless power of propaganda, would be hard put to it to beat the *Chronicle*'s opening sentence for the events of the year 876: 'In this year the enemy army slipped past the army of the West Saxons into Wareham.' For sheer nerve, this statement makes one think of the immortal British press communiqué of December 1941, when the British were being thrown out of Malaya by the Japanese: 'Our forces successfully disengaged from the enemy.' This was a superb march that totally outwitted Alfred and revealed the flimsiness of the West Saxon defences. From Cambridge to Wareham today is over 140 miles as the crow flies, and on foot in 876 it would have been nearer to 250. Assuming that Guthrum's Danes took the best possible route, they obviously gained a total surprise over the watchers on the West Saxon frontier along the Thames. Let us assume that the Army took the natural – indeed, the prehistoric – route along the uplands: south-west along the Icknield Way and the crest of the Chilterns to the Goring Gap on the Thames, west along the Berkshire Downs to Avebury; south south-west across Salisbury Plain to Wareham in southern Dorsetshire. No Danish forces had ever taken this route, and Guthrum must have been helped by inside information – either from the cowed East Angles or from terrified locals encountered *en route*. Certainly the Danes met with no opposition worthy of record from the English point of view. Taking the most charitable attitude, and assuming that the *Chronicle*'s reference to 'the army of the West Saxons' is not total fabrication, we must accept that, when it came to the arts of manœuvre, Alfred had certainly met his match for this year at least. By the time Guthrum's forces dug in at Wareham it was far too late for the West Saxons to have a chance of intercepting their invaders in open country. The Danes certainly had time to select the site for their new lair: Asser says that it was the site of an

English nunnery, between the Frome and Tarrant rivers, on an easily defensible peninsula.

Five years before, Alfred had agreed a truce with the Army after a non-stop year of fighting in which the West Saxon forces had given as good as they got. Now, with the enemy army safely ensconced in the heart of Wessex, Alfred again sought for terms, which alone is proof that there was nothing else for him to do. Conversely, it must be pointed out that this was the first time that the Danes had ever agreed a truce and condescended to bind themselves by oath to observe it. 'And they gave him hostages, who were the most important men next to their king in the army, and swore oaths to him on the holy ring – a thing which they would not do before for any nation – that they would speedily leave his kingdom.' For the first time, diplomacy became a vital factor in the Danish wars. Alfred needed time; Guthrum obviously knew it and wanted to get him off guard. These were unprecedented negotiations. The scribes of the *Chronicle* drew obvious satisfaction from the fact that this was the first time that the Danes had pledged themselves on their holy ring. But it was also the first time that a king of Wessex had bought time from the 'heathen'. Both sides needed this treaty; neither side had any intention of regarding it as anything more than a purchaser of time.

This was proved to the hilt by the events of 877. Guthrum's army broke camp at Wareham, but it did not quit Wessex. Instead it made another surprise march, pushing even further away from its base and flinging itself into the old city of Exeter. The six texts of the *Chronicle* are contradictory as to what happened: two of them omit the statement that a viking fleet accompanied the progress of the Danish army, and that Alfred's army could not overtake the Army before it had ensconced itself in Exeter, where it 'could not be reached'. It is certain that this time Alfred had a mounted army and wasted no time in putting Exeter under siege. This is an interesting moment in the story, for this was the second time that Alfred had been in such a position. The first had been in 868, when he and his brother King Ethelred had joined the Mercians in blockading Nottingham. Since that siege was raised, Alfred must have had many a bitter moment in which to reflect on the wasted opportunity of Nottingham. Certainly he never forgot a lesson; and it is only fair to deduce that his army before Exeter was melting away from desertions. After all, from

Wareham in Dorsetshire, as the *Chronicle* says, Alfred 'rode after the mounted army with the English army as far as Exeter' – by the standards of the day a considerable imposition on the *fyrdmen* of Dorset, especially when they found themselves expected to sit down in front of Exeter for a time-wasting siege.

Once again, Alfred came to terms with Guthrum for the evacuation of West Saxon territory by the Danes. Oaths and hostages were again exchanged, and this time the Danes seemed to adhere to their part of the bargain. They 'went away into Mercia and shared out some of it, and gave some to Ceolwulf'. And the argument that Alfred's main trouble at the time was the recalcitrance of the *fyrd* is backed up by the unusually precise timing provided by the *Chronicle*: the truce had been agreed by harvest-time (7 August), which must have delighted Alfred's soldiers as they headed home.

It was now over eleven years since the Great Army had first landed in East Anglia, and what happened next suggests that the English had at last fallen into the trap of believing that their mortal enemy only had one way of fighting: campaigning in the summer, and holing up in a fortified lair for the winter. Guthrum and his army left Exeter in early August 877. Five months passed; and then, 'in midwinter after twelfth night the enemy army came stealthily to Chippenham, and occupied the land of the West Saxons and settled there, and drove a great part of the people across the sea, and conquered most of the others; and the people submitted to them, except King Alfred'. This was something totally new. It shows what a remarkable war-leader Guthrum was, to wage the first ever Danish winter campaign on English soil with such an incredible reward. Effectively, the land of Wessex had hibernated for the winter. Certainly its army had been long dispersed. Even if the watch on the frontiers had been maintained after the August peace, it had obviously lapsed. But why did the Danes strike at Chippenham? Asser gives a clue which demands much respect: it was 'a royal residence'. It must have been an attempt to eliminate Alfred and his councillors at a stroke. Although it failed, and Alfred escaped, 'he journeyed in difficulties through the woods and fen-fastnesses with a small force'. This winter descent of the Danes, while their West Saxon foes were completely off-guard, succeeded where the Great Army's previous attacks had been repulsed. Wessex, surprised, confused, and appalled, lay at the mercy of the Great Army, with her king a vanished fugitive.

In that dreadful winter of 877–8, the fortunes of the English hit rock-bottom as the news spread from Chippenham that Guthrum was the new master of Wessex. King Alfred had vanished; most believed him dead. He had in fact fled south-east into the heart of Somerset and set up a guerilla base on the Isle of Athelney (now drained and reclaimed); 'and he and that section of the people of Somerset which was nearest to it proceeded to fight from that stronghold against the enemy'. The English chronicler Æthelweard says that he had no helpers save the members of his own household. In the beginning this was almost certainly the case, but very soon he would have been relying on the ealdorman of Somerset, as the wonderful news spread out from Athelney that the king was still alive and fighting.

These months as a fugitive, with his whereabouts unknown to the majority of his subjects, were a fertile seed-bed for the legends by which Alfred is best remembered; how he was set to watching the baking bread of a woman who gave him shelter, allowed it to burn, and was reviled for a stupid lout by his hostess; how he disguised himself, ventured into the Danish camp, and played the harp before Guthrum. But it is certain that beyond the immediate crisis Alfred sensed that the destruction of the Danes had changed all England for ever, and that the old order could never be restored. After all, Chesterton, in his superb poem *The Ballad of the White Horse*, put the position of the English in a nutshell when he wrote:

'There was not English armour left,
    Nor any English thing,
When Alfred came to Athelney
    To be an English king. . . .

In the island in the river
    He was broken to his knee:
And he read, writ with an iron pen,
That God had wearied of Wessex men
And given their country, field and fen,
    To the devils of the sea.'

Alfred's true strength, his resilience, was never tested more than during his months on Athelney. Nor were his patience and powers of judgment. He had had plenty of examples of how much the Danes could achieve if they were given time; only a swift counter-blow when they were least expecting it could break their hold on Wessex now – but he dare not launch it prematurely. He had no chance of raising the full muster of Wessex, but decided to see what could be done with the *fyrds* of Somerset, Wiltshire, and western Hampshire. His messengers headed east and set the fur-tive, initial stages of mobilization in progress; and finally, 'in the seventh week after Easter he rode to "Egbert's stone" east of Selwood' to meet his people and take command of the host for what he knew must be the decisive campaign.

'Egbert's stone' cannot be located precisely, but it must have been in the neighbourhood of Frome. It is not difficult to imagine the hysterical delight of the men of Wessex when they saw their king again, but Alfred gave them little time for rejoicing. Within twenty-four hours he was leading his army towards the northern fringe of Salisbury Plain, where Guthrum's army had paused on what was presumably the first leg of a triumphal march through Wessex. And at *Ethandune* – Edington – the armies came to grips.

There is always something larger than life about a battle which the underdog wins against all odds. Obviously Alfred had the advantage of surprise, but just as obviously the Wessex men had gained a total moral superiority over their enemies. About the battle itself the *Chronicle* says simply that Alfred 'fought against the whole army and put it to flight'. This was not the first battle which had gone against a viking force, or even against the Great Army; but the events which followed the West Saxon victory at Edington were unprecedented.

And then the enemy gave him preliminary hostages and great oaths that they would leave his kingdom, and promised also that their king should receive baptism, and they kept their promise. Three weeks later King Guthrum with 30 of the men who were the most important in the army came [to him] at Aller, which is near Athelney, and the king stood sponsor to him at his baptism there; and the unbinding of the chrism* took place at Wedmore. And he was twelve days with the king, and he honoured him and his companions greatly with gifts.

* The symbolic white cloth worn round the head for eight days after baptism.

Why Guthrum consented to this extraordinary step we can only imagine: Alfred's motives are easy to reconstruct. Almost certainly the defeat at Edington was followed by intense high-level discussions between Guthrum and his earls, which resulted in the decision to come to formal terms with Alfred and abandon the assault on Wessex. Guthrum may have been facing growing unrest that his branch of the Great Army was still soldiering on in the field while Halfdan's followers were happily settling Northumbria. A peace with the Christians of the south would leave them free to consolidate their hold on East Anglia and southern Mercia.

The following year, 879, was clearly a period of great tension, with Alfred keeping as many of his forces as he could in the field in case Guthrum broke his word again. The Danish army pulled back to the north and spent the year at Cirencester in the Cotswolds. Alfred was still in a perilous position, for in 879 a viking fleet swept up the Thames and built a camp at Fulham. This was clearly a terrifying new situation, for at first sight there was nothing to suggest that the two viking forces would not combine against Wessex, and certainly no reason to believe that the new viking fleet's arrival was anything else but a deliberate reinforcement. Such a frightening prospect was in fact dispelled within twelve months. Alfred's forces headed for London, ready for a showdown against the new invaders; but the viking army at Fulham broke camp and sailed for France. In the meantime Guthrum led his own army back into East Anglia and began the formal Danish settlement of that kingdom.

Wessex had been spared another fight for survival immediately after the momentous year of Athelney and Edington, but Alfred knew that there was no cause for any relaxation of vigilance. This is proved by a remarkable change in the information provided by the *Chronicle* for the years 880–5, when Alfred was beginning the reconstruction of Wessex. The most obvious fact is the wealth of information which the English clearly had on the movements of the Danish army on the Continent, which were traced in detail as it roamed its way through Flanders, using the river-lines of the Meuse, the Scheldt, and the Somme. For the first time in their history, here were the English keeping a close watch on a potential menace on the far side of the English Channel. This was certainly Alfred's work. We know that he was desperately adding to the West Saxon navy, for in 882 the *Chronicle* records:

And the same year King Alfred went out with ships to sea and fought against four crews of Danish men, and captured two of the ships – and the men were killed who were on them [presumably after capture] – and two crews surrendered to him. And they had great losses in killed or wounded before they surrendered.

However, it was simply impossible for Alfred to concentrate on building up an impregnable coast defence force and Channel fleet to intercept all future mass descents from across the Channel. He was faced with a threat on two fronts, for north of the line of the Thames the Danes in Mercia and East Anglia, despite the rapidity of their settlement, still posed an equal danger. Alfred's potential military dilemma became reality in 885. The Danish army on the Continent split, and one half returned to Kent, pushing up the Medway river and besieging Rochester. Another facet of Alfred's defence strategy paid dividends in the crisis, for 'the English defended the city until King Alfred came up with his army'. Together with the maintenance of a strong fleet, the fortification of the key English towns was another cardinal factor in Alfred's fight for survival. A fortified *burh* or town whose garrison could stand a siege could deprive the enemy army of mobility, pinning it down until the main English field army could close with it. At Rochester in 885 these tactics won the English victory on land: 'Then the enemy went to their ships and abandoned their fortification, and they were deprived of their horses there, and immediately that same summer they went back across the sea.'

Alfred followed up his success at Rochester with a naval sweep along the East Anglian coast which met with mixed fortunes. He fought a furious battle off the mouth of the Stour with sixteen viking ships, 'and seized all the ships and killed the men'. But 'when they turned homeward with the booty, they met a large naval force of vikings and fought against them on the same day, and the Danes had the victory'. Here was another painful lesson for Alfred: he had forgotten that the Great Army had originally been landed in East Anglia by a powerful fleet, and now he found, the hard way, that the vikings were adept at keeping their warships cocooned on land but preserving them in a state of instant readiness. In addition to these dramatic events at sea, he also had to take notice of repeated violations of the peace treaty on the part of Guthrum's Danes across the lower Thames.

In the following year, therefore, Alfred made a move which was momentous for the history of the English. Determined to prevent the sporadic raiding on the lower Thames from escalating into full-blown trouble, he took London and fortified it. The effect was tremendous. London had never been a West Saxon town – it had marked the south-eastern limit of Mercian power – and it had never been a capital town in the political sense of the word. But now Alfred had made of London a truly national symbol of defiance and aggression, of the determination of the English to hold all they had and recover all they could.

Alfred's capture of London in 886 heightened his already matchless reputation as the leader of English resistance to the Danes, but it went much further than that. The white-hot danger posed by the heathen invaders from across the sea had melted away the traditional loyalties to the old kingdoms of the Heptarchy. One of the most important sentences in the *Chronicle* is also the simplest: 'That same year King Alfred occupied London; and all the English people that were not under subjection to the Danes submitted to him.' The capture of London made him nothing less than the first king of *England*. There were no other English contenders for the honour.

This was proved by the loyalty and generosity to the English cause of a new character to appear on the scene: Ethelred of Mercia. Ceolwulf 'the foolish king's thegn', whom the Danes had sought to make their puppet in Mercia, had faded from the scene by 880; and the Mercians, cheered by the splendid example of their southern neighbours in Wessex, began to fight back. Their leader, Ethelred, took the title of 'ealdorman of Mercia'. He never pretended to the kingship but threw himself into the struggle as a loyal ally and subject of Alfred; and one of the first tasks which Alfred entrusted to his new viceroy north of the Thames was the defence of London.

Alfred's reassertion of West Saxon military power on the lower Thames was followed by another act which had never occurred before in the viking wars: a formal treaty delineating a frontier between English and Dane. But the treaty went beyond the mere issue of the frontier. Its terms accepted that for better or worse a new order had come into being in England, and that the future rights of the new Danish population and of the surviving English both needed definition and mutual guarantee:

PROLOGUE. This is the peace which King Alfred and King Guthrum and the councillors of all the English race and all the people which is in East Anglia have all agreed on and confirmed with oaths, for themselves and for their subjects, both for the living and those yet unborn, who care to have God's grace or ours.

1 First concerning our boundaries: up the Thames, and then up the Lea, and along the Lea to its source, then in a straight line to Bedford, then up the Ouse to the Watling Street.

2 This is next, if a man is slain, all of us estimate Englishman and Dane at the same amount, at eight half-marks of refined gold, except the *ceorl* who occupies rented land, and their [the Danes'] freedmen; these also are estimated at the same amount, both at 200 shillings.

3 And if anyone accuses a king's thegn of manslaughter, if he dares to clear himself by oath, he is to do it with 12 king's thegns; if anyone accuses a man who is less powerful than a king's thegn, he is to clear himself with 12 of his equals and with one king's thegn – and so in every suit which involves more than four mancuses – and if he dare not [clear himself], he is to pay three-fold compensation, according as it is valued.

4 And that each man is to know his warrantor at [the purchase of] men or horses or oxen.

5 And we all agreed on the day when the oaths were sworn, that no slaves nor freemen might go without permission into the army of the Danes, any more than any of theirs to us. But if it happens that from necessity any one of them wishes to have traffic with us, or we with them, for cattle or goods, it is to be permitted on condition that hostages shall be given as a pledge of peace and as evidence so that one may know no fraud is intended.

The treaty with Guthrum ranks as one of Alfred's most important long-term achievements, in that it was the first attempt to agree on the basics of day-to-day co-existence between the two races. In the short term it gave Alfred five invaluable years in which he did not have to watch his northern frontier. King Guthrum died in 890 and the treaty was honoured by his successor or successors, whoever they may have been. In the years 886–91, meanwhile, Alfred's 'intelligence men' continued to keep a watchful eye on the movements of the viking army across the Channel. This vigilance was well worth the effort. In 892, having plundered the Seine valley bare, the army massed at Boulogne with its ships, then swept across the Channel, 250 vessels strong, and descended on Kent. They rowed up the Lympne estuary until they reached the eastern end of the natural barrier of the forest of the Weald and dug in there. Clearly Alfred had already marked this down as a crucial sector, for the *Chronicle* makes special mention of the fact that the viking host stormed an unfinished fortress: 'Inside that fortification there were a few peasants, and it was only half made.' The Danes had had the luck to catch one of Alfred's new *burhs* before its completion, and they made full use of the fact. But apart from the Danish army down near Lympne, Alfred was faced with a pincer-movement, for almost immediately 'Hæsten came with 80 ships up the Thames estuary and made himself a fortress at Milton, and the other army made one at Appledore.' As at the time of Guthrum's invasion in 876, Alfred was faced with the *fait accompli* of enemy forces dug in on his territory, and waiting for him.

Alfred's handling of the situation, however, showed just how much had changed since Guthrum ran rings round the West Saxon army in 876–7. Alfred, having raised his army, positioned it midway between the two Danish bases 'so that he could reach either army, if they chose to come into the open country'. He then prepared to sit it out, and by now he was prepared for a long campaign, having 'divided his army into two, so that always half its men were at home, half on service, apart from the men who guarded the boroughs'. Weeks of sparring ensued, with Danish war-parties sounding out the strength of Alfred's position and the defences of the *burhs*.

It is clear that, for all his control of the 'interior lines', Alfred was not able to prevent the Danes from breaking out of their twin bases in Kent. 'Then they captured much booty, and wished to carry it north across the Thames into Essex, to meet the ships.' This time, however, Alfred had not put all his eggs in one basket. While he had raced east to contain the Danes in Kent, his son and heir, the atheling Edward, had been raising a second English army, which now intercepted the Danish host at Farnham. This was Edward's first recorded battle, and a smashing victory. As the Danes retreated from Farnham they left their spoils to the English. Edward's education by his father had obviously been thorough, for he gave his beaten enemy no respite. His army followed on the heels of the Danes and penned them on an island in the River Colne until Alfred came up with his force and took over the siege from Edward's men.

These beaten survivors from the Danish army which had been the terror of Western Europe for the last twelve years were now saved from capitulation by their brethren in East Anglia and Northumbria. A viking fleet of over a hundred ships swept down the east coast, rounded the North Foreland, and headed down the Channel to make landfall at the other end of Wessex, in Devon. One division of this fleet rounded the toe of Cornwall and landed on the north coast of Devon; the other laid siege to Exeter. The scope of Alfred's military worries could not have been widened further: they now stretched from Devon to the lower Thames. Once again, it was impossible for the English to bring their main strength to bear at any one point.

Alfred decided to go west and tackle the force at Exeter, leaving Ethelred and Edward to contend with Hæsten, who had rallied the eastern Danes from a new fortified base at Benfleet on the Essex coast. The English commanders waited until Hæsten was out on a raid, then struck at the bulk of the Danish army in the Benfleet camp. They scattered the Danish force, destroyed its ships, and brought all its goods, women, and children to London and Rochester. But the Danes were far from finished. Their army besieging Exeter took to their ships when the king arrived and headed back to the Thames estuary, where Hæsten had established yet another base at Shoebury. Together with more reinforcements from East Anglia and Northumbria, the combined Danish forces quit Shoebury and swarmed up the Thames valley, west across Worcestershire to the upper waters of the Severn.

The English replied to this tremendous march with a wide-sweeping *fyrd* 'from every borough east of the Parret, and both west and east of Selwood, and also north of the Thames and west of the Severn, and also some portion of the Welsh people'. This English army, under the supreme command of Ealdorman Ethelred, then blockaded the Danes in their base at Buttington until famine drove them to a desperate sortie and defeat in pitched battle. Back to Essex went the survivors, where they met still more reinforcements from the north. Still the offensive energy of the Danes had not been quenched. They 'placed their women and ships and property in safety in East Anglia, and went continuously by day and night till they reached a deserted city in Wirral, which is called Chester'. Ethelred repeated his starvation-tactics as he besieged Chester. He could not keep the Danes blockaded throughout the winter, but 'seized all the cattle that was outside, and killed the men whom they could cut off outside the fortress, and burnt all the corn, or consumed it by means of their horses, in all the surrounding districts'.

The second year of this great war saw the scales begin to tip in favour of the English. The Danish army, desperate and starving, quit Chester and flung itself into north Wales to glut itself on the country. Refreshed and rich with spoils, it then made an enormous route-march to the north and east, 'so that the English army could not reach them', back to Essex, where the new Danish base was established on Mersea island. Meanwhile, Alfred's dogged blocking tactics in the west finally induced the Danish forces there to cut their losses and join up with the main body. Devon was saved, and now another heartening example was given of the effectiveness of Alfred's defences: 'And when the Danish army which had besieged Exeter turned homewards, they ravaged up in Sussex near Chichester, and the citizens put them to flight and killed many hundreds of them, and captured some of their ships.' The year 894 ended with another classic Danish shift at the end of the 'campaigning season', when the Mersea army sailed up the Thames and camped for the winter on the upper Lea.

Spring brought a setback for the English, when an attempt to budge the Danes from their camp on the Lea, twenty miles upstream from London, was beaten off with heavy losses. Alfred came up with an army. His first move was to safeguard the local English while they gathered their harvest. Then he planted two fortresses on the river which were so well sited that the Danes accepted that they would be unable to extricate their ships. They took to the land and again headed for the upper Severn, abandoning their ships as trophies for the Londoners, and dug in at Bridgnorth for the winter. But it was their last card. In the summer of 896 the army split, one force going into East Anglia and one into Northumbria; and those that were moneyless got themselves ships and went south across the sea to the Seine'. The crisis was over.

This tremendous three-year campaign tested to the utmost the defences that Alfred and his people had built. Those defences held, and for all the energy, endurance, and constantly replenished strength of the Danes, their efforts came to resemble the plunging of a wild buffalo in a net. The over-all resilience of that net was the secret of its strength. Nowhere did its fabric suffer crucial damage. As the *Chronicle* puts it: 'By the grace of God, the army had not on the whole afflicted the English people very greatly; but they were much more seriously afflicted in those three years by the mortality of cattle and men, and most of all in that many of the best king's thegns who were in the land died in those three years.' For a country fighting for its life, this was a generous tribute to the economy of Alfred's measures.

This, the last of Alfred's long wars against the vikings, ended with repeated heavy raids along the south coast, and the onus passed from the foot-soldiers of the *fyrd* to the sailors of Alfred's fleet. Alfred had developed a type of warship which he intended to outclass the viking long-ships. 'They were almost twice as long as the others. Some had sixty oars, some more. They were both swifter and steadier and also higher than the others. They were built neither on the Frisian nor the Danish pattern, but as it seemed to him himself that they could be most useful.' Alfred's new fleet was obviously made up of the 'super-Dreadnoughts' of the viking age, but the English still had a lot to learn about seamanship. This was made painfully obvious by a celebrated battle off the south coast in 896, which seems to have been remembered in Saxon England in the same way that the last battle of Sir Richard Grenville and the *Revenge* caught the imagination of Tudor England:

Then on a certain occasion of the same year, six ships came to the Isle of Wight and did great harm there, both in Devon and everywhere along the coast. Then the king ordered (a force) to go there with nine of the new ships, and they blocked the estuary from the seaward end. Then the Danes went out against them with three ships, and three were on dry land farther up the estuary; the men from them had gone up on land. Then the

English captured two of those three ships at the entrance to the estuary, and killed the men, and the one ship escaped. On it also the men were killed except five. These got away because the ships of their opponents ran aground. Moreover, they had run aground very awkwardly: three were aground on that side of the channel on which the Danish ships were aground, and all [the others] on the other side, so that none of them could get to the others. But when the water had ebbed many furlongs from the ships, the Danes from the remaining three ships went to the other three which were stranded on their side, and they then fought there. And there were killed . . . in all 62 Frisians and English and 120 of the Danes. Then, however, the tide reached the Danish ships before the Christians could launch theirs, and therefore they rowed away out. They were then so wounded that they could not row past Sussex, but the sea cast two of them on to the land, and the men were brought to Winchester to the king, and he ordered them to be hanged. And the men who were on the one ship reached East Anglia greatly wounded. That same summer no fewer than 20 ships, men and all, perished along the south coast.

This was the last recorded fighting of Alfred's great reign. He died on 26 October 899, and was succeeded by Edward. For twenty-eight and a half years he had fought off the full weight of the Danish invasions, succeeding against all odds. But in all these constant wars he did not lose sight of the fact that a new order was beginning, a new order to which he alone could give direction and order. The *Chronicle* wrote of Alfred: 'He was king over the whole English people except for that part which was under Danish rule. . . .' It is now time to examine what the first king of England did for his people apart from preserving their liberty.

## Chapter 5

In the days of the rest of Alfred,
    When all these things were done,
And Wessex lay in a patch of peace,
    Like a dog in a patch of sun . . .

And he gat good laws of the ancient kings,
    Like treasure out of the tombs;
And many a thief in thorny nook,
Or noble in sea-stained turret shook,
For the opening of his iron book,
    And the gathering of the dooms.

G. K. Chesterton, *The Ballad of the White Horse.*

# Alfred's achievement

From any study of the violent ups and downs of Alfred's twenty-eight and a half years on the throne of Wessex, it would be quite reasonable to suspect that he died an embittered and emotionally exhausted man who could think only of fighting Danes and surviving the next campaign. But nothing is further from the truth. The real paradox of Alfred – the paradox which entitles him to be remembered as 'the Great' – lies in the fact that for him wars became an increasing distraction from the proper duties of his kingship. Alfred remains one of the very few characters in the whole of history whom it is impossible to 'debunk'. Nothing can decry his modest and realistic approach to the most depressing problem, his deep awareness of his own shortcomings, his constant willingness to learn from any man and pass on his knowledge for the benefit of his subjects. With all this, he can be described as the most human character ever to wear a crown.

Of course, Alfred's biographer Asser, to whom we owe virtually everything we know about the king's character, had not sat down to pick holes in the character of his royal subject – this cannot be denied. The disarming fact is that Asser's life of Alfred contains a wealth of criticism of the king – all of it made by Alfred himself.

It is possible to isolate five major achievements which were Alfred's legacy to his people. The first we have already covered: their survival, won at surprisingly low cost, and military security. The second is a uniform code of laws for the good order of the English kingdom. The third is his restoration of the shattered monastic life of the Church in England. The fourth is the sequel: enthusiastic patronage of the arts and learning. And the fifth was international respect. When Alfred died, England had not enjoyed such a reputation overseas since the palmy days of Offa of Mercia a century before.

Alfred's method of getting things done was a simple and worka-day one which we have already seen beautifully defined in the *Chronicle*'s description of his new warships. In trying to produce a warship which would enable the English to beat the vikings at their own game, he did not slavishly follow any one model, or introduce unworkable changes for the mere sake of change, but 'as it seemed to him himself that they could be most useful'. And he used precisely the same approach when he drew up a new code of laws for the English. This cannot be dated precisely, but it almost certainly happened in the 'reconstruction period' between 880 and 885, after Guthrum's Army returned to East Anglia and before the later wars began. In the introduction to his law code, Alfred gives his own motives for their formation:

After it came about that many peoples had received the faith of Christ, many synods were assembled throughout all the earth, and likewise throughout England, after they had received the faith of Christ, of holy bishops and also of other distinguished wise men; they then established, for that mercy which Christ taught, that secular lords might with their permission receive without sin compensation in money for almost every misdeed at the first offence, which compensation they then fixed; only for treachery to a lord they dared not declare any mercy, because Almighty God adjudged none for those who scorned him, nor did Christ, the Son of God, adjudge any for him who gave him over to death; and he charged [everyone] to love his lord as himself.

They then in many synods fixed the compensations for many human misdeeds, and they wrote them in many synod-books, here one law, there another.

Then I, King Alfred, collected these together and ordered to be written many of them which our forefathers observed, those which I liked; and many of those which I did not like, I rejected with the advice of my councillors, and ordered them to be differently observed. For I dared not presume to set in writing at all many of my own, because it was unknown to me what would please those who should come after us. But those which I found anywhere, which seemed to me most just, either of the time of my kinsman, King Ine, or of Offa, king of the Mercians, or of Ethelbert, who first among the English re-ceived baptism, I collected herein, and omitted the others.

Then I, Alfred, king of the West Saxons, showed these to all my councillors, and they then said that they were all pleased to observe them.

Alfred's code was basically conservative, then, relying heavily on previous legislation; and in traditional style his code is replete with laws against every conceivable expression of violence. Alfred's era was still one in which the king and his councillors considered it necessary to legislate against crimes such as the following examples, which seem impossibly bizarre today but which were clearly an unpleasant reality in Saxon times:

If in insult he disfigures him by cutting his hair, he is to pay him 10 shillings compensation.
If, without binding him, he cuts his hair like a priest's, he is to pay 30 shillings compensation.
If he cuts off his beard, he is to pay 20 shillings compensation.
If he binds him and then cuts his hair like a priest, he is to pay 60 shillings compensation.
Moreover, it is established: if anyone has a spear over his shoulder, and a man is transfixed on it, the wergild is to be paid without the fine. . . .
If they are both level, the point and the butt end, that is to be [considered] without risk.
If anyone binds an innocent *ceorl*, he is to pay him six shillings compensation.
If anyone scourges him, he is to pay him 20 shillings compensation.
If he places him in the stocks, he is to pay him 30 shillings compensation.

Yet although such measures must appear vaguely comic to twentieth-century eyes, they represent one of the most important aims of Alfred's law-code: to strengthen the rights and protection of all levels of English society, and at the same time to tighten up a man's loyalty to his lord. 'Thus also we determine concerning all ranks, both *ceorl* and noble: he who plots against his lord's life is to be liable to forfeit his life and all that he owns, or to clear himself by his lord's wergild.' Alfred took Ine's law that fighting in the presence of the ealdorman was a serious offence, and doubled the penalty: 'If anyone fights in a meeting in the presence of the

king's ealdorman, he is to pay wergild and fine, as it is fitting, and
before that, 120 shillings to the ealdorman as a fine. If he disturbs
a public meeting by drawing a weapon, [he is to pay] 120 shillings
to the ealdorman as a fine.' Alfred's efforts to prevent breaches
of his peace were wide-ranging, however: even drawing a weapon
in a *ceorl*'s house meant a three-shilling fine, while actually starting a fight beneath a *ceorl*'s roof cost double.

Such measures were necessary for an embattled people, and
Alfred made a breach of the peace while the army was called out
cost the offender double. But he and his councillors still did not
do away with the ancient right to carry on a just feud. Nevertheless
they tightened the regulations:

> Moreover we declare that a man may fight on behalf of his lord,
> if the lord is being attacked, without incurring a vendetta.
> Similarly the lord may fight on behalf of his man.
> In the same way, a man may fight on behalf of his born kins-
> man, if he is being wrongfully attacked, except against his lord;
> that we do not allow.
> And a man may fight without incurring a vendetta if he finds
> another man with his wedded wife, within closed doors or
> under the same blanket, or with his legitimate daughter or his
> legitimate sister, or with his mother who was given as a lawful
> wife to his father.

But although Alfred's laws were cautious and conservative in
themselves, their compilation was very new. Alfred's law-code
was the first compendium of regional English law, which was now
to be observed in Kent, Wessex, and Mercia alike. The Danish
wars had left Alfred as the only English king to whom a free
Englishman could give his allegiance; and Alfred's laws were an
official recognition of that fact.

When Roman Britain had gone under to the invading English,
the established Church had vanished as well. This did not happen
to Saxon England during the Danish wars; the Church survived,
but severely buckled and with a considerable amount of super-
ficial damage. To Alfred, the most serious aspect of this damage
was the setback to the monastic life, which had given so much to
the culture of the English in previous centuries; and he made
strenuous efforts to repair the fabric of the Church. As with the
laws, Alfred's Church reconstruction programme relied heavily

on *English* rather than West Saxon resources, particularly from
English Mercia.

The king's biographer, Asser, had very good reason to bear
witness to Alfred's concern for the spiritual welfare of his subjects, and to describe the key churchmen on whom the king
relied. For Asser himself was one of the men whom Alfred roped
into his service after persistent requests. (Asser was a priest from
St David's in Wales, and he took a good deal of persuading before
he agreed to move into a closer orbit in Alfred's service. The king
rewarded him by promoting him to the bishopric of Sherborne
in Dorset.) Asser says of Alfred:

. . . he complained in anxious sadness by day and night to God
and all who were bound to him in close affection, and lamented
with repeated sighs, that Almighty God had not made him
skilled in divine wisdom and the liberal arts. . . . Whenever he
could, he would acquire assistants in his good design, who could
help him to the desired wisdom, that he might obtain what he
longed for. Forthwith, like the prudent bee, which arises in the
summer-time at dawn from its beloved cells and, directing its
course in swift flight through the unknown ways of the air,
alights upon many and various blossoms of herbs, plants and
fruits, and finds and carries home what pleases it most, he
turned afar the gaze of his mind, seeking abroad what he had
not at home, that is, in his own kingdom.

And then God, suffering no longer his so good and just
complaint, sent for the king's goodwill some consolations, certain lights, as it were, namely Wærferth, bishop of the church of
Worcester, a man well versed in the divine Scripture, who at the
king's command first translated clearly and beautifully from
Latin into the Saxon language the books of the 'Dialogues' of
Pope Gregory and his disciple Peter, sometimes giving a paraphrase; and then Plegmund, a Mercian by race, archbishop of
the church of Canterbury, a venerable man, endowed with
wisdom; also Athelstan and Wærwulf, priests and chaplains,
learned men, of Mercian race. King Alfred summoned these
four to him from Mercia, and advanced them with great
honours and authority in the kingdom of the West Saxons, in
addition to those which Archbishop Plegmund and Bishop
Wærferth possessed in Mercia. . . .

But, since in this matter the royal avarice, praiseworthy as it was, was still unsatisfied, he sent messengers across the sea to Gaul to acquire teachers. From there he summoned Grimbald, priest and monk, a venerable man, an excellent singer, most learned in every way in ecclesiastical studies and the divine Scriptures, and adorned with all good qualities; and also John, likewise a priest and monk, a man of very keen intelligence and most learned in all branches of the art of literature, and skilled in many other arts. By their teaching the king's mind was much enriched, and he endowed and honoured them with great authority.

This was the formidable battery of talent which Alfred built to draw on. The basic layout of the bishoprics had survived in the English shires, and apart from the appointment of some 'new blood' – men like Bishop Asser – Alfred left it alone. His biggest worry was the virtual collapse of monasticism, which had set in long before the invasion of the Great Army. It has been claimed that Alfred painted a deliberately gloomy picture of England's illiteracy and that English learning had certainly not died out in Mercia, but he certainly did no harm in so doing. Organized monastic life, as Alfred fully realized, was the only source of widespread learning in the island – there were no schools or universities to take its place. He therefore did everything in his power to encourage the regeneration of monasticism, his own two most famous foundations being a monastery at Athelney and a nunnery at Shaftesbury.

What really counted, however, were his personal efforts to restore learning to the English. As in every other sphere, he was a realist when it came to the education of his people – not trying to turn back the clock to the great days of English Latin scholarship, but rather seeking to improve on the existing *status quo*. As he saw it, Latin learning had largely vanished from England; it would therefore be quicker and easier to harness the English language as a new medium in the dissemination of learning, and in this, too, he took the leading part. Aided by his coterie of learned men, he set himself to his lessons and became England's first scholar-king.

Alfred's efforts are summed up in his own words in the prose preface to a new version of Pope Gregory's *Pastoral Care* – a famous textbook which Alfred translated into English, and then circulated throughout his lands. It enables us, once again, to hear the king speaking his mind:

. . . So completely had learning decayed in England that there were very few men on this side of the Humber who could apprehend their services in English or even translate a letter from Latin into English, and I think that there were not many beyond the Humber. There were so few of them that I cannot even recollect a single one south of the Thames when I succeeded to the kingdom. Thanks be to God Almighty that we now have any provision of teachers. . . . Remember what temporal punishments came upon us, when we neither loved wisdom ourselves nor allowed it to other men; we possessed only the name of Christians, and very few possessed the virtues.

When I remembered all this, I also remembered how, before everything was ravaged and burnt, the churches throughout all England stood filled with treasures and books, and likewise there was a great multitude of the servants of God. And they had very little benefit from those books, for they could not understand anything in them, because they were not written in their own language. . . . Therefore it seems better to me, if it seems so to you, that we also should turn into the language that we can all understand some books, which may be most necessary for all men to know; and bring it to pass, as we can very easily with God's help, if we have the peace, that all the youth now in England, born of free men who have the means that they can apply to it, may be devoted to learning as long as they cannot be of use in any other employment, until such time as they can read well what is written in English. One may then teach further in the Latin language those whom one wishes to teach further and to bring to holy orders.

When I remembered how the knowledge of the Latin language had previously decayed throughout England, and yet many could read things written in English, I began in the midst of the other various and manifold cares of this kingdom to turn into English the book which is called in Latin *Pastoralis* and in English 'Shepherd-book', sometimes word for word, sometimes by a paraphrase; as I had learnt it from my Archbishop Plegmund, and by Bishop Asser, and my priest Grimbald and my priest John. When I had learnt it, I turned it into English according as I understood it and as I could render it most intelligibly; and I will send one to every see in my kingdom; and in each will be a book-marker [?] worth 50 mancuses.*

And I command in God's name, that no one take that book-marker from the book, nor the book from the church. It is unknown how long there may be such learned bishops, as now, thanks be to God, are almost everywhere; therefore I would like them always to be at that place, unless the bishop wish to have it with him, or it is anywhere on loan, or someone is copying it.

Alfred the self-made scholar, sitting down to translate Pope Gregory's *Pastoral Care*, identified himself completely with his subject, which stressed that the ideal bishop must be a teacher as well as a ruler. It was by no means his only literary achievement. He and his team went on to translate Bede's *Ecclesiastical History* and Orosius' *History of the Ancient World*. To the Orosius translation, Alfred added much material from his own experiences and from interviews with travellers familiar with central and northern Europe. One of his most important consultants was a Norwegian merchant from Halogaland named Ohthere, who told the royal author of his regular voyages down the coast of Norway to Danish Hedeby, and also of his voyage of exploration northward, round the North Cape, and on to the White Sea. From another experienced sea traveller, Wulfstan, Alfred received details of voyaging in the Baltic between Schleswig and the region of modern Danzig. Then came the king's translation of an elaborate work of philosophy, *De Consolatione Philosophiæ* by Boethius. This, like the *Pastoral Care*, struck a sympathetic chord in Alfred's thinking. Out of this original dissertation 'On the Consolations of Philosophy', Alfred drew a picture of a new, Christian stoicism enabling mankind, through faith and strength of will, to survive every blow of fate. And finally there was his 'collection of blossoms' – an anthology drawn from St Augustine's *Soliloquies*. Here again Alfred puts his own personal touch on his subject, constantly using examples from everyday life. To this, as to the *Pastoral Care*, Alfred wrote an important preface in which he used a metaphor which was certainly apt for himself: a man

---

* A de luxe present. This would buy 300 sheep or 50 oxen.

gathering timber in a great wood, where others too might find material for what they wanted to build. If ever a man wrote his own epitaph, Alfred did when he wrote:

Then I gathered for myself staves and props and bars and handles for all the tools I knew how to use, and cross-bars and beams for all the structures which I knew how to build, the fairest pieces of timber, as many as I could carry. I neither came home with a single load, nor did it suit me to bring home all the wood, even if I could have carried it. In each tree I saw something that I required at home. For I advise each of those who is strong and has many wagons, to plan to go to the same wood where I cut these props, and fetch for himself more there, and load his wagons with fair rods, so that he can plait many a fair wall, and put up many a peerless building, and build a fair enclosure with them; and may dwell therein pleasantly and at his ease winter and summer, as I have not yet done. . . .

Alfred's international outlook had been moulded in his youth, for he had been twice to Rome (in 853 and 855). The *Chronicle* records in detail that one of the first acts of foreign policy which Alfred brought about after weathering the crisis of 877–8 was the annual dispatch of the alms of Wessex to Rome, with an ealdorman as an escorting ambassador. Alfred's relationship with the papacy was naturally helped by the fact that he was practically the last successful Christian warrior-king in the West to hold out against the 'heathen men'. Pope Marinus I (882–4) granted Alfred's request to free the English quarter in Rome from taxation, and he also honoured the king by sending him a fragment of the True Cross. Archbishop Fulk of Rheims wrote regularly to Alfred, full of praises for his legal measures to tighten up monastic life and to refuse to allow 'bishops and priests to have women living near them, and anyone, who wished, to approach kinswomen of his own stock, and, moreover, to defile women consecrated to God, and, although married, to have at the same time a concubine'.

Even in his own lifetime, therefore, Alfred's reputation as an English king almost matched that of Offa of Mercia before him. Neither was it insular, nor restricted to making the correct monetary payments to Rome every year. Alfred was acutely aware of how much England could learn from overseas, and it was no accident that he 'plundered' wise councillors from France. In

D

speaking of the king's interest of the outside world despite the terrible distractions at home, Asser writes:

'What shall I say of his frequent expeditions and battles against the pagans and the incessant cares of government? What of his daily [solicitude] for the nations, which dwell from the Tyrrhenian Sea to the farthest end of Ireland? Indeed, we have even seen and read letters sent to him along with gifts by the patriarch Elias.'

The last word on Alfred may very well be left to Archbishop Fulk of Rheims, who in the conclusion of one of his letters to Alfred paid tribute to the three qualities which stamped everything to which Alfred ever set his hand: 'May your most noble dignity, your most holy piety, and also most unconquered fortitude, ever rejoice and flourish in Christ the King of Kings and Lord of Lords.'

## Chapter 6

In this year King Athelstan, lord of nobles, dispenser of treasure to men, and his brother also, Edmund atheling, won by the sword's edge undying glory in battle round *Brunanburh*.

*Anglo-Saxon Chronicle*: 937.

# Edward and Athelstan

The reign of Alfred's son, Edward the Elder (899–924), began with a crisis – a crisis, ironically, bred from the very security which Alfred had won for his kingdom. No sooner had he died than the West Saxon ruling line treated itself to a long-unaccustomed luxury: a bid for the throne and a brisk civil war, something that had not been seen in Wessex for over a hundred years.

The culprit was the atheling Æthelwold, Alfred's nephew – the son of the King Ethelred who had insisted on finishing his prayers while Alfred opened the battle of Ashdown, back in 871. When his father died later that year, Æthelwold was a mere boy and there could be no question of entrusting the fortunes of embattled Wessex to him – Alfred was the obvious choice. When Alfred finally died, Æthelwold (by now he would have been about thirty-five years old) decided that the time had come to assert himself at the expense of his rival, Edward.

Æthelwold started by seizing two royal residences, at Wimborne (where his father was buried) and Christchurch; and he succeeded in winning over a few adherents. He put himself further beyond the pale by making off with a nun. But the new king's reaction was prompt and effective. Edward raced an army down into Dorsetshire and blockaded his obstreperous cousin in Wimborne. As the *Chronicle* has it:

> . . . Æthelwold stayed inside the residence with the men who had given allegiance to him; and he had barricaded all the gates against him, and said that he would either live there or die there. Then meanwhile the atheling rode away by night, and went to the Danish army in Northumbria, and they accepted him as king and gave allegiance to him. Then the woman was seized whom he had taken without the king's permission and contrary to the bishop's orders – for she had been consecrated a nun.

So the tenth century opened for Saxon England, with the heir of the great Alfred faced with imminent war against the Danes and the exiled Æthelwold. He was the first English renegade to turn to the Danes for help – and he would not be the last. Æthelwold spent the year 901 raising an invasion fleet in Northumbria. In the south, King Edward found himself deprived of three of his father's faithful helpers: the ealdormen Ethelred and Æthelwulf and the priest Grimbald died. However, Alfred's great lieutenant, Ethelred of Mercia, lived on. He was Edward's brother-in-law by virtue of his marriage to the spirited Æthelflæd, and the close co-operation between Wessex and English Mercia was not threatened by the defection of Æthelwold.

The war began in 902, when Æthelwold sailed down the east coast 'with all the fleet he could procure' and accepted the submission of the men of Essex. His next move was to win over King Eohric of East Anglia, thus bringing a formidable coalition to bear against the English. In 903 an East Anglian host flung itself upon English Mercia and plundered its way towards the upper Thames at Cricklade. Edward's reaction was sluggish, and the Danish force was able to make a sweep south of the Thames before it retraced its steps homeward. When Edward had finally raised his own army he retaliated with a spirited raid deep into Danish Mercia as far as the Fens. Then the *Chronicle* records an odd incident that suggests that the new king's authority was not yet as complete as Alfred's had been: 'When he wished to go back from there he had it announced over the whole army that they were all to set out together. Then the men of Kent lingered behind there against his command – and he had sent seven messengers to them.' This flicker of disaffection in the English army was speedily ended by the appearance of Æthelwold and the main Danish army. Battle was joined on the Holme river – a pounding-match in the old style. Edward lost two ealdormen and a king's thegn in the fight, but on the Danish side Æthelwold and King Eohric fell, effectively ending the whole civil war. The battle of the Holme was a fight to the finish; it ended with the Danes still holding their ground, but they had lost the more casualties. Intermittent fighting continued over the next two years before Edward agreed a peace with the East Anglians and Northumbrians. The 'E' text of the *Chronicle* says he did this 'from necessity'. Whatever the reason, the next three years saw no large-scale operations on either side.

It is certain, however, that in this period Edward made his decision to go over to the offensive and recover as much territory from the Danes as he could. By taking and fortifying London, Alfred had made the town the key strategic pivot in the south-east, vital for both defensive and offensive operations. And in 907 Edward repeated the process at the other end of his long frontier with the Danes, up in Mercia, by taking and restoring Chester, which in past years had served the Danes well as a base. Now the English frontier was securely pegged by fortified *burhs* at its north-western and south-eastern extremities.

About this time, too, Edward and Ethelred began to encourage their thegns to buy land from the Danes. Times were changing fast. A generation had passed since the invaders had begun their settlement in England. But as early as Alfred's treaty with Guthrum it had been obvious that the English had accepted them, at least, as people with whom one could do business. With the official encouragement of the West Saxon leaders, therefore, land-trading began about 906-9. We know this from a land grant by Edward's successor, Athelstan, which was made in 926. This put the official seal on the private land deal made twenty-odd years before in his father's time:

. . . I, Athelstan, king of the Anglo-Saxons, adorned and elevated with no small dignity, prompted by desire from on high, will grant to my faithful thegn Ealdred the land of five hides* which is called Chalgrave and Tebworth, which he bought with sufficient money of his own, namely ten pounds of gold and silver, from the pagans by the order of King Edward and also of Ealdorman Ethelred along with the other ealdormen and thegns; conceding with it the freedom of hereditary right, to have and possess as long as he lives, and to give after his death to whatever heirs, acceptable to himself, he shall wish.

Such were the beginnings of the great English recovery of the tenth century, which would end by sweeping away the last vestige of independent Scandinavian power in England.

It had been heralded by a small but highly significant change in the king's title. Alfred had styled himself merely 'King of the

---

* Basic unit of Saxon land measurement. Originally the amount of land required to support a peasant household, the hide varied in size from place to place.

West Saxons'. But Edward adopted the title of 'King of Anglo-Saxons' right from the start – it appears in a royal land grant for 901. Now Wessex, too, by its own king's will, had been reduced to the status of a regional province of the new English kingdom which was painfully taking shape.

Edward finally reopened hostilities in 909, sending a powerful Wessex–Mercian task force on a five-week raid deep into Northumbria, where 'it ravaged very seriously the territory of the northern army, both men and all kinds of cattle, and they killed many men of those Danes. . . . Blow was rapidly followed by counter-blow. Although the English were now the aggressors, the *Chronicle* found no difficulty in giving a propaganda-flavoured twist to its account of the year 910: 'In this year the army in Northumbria broke the peace, and scorned every privilege that King Edward and his councillors offered them, and ravaged over Mercia.' In the opening stages of this campaign Edward was engaged in mustering a fleet in Kent, and was waiting for the last naval contingents to join up with the main body. The Danish leaders, Kings Halfdan and Eowils, made a fatal miscalculation. Assuming that Edward's main army was embarking in the fleet, they deepened their raids in western Mercia, probing far across the Severn. This, however, gave Edward and Ethelred the time they needed to raise a centrally placed Wessex–Mercian army, which overtook the Danish army and smashed it in a battle near Tettenhall in Staffordshire. Both Danish kings and two earls were killed and their army virtually destroyed. It was the last time that the Danes in Mercia and East Anglia got any help from their kinsmen north of the Humber.

In the same year as this dramatic campaign, Edward's sister, Æthelflæd, added another link to the English chain of *burhs* by building another at a place called *Bremesbyrig*. It was another small but inexorable step forward into former Danish territory. Ealdorman Ethelred died shortly after the battle of Tettenhall, but his remarkable wife's spirit was not crushed by widowhood. Although Edward 'succeeded to London and Oxford and all the lands which belonged to them' in English Mercia, Æthelflæd continued to lead her people with the honorary title of 'lady of the Mercians'. She not only continued to plan the siting of new *burhs* but frequently led the Mercian host out to battle. Edward was therefore spared the distraction of having to worry about

Mercia. It enabled him to concentrate on his plan to reduce the Danes in the south.

Edward and Æthelflæd laid the firm foundation for the advance in the year 912. Edward built a *burh* at Hertford, then pushed into Essex and built another at Witham. Æthelflæd added to the Mercian defences on the upper Severn with a *burh* at Bridgnorth and another at *Scergeat*. This pattern fell into a routine during the next four years, in which Æthelflæd personally secured new *burhs* at Tamworth and Stafford (913), Eddisbury and Warwick (914), Chirbury, *Weardbyrig*, and Runcorn (915), launching a punitive raid against the Welsh in the Brecon region in 916. In 916 Æthelflæd added to her laurels by taking Derby, far to the north of the frontier with Danish Mercia settled by her father. In early 918, according to the *Mercian Register*:

'. . . she peacefully obtained control of the borough of Leicester . . . and the greater part of the army which belonged to it was subjected. And also the people of York had promised her – and some had given pledges, some had confirmed it with oaths – that they would be under her direction. But very soon after they had agreed to this, she died twelve days before midsummer in Tamworth, in the eighth year in which with lawful authority she was holding dominion over the Mercians. And her body is buried in Gloucester in the east chapel of St Peter's Church.

By any criterion, the achievements of the remarkable lady of the Mercians matched those of her father Alfred as far as territorial expansion was concerned. Æthelflæd left a daughter, Ælfwyn, but Edward did not try to keep the previous semi-autonomy of English Mercia in being. He took over himself. Ælfwyn 'was deprived of all authority in Mercia and taken into Wessex, three weeks before Christmas'. Her mother's achievements had pushed English authority far beyond Alfred's former Watling Street frontier. Now it reached north to the line of the Humber and the threshold of Northumbria.

During the years 913–18, while Æthelflæd's Mercians sapped their way steadily deeper into Danish-held territory, Edward and the people of the south were weathering dramatic events.

In 913, the Danes started with a hit-and-run raid across the border after Easter, from the Leicester–Northampton area, which did a good deal of damage around Hook Norton. Apparently encouraged by the lack of opposition encountered by these raiders, a second force attacked Luton shortly afterwards, but was routed by the spirited defence of the local *fyrd*, which not only recovered all the loot initially taken by the raiders but captured many Danish horses and weapons as spoils of war.

The following year saw more trouble in the Severn valley. A viking fleet from Brittany entered the estuary and pushed up river, 'and ravaged in Wales everywhere along the coast where it suited them'. Then there occurred an incident which showed how much the 'pagans' had learned of the benefits of civilization since their early days as the scourge of God and man. They captured Cyfeiliog, bishop of Archenfield in Herefordshire, and instead of treating him to an unsavoury and violent martyrdom hauled him off to their ships and started haggling with King Edward for ransom. Edward settled for forty pounds, the bishop was handed over, and the raiders prepared to continue with the job of ravaging Herefordshire. But again the dead hand of Alfred proved too strong for the raiders: 'Then the men from Hereford and Gloucester and from the nearest boroughs met them and fought against them and put them to flight. . . .' The survivors did not escape to their ships, but were hopelessly trapped in 'an enclosure' and forced to sue for terms. Hostages were handed over as surety for the Danes' promise to quit the king's dominions. Meanwhile, however, Edward had not been idle. He had mobilized the entire local manpower from Cornwall to Avonmouth to seal in the Danish force – a wise precaution. The Danes made two attempts to break out to the south, but were beaten back on both occasions. Eventually, in autumn 914, they gave up, headed into Wales, and finally sailed for Ireland. The close of the year found Edward at the other end of his kingdom, in southern Mercia, building twin *burhs* on the Ouse at Buckingham. And the successes in east and west that year were crowned when 'Earl Thurcetel came and accepted him as his lord, and so did all the earls and principal men who belonged to Bedford, and also many of those who belonged to Northampton.'

These latter events are particularly interesting because of the light they shed on the state of the frontier since its definition by Alfred and Guthrum. Buckingham, Luton, and Bedford all belonged to the southern sector, which ran 'along the Lea to its source, then in a straight line to Bedford, then up the Ouse to the

Watling Street'. Bedford, straddling the River Ouse, had obviously developed into a key frontier-town with the English and Danish halves separated by the river. Tension would always have existed between the two; and now the Danish leader, impressed by the energy of the English king, had made a voluntary surrender of his independence. Edward made quite sure of his supremacy in Bedford by going there with his army in 915, occupying it all, and building a new *burh* there. It seems that not all of the Bedford Danes welcomed their new lord with open arms; even the *Chronicle* has to admit that it was only 'almost' all the citizens who submitted to him.

Edward had no dramatic campaigning to do in 916, but he strengthened his hold on central Essex by building a new *burh* at Maldon. He also gave his approval and support to his new Danish vassal, Earl Thurcetel of Bedford, who now chose to go 'across the sea to France, along with the men who were willing to serve him. . . .' Here again, Edward was relying on the practical politics of his father, who had never attempted to overstrain Anglo-Danish relations when it came to changing loyalties. Edward's take-over of Bedford had been a peaceful one, with no witch-hunt against those who resented his coming. Nor did he put any obstacles in the way of Earl Thurcetel when the latter saw fit to take his adherents off to France – even though the risk of their returning as part of a hostile viking fleet was an obvious one.

The secret of this patient, step-by-step *revanche* by the English lay in the establishment of the *burhs*, not in the march of armies, and the fact was not ignored by the Danes. After all, fortified posititions had always played a key role in their waging of war; and by 917 the Danish leaders knew only too well what was afoot when an English army stopped marching and started digging. The cut-and-thrust campaign of 917 centred exclusively around the capture and defence of fortified positions on both sides; and thus it may be taken as symptomatic of a new form of warfare – one of march, and counter-march, and siege, and relief – that was destined to endure for over eight and a half centuries. It lasted right through the Middle Ages to the post-Renaissance wars of religion; through the Thirty Years War until the art of fortification was brought to its peak by Vauban; through Marlborough and Saxe and Frederick the Great; until it was swept away by the French Revolutionary Wars and the genius of Napoleon. In all this immense period of time, the basic elements of every campaign fought by any European army are reflected in miniature by the Anglo-Danish campaign of 917.

It started before Easter, when Edward planted two new *burhs*: one at Towcester on Watling Street, and another unidentified one at *Wigingamere*. The Danes of Northampton and Leicester concentrated an army and struck at the Towcester *burh*, whose defences could hardly have been completed. Although hard pressed, the Towcester garrison held out until Edward sent up reinforcements. The Danes then adopted the tactics of the English, moving up from Huntingdon and building an advanced base of their own at Tempsford. From this base they then marched on Bedford – but were met in open country by the Bedford defence forces and beaten off with heavy losses. Another Danish army was raised in East Anglia and Mercia and hurled against the other new English *burh* at *Wigingamere*, but this, too, held out. Having proved the value of his defences, Edward now went over to the attack and fell upon the Danish fortifications at Tempsford. Here, too, no quarter was given or taken. The English 'took it by storm; and they killed the king* and Earl Toglos and his son Earl Manna, and his brother and all those who were inside and chose to defend themselves. . . .' The Danes, who only fifty years before had proved themselves invincible once they dug in behind fixed defences, had met their match at last.

The action now shifted rapidly to Essex. Edward, a master of retaining the initiative once he had won it, raised a field army from the men of Kent, Surrey, 'English' Essex, 'and from the nearest boroughs on all sides', and flung it north-eastwards to take Colchester by storm. The East Anglian Danes riposted by sending a sea-borne force down the coast to take Maldon and cut off the English in Colchester. It was a good plan, but it was wrecked by the stubborn defence of the Maldon garrison which held out until a relief force made contact and the besiegers drew off. A vigorous sortie by the Maldon garrison then caught the discomforted Danes between hammer and anvil and routed them. Essex had been returned to the rule of the English in one smashing campaign.

Edward, however, had not been diverted from the basic strategy with which he had begun the year. He returned to

---

* The current Danish king of East Anglia.

Towcester with his army, which stood by until the *burh* there had been given a sound stone wall. The Danes of Northampton had had enough: 'And Earl Thurferth . . . submitted to him, and so did all the army which belonged to Northampton, as far north as the Welland, and sought to have him as their lord and protector.' Edward now proved that his father's army rota-system, no less than the *burhs*, was as useful in attack as it was in defence. The troops in the field were relieved and went home, and Edward marched the replacements forward to Huntingdon, fortified it, and received the submission of the entire district.

Finally, Edward returned to Colchester and repaired the defences of the *burh*. Once again, the diplomatic consequences of this deliberate advance were immense. He received the total submission of the surviving Danish leaders in Essex and East Anglia, together with that of the Danish army of Cambridge – a mere fifty-one years after the Great Army of the Danes had launched its invasion of Saxon England by receiving the submission of East Anglia.

This was the last great campaign which Edward (later remembered as Edward the Elder) had to fight. In early 918 he commenced operations in Lincolnshire by establishing a new *burh* at Stamford, but on the death of his sister Æthelflæd in midsummer he concentrated on cementing his authority over Mercia. Edward also benefited from the 916 campaign of his sister in Wales, for when he took over in Mercia 'the kings in Wales . . . and all the race of the Welsh, sought to have him as lord'. When he took and fortified Nottingham later in the year, all Mercia was his, 'both Danish and English'.

Six years of life remained for Edward the Elder, in which he expanded his domains still further by taking Thelwall, Manchester, and Bakewell on the upper Derwent. By the time he died in 924, he was master of all England south of the Humber and had received token submission at least from 'the king of the Scots and all the people of the Scots, and Ragnald* and the sons of Eadwulf and all who live in Northumbria, both English and Danish, Norsemen and others, and also the king of the Strathclyde Welsh and all the Strathclyde Welsh. . . .' Great though it was, Edward's achievement relied completely on the massive strength of the foundations built by Alfred. Even when this is accepted, however, Edward and

* The Norse king of York.

Æthelflæd were certainly not pygmies standing on giant shoulders. Their patient, skilful expansion of Alfred's chain of *burhs* is matched only in British history by the Roman general Agricola in the first century, whose lengthening chain of interdependent forts brought Wales, the Pennines, Cumberland, and all southern Scotland, under the control of Rome.

Edward's son, the atheling Athelstan, was the new king. (His elder brother, Ælfweard, had died within weeks of their father.) Like Edward, Athelstan claimed the title of 'King of the Anglo-Saxons'. During Athelstan's sixteen-year reign the frontier of the English kingdom widened still further, and at its close England had been firmly established as the dominant power in Britain.

During the last ten years of Edward the Elder, a new viking power had established itself north of the Humber. The founder of this new Scandinavian kingdom of York was a leader of the vikings who had colonized the eastern Irish coast named Ragnald, who first landed in Northumbria between 913 and 915. Ragnald's main quarrel lay not with the southern English but with the north, and Constantine, king of Scotland, was his main adversary. The isolated pocket of 'English' Northumbria, centred on Bamburgh, was caught up in the ensuing struggle. English ecclesiastical records from Durham say that Ragnald defeated Constantine soon after his initial landing, up at Corbridge on the line of Hadrian's Wall, and add that the English Northumbrians under Ealdorman Ealdred of Bernicia fought with Constantine and were beaten with him.

Ragnald's next venture came in 918, when he sailed north against Constantine with a big viking fleet from Waterford in Ireland. They clashed again on the River Tyne, and Ragnald's army won; he wintered in Northumbria, and in the following year he conquered the city of York and set himself up as king there.

Ragnald's success opened up a wide bridgehead in England of which viking adventurers from Ireland proceeded to make the fullest use. The Mersey and Dee estuaries gave them easy access to north-western Mercia, and this was why Edward the Elder's last *burhs* were built. Then, in 920, came a full-scale 'raid in force' led by Sihtric, a cousin of Ragnald, with an army from Dublin. English sources do not cover this, and all we know from other sources is that Sihtric destroyed Davenport in Cheshire. But this raid certainly inspired Edward the Elder's energetic northern drive of 920, which culminated in the English king's obtaining the homage of all leading rulers in northern Britain, as we have seen. It was a thoroughly acceptable establishment of the balance of power. It suited the English of Northumberland as well as England proper; it recognized the power of Ragnald in York; and for Constantine of Scotland it gave an English guarantee of potential aid against any further trouble from Ragnald. For the smaller fry in the north, this general acceptance of English supremacy was equally welcome as a warning to any of their direct neighbours who might otherwise feel tempted to indulge in military adventures.

Broadly speaking, this was the *status quo* in the north when Athelstan became king of England, except that Ragnald of York had died in 921 and his cousin Sihtric was the new king there.

Athelstan's accession is interesting on two counts. First, he had been brought up as a child in the household of Ealdorman Ethelred and Æthelflæd, which meant that he was *simpatico* to the Mercians as neither Alfred nor Edward had been. And second, he was the first English king since Offa of Mercia's son Ecgfrith to have a recorded coronation to his name. This took place at Kingston on 4 September 925.

To start with, the good relations with the Norse kingdom of York were maintained. Sihtric and Athelstan continued the alliance, and Sihtric was given one of Athelstan's sisters in marriage at the end of January 926 after a meeting with Sihtric at Tamworth. But the trouble really started with Sihtric's death in 927. His brother Guthfrith came over from Dublin with an army to support Sihtric's son, Olaf, in Northumbria, and Athelstan invaded Northumbria at once. Olaf fled to Ireland, Guthfrith to Constantine of Scotland. Athelstan entered York in triumph, the first southern English king to take possession of the ancient Northumbrian capital; and at Eamont, near Penrith, Constantine of the Scots came to terms with the English king on 12 July 927. Athelstan received the homage of the kings of Scotland and Strathclyde, and of Ealdorman Aldred of Bernicia. Guthfrith escaped with a die-hard band of loyalists and tried to take York, but finally surrendered to Athelstan, who let him go back to Ireland.

Twenty-seven years after the death of Alfred, the great king's grandson had carried English supremacy as far north as the banks of the Tweed and the Scots frontier – an amazing recovery from the black winter of 877–8, when it seemed that viking military power had crushed the last sparks of English resistance. Athelstan rounded out his achievement by turning west. His power was accepted by the kings of Wales – particularly Hywel of Dyfed, who struck English-style silver pennies and issued a law-code on the basic English model – and the tributary status of the rulers of Wales in Athelstan's reign showed itself in the number of charters they witnessed at Athelstan's court. Athelstan also put an end to a resurgence of trouble from Cornwall, refortifying Exeter, pushing the effective power of the Cornishmen back behind the Tamar river, and founding a new bishopric at St Germans.

Athelstan's place in the north lasted until 934, when he was once again forced to use the mailed fist against Constantine. What the Scots king's offence had been is not known, but Athelstan's response was overwhelming. It took the form of a combined land invasion and naval sweep along the coast, with the English ships raiding as far north as Caithness. Certainly Constantine was unable to resist Athelstan on this occasion. But three years later the Scots formed the keystone of a formidable coalition of Athelstan's northern enemies.

The key troublemaker was the son of Guthfrith whom Athelstan had expelled from York in 927: Olaf Guthfrithson. Guthfrith himself died in 934 and Olaf was accepted as the leader of all the viking communities in Ireland. He proposed a tripartite alliance between himself, Strathclyde, and Scotland, with the aim of defeating Athelstan and recovering York for himself. This certainly appealed to the northern British powers, who welcomed the prospect of a buffer-state between themselves and the southern English; the pact was made, and the three powers invaded England in 937.

The result was the Battle of *Brunanburh*, one of the most celebrated events in the history of Anglo-Saxon England. The coalition army was routed by Athelstan's Wessex–Mercian host. Although the site of the battle remains unconfirmed, it was in northern Northumbria. Anglo-Saxon historians gave the battle unusual prominence in their writings, and even the *Chronicle* broke into a poetic fanfare in its entry on the victory:

The whole day long the West Saxons with mounted companies kept in pursuit of the hostile peoples, grievously they cut down the fugitives from behind with their whetted swords. The Mercians refused not hard conflict to any men who with Olaf had sought this land in the bosom of a ship over the tumult of waters, coming doomed to the fight. Five young kings lay on that field of battle, slain by the swords, and also seven of Olaf's earls, and a countless host of seamen and Scots. There the prince of the Norsemen was put to flight, driven perforce to the prow of his ship with a small company; the vessel pressed on in the water, the king set out over the fallow flood and saved his life.

There also the aged Constantine, the hoary-headed warrior, came north to his own land by flight. He had no cause to exult in that crossing of swords. He was shorn of his kinsmen and deprived of his friends at that meeting-place, bereaved in the battle, and he left his young son on the field of slaughter, brought low by wounds in the battle. The grey-haired warrior, the old and wily one, had no cause to vaunt of that sword-clash; no more had Olaf. They had no need to gloat with the remnants of their armies, that they were superior in warlike deeds on the field of battle, in the clash of standards, the meeting of spears, the encounter of men, and the crossing of weapons, after they had contended on the field of slaughter with the sons of Edward.

. . . Never yet in this island before this, by what books tell us and our ancient sages, was a greater slaughter of a host made by the edge of the sword, since the Angles and the Saxons came hither from the east, invading Britain over the broad seas, and the proud assailants, warriors eager for glory, overcame the Britons and won a country.

As the years rolled by, Athelstan's triumph at *Brunanburgh* became treasured in a way that applied to none of the victories of Alfred. *Brunanburh* became a national symbol, like the Armada, Trafalgar, Waterloo, and Alamein in later centuries: a symbol of the people's pride in a joint achievement, and a prominent milestone, for that reason alone, in the evolution of England.

However, Athelstan's conquest of Northumbria and his great victory at *Brunanburh* were by no means his only claims to fame. While on campaign in the north he certainly displayed all the military energy of his father and grandfather; but when he was at peace he was content to limit his travels to the confines of Wessex. At Grately in Hampshire he issued an important code of laws

which do much to show how fast English society had been changing since Alfred issued his. There is a welter of legislation against
every form of fraud and thievery – much more than in Alfred's
laws. For the first time, too, an English king issued laws against
lords whose establishments and acts broke the king's law – showing how early Saxon society was tending to 'jell' into feudalism.
Athelstan was also the first king to give a deliberate boost to the
development of towns. The military *burhs* of Alfred, Edward, and
Æthelflæd had been sited to get the best advantage out of the
local terrain, and those sites naturally coincided with provincial
trade-routes. Athelstan laid it down that all buying and selling
was to be conducted in towns.

Towns also had an important role in Athelstan's overhaul of the
English coinage, which must have been chaotic at the beginning
of his realm. He ordered that 'there is to be one coinage over all
the king's dominion, and no one is to mint money except in a
town'. Athelstan also decreed where this was to be done:

> In Canterbury [there are to be] seven moneyers; four of the
> king, two of the bishop, one of the abbot; in Rochester three,
> two of the king, one of the bishop; in London eight; in Win-
> chester six; in Lewes two; in Hastings one; another at Chich-
> ester; at Southampton two; at Wareham two; [at Dorchester
> one]; at Exeter two; at Shaftesbury two; otherwise in the
> other boroughs one.

This again shows the predominance of the ancient kingdom of
Wessex in the new English kingdom.

The tremendous expansion of that kingdom under Edward and
Athelstan had also created formidable problems for the royal
administration. Athelstan's reign is therefore important in that it
saw the first embryonic attempts to produce a civil service close
to the king's person. This is obvious from the remarkable change
that came over the wording of royal charters. It was no longer
considered fit for the royal dignity to issue the laconic, straightforward grants of the ninth century, perhaps no longer than two
or three paragraphs over all and witnessed by a couple of bishops
and a handful of thanes and ealdormen. Now professional clerks
drafted copious and florid documents in Latin – ludicrously over-
stated, dripping with verbosity, and all in all the direct ancestors

of that civil service 'officialese' which still murders the English language today.

The prologue of a grant of land by Athelstan to the church of York in 934 is an excellent example:

The wanton fortune of this deceiving world, not lovely with the milk-white radiance of unfading lilies, but odious with the gall-steeped bitterness of lamentable corruption, raging with venomous wide-stretched jaws, bitingly rends the sons of stinking flesh in this vale of tears; and although by its smiles it may be able to draw unfortunates to the bosom of Acherontic Cocytus, unless the Creator of the roaring deep lend his aid, it is shamelessly fickle; and therefore, because this ruinous fortune falls and mortally decays, one should chiefly hasten to the pleasant fields of indescribable joy, where are the angelic instruments of hymn-singing jubilation and the mellifluous scents of blooming roses are perceived with inconceivable sweetness by the nostrils of the good and blessed and harmonies are heard by their ears for ever. Allured by love of that felicity – when now depths disgust, heights grow sweet – and in order to perceive and enjoy them always in unfailing beauty, I, Athelstan, king of the English, elevated by the right hand of the Almighty, which is Christ, to the throne of the whole kingdom of Britain, assign willingly in fear of God to Almighty God and the blessed Apostle Peter, at his church in the city of York, at the time when I constituted Wulfstan its archbishop, a certain portion of land of no small size, in the place which the inhabitants call Amounderness. . . .

Even the conventional curse pronounced on anyone who dared tamper with the king's grant was inflated to the point of bathos:

If, however – which God forbid – anyone puffed up with the pride of arrogance shall try to destroy or infringe this little document of my agreement and confirmation, let him know that on the last and fearful day of assembly, when the trumpet of the archangel is clanging the call and bodies are leaving the foul graveyards, he will burn with Judas the committor of impious treachery and also with the miserable Jews, blaspheming with sacrilegious mouth Christ on the altar of the Cross, in eternal confusion in the devouring flames of blazing torments in punishment without end.

The nub and gist of the document – precisely how much land Athelstan was handing over to the church – is dealt with in the final sentence – nine-tenths of the total wording is pious verbiage. This was not the way King Alfred had got through his 'paper-work' – not only did he prefer to get straight to the point in the simplest possible wording, but he did not have the time or clerical staff.

But what makes this land-grant really impressive is the list of witnesses. First come the archbishops of Canterbury and York; then three Welsh sub-kings; then no less than sixteen bishops. The next lay witnesses are particularly interesting because they show that the lords of what would soon be called the Danelaw – Guth-rum's share of England at the time of his treaty with Alfred – were regarded as no less essential to the good order of the realm than the English ealdormen. In this case there are seven ealdormen and six Danish earls. Eleven king's thegns and thirteen unidenti-fiable names conclude the list of the king's witnesses.

Here, on a national scale – representative of *all* England – are the magnates of Church and State, the king's councillors, witness-ing a royal decree. It is the direct forbear of the medieval king's council, and of the later English Parliament – but in essence it is only the old, limited Witan of Wessex writ large. And what had made such an important assembly not only possible but essential was the expansion of England under Edward and Athelstan.

Athelstan's achievements as war-leader, lawgiver, overlord of Britain, and generous-handed maintainer of the peace were no-table enough. But in his extensive relations with the major powers of Western Europe, Athelstan was only matched by Offa of Mercia before him; and he was the most 'European' king of England until Cnut built up his Anglo-Danish-Norwegian empire some eighty years later. The marriages of royal princesses have sealed more diplomatic alignments than anything else in history; and one of Edward the Elder's most useful legacies to Athelstan was a generous crop of sisters.

One of these sisters had been married off before Athelstan be-came king. Her name was Eadgifu, and Edward had married her to the most powerful ruler just across the Channel – Charle-magne's great-great-grandson, Charles the Simple, king of the West Franks. Usurpers threw Charles off his throne, jailed him, and replaced him with Rudolf of Burgundy; but Queen Eadgifu and the Carolingian heir, Prince Louis, came to England where Athelstan gave them asylum. In 926 Athelstan was approached by Hugh, duke of the Franks, the power behind King Rudolf's throne. Hugh wanted a marriage alliance with the English king who was playing host to the exiled Frankish heir. After long negotiations and the exchange of the most lavish gifts – the Frankish contributions included Constantine the Great's sword with a nail from the Cross set in its hilt, and the reputed lance with which the centurion had stabbed Jesus on the Cross – Hugh married Athelstan's sister Eadhild at the close of 926.

Athelstan's close ties with the West Franks did not end there. Rudolf died in early 936, and Hugh was the prime mover for the restoration of Prince Louis to his rightful throne. This was masterminded by Athelstan, who sent over Bishop Oda of Ramsbury to arrange the details before shipping Louis across the Channel with a royal retinue.

Athelstan had also been approached by the ruler of the German section of Charlemagne's old empire, Henry the Fowler of Germany. In 928, King Henry had asked Athelstan for an English princess to marry his son Otto, and Athelstan had replied by sending over two candidates for Otto to choose between. Otto picked the elder princess, Edith, and the marriage opened up decades of a close *entente* between England and Germany.

In 939, however, Athelstan found himself holding the balance of power in yet another clash between Germany and the West Franks. Louis' domains were invaded by Otto of Germany and Athelstan sent the English fleet across the Channel to raid Otto's coastal domains. It was not a major commitment of force, but it was certainly the first recorded instance of an English king sending military aid to a Continental ally.

Nor was this all. It was in Athelstan's reign that the English made their first contact with the new Scandinavian masters of Normandy – the first link in a fateful chain of events. England had always maintained good relations with the rulers of Brittany and, when viking settlers overran it, Athelstan found himself playing host to the refugee Breton ruler, Alan, to whom he stood godfather. When Count Alan returned to Brittany in 936, he went with English assistance; and, although Alan's principal foes were the vikings of the Loire, he also had to worry about the increasing viking control of the Norman coast,

But nothing bears such eloquent witness to Athelstan's international reputation as the diplomatic mission sent to him by the greatest Scandinavian ruler of the age: Harold Fairhair, king of Norway. We know nothing more about Harold's mission than that it was a positive demonstration of goodwill from across the North Sea which was reciprocated in kind. Both Harold and Athelstan had every reason to come to a common agreement for mutual co-operation against independent viking pirate raiders in the North Sea, although there is no record that this was actually discussed. The mission came to York, bringing a magnificent ceremonial Norwegian long-ship; and William of Malmesbury, who gave Athelstan extensive coverage in his book *Concerning the Acts of the Kings of the English*, described it as follows:

> A certain Harold, king of the Norwegians, sent him a ship which had a gold beak and a purple sail, surrounded inside with a dense rank of gilded shields. The names of his envoys were Helgrim and Osfrid; who, being royally entertained in the city of York, were compensated for the labours of their journey with fitting gifts.

This impressive demonstration of 'hands across the North Sea' epitomizes the heights to which Athelstan had raised the status of England by his efforts at home and abroad. Athelstan's great reign had finished the creation of the kingdom of England; and by its close, as William of Malmesbury wrote: '. . . all Europe proclaimed his praises, extolled his excellence to the skies; foreign kings rightly considered themselves fortunate if they could buy his friendship either by marriage alliance or gifts.'

## Chapter 7

In this year died Edgar, ruler of the Angles, friend of the West Saxons and protector of the Mercians. It was widely known throughout many nations across the gannet's bath, that kings honoured Edmund's son far and wide, and paid homage to this king as was his due by birth. Nor was there fleet so proud nor host so strong that it got itself prey in England as long as the noble king held the throne.

*Anglo-Saxon Chronicle*: 975.

# The new England

The charisma of Athelstan's reign was heightened by the setbacks experienced by his short-lived successors. Long-reigning kings had been an immense help in accelerating the English recovery from the onslaught of the Great Army: Alfred had reigned for twenty-eight years, Edward the Elder for twenty-five, Athelstan for sixteen. But after Athelstan's death in 940 there were four kings of England in seventeen years, and the resultant failure to achieve security led directly to new trouble from the Norsemen of Ireland – trouble that exploded as soon as the news of Athelstan's death was spread.

Edmund the Atheling was the new king of England – only eighteen years old, but a prince who had won full battle honours fighting with Athelstan at *Brunanburh*. But no sooner had he been accepted as king than the fatal legacy of that battle came home to roost.

Olaf Guthfrithson, who had fled back to Ireland from the defeat at *Brunanburh* with the remnants of his army, was still the unchallenged viking overlord across the Irish Sea; and he proved it by making another bid for a Norse kingdom in England almost before Athelstan had been laid to rest in Winchester. He took York with ease and turned south to subdue Mercia. Here he met with mixed fortunes. He could not take the *burh* at Northampton but managed to storm Tamworth before Edward came up with the English army and intercepted him at Leicester. But the two armies did not fight – an extraordinary thing happened. The archbishops of York and Canterbury negotiated a treaty between Edmund and Olaf in which the latter was granted not only York but all English territory between Watling Street and the Humber. Olaf had got his kingdom without having to fight a second *Brunanburh*.

Nothing more humiliating had happened to the English since the surprise Danish attack on Alfred's Wessex in the winter of 877. The English were led by a proven warrior king who had obviously led his army out to fight. What had happened? The only clue we have is in Roger of Wendover's *Flowers of the Histories* for 940, in which he says: 'Then Olaf married Aldgyth, daughter of Earl Orm, with the support of whose aid and counsel he had obtained the aforesaid victory.' Now an 'Urm' crops up as a witness in not a few of Athelstan's charters. Here we have a Danish earl of similar name whose daughter had been given an English name – presumably because he had married an Englishwoman himself – not only going over to the invader but giving him 'aid and counsel'. It must have been a double-cross which left Edmund in an impossible position: deserted by one of the key Danelaw earls on the eve of the all-important battle with Olaf, and put in much the same position as Richard III on Bosworth Field when Stanley went over to Richmond. Rather than risk total disaster, Edmund decided to eat humble pie until he was strong enough to reverse the situation. Alfred himself would have done no less.

Edmund was immensely helped by the early death of Olaf, who was replaced by his cousin Olaf Sihtricson. Within months, Edmund launched a successful invasion of the territory ceded at Leicester and recovered the lot. The Northumbrians threw out Olaf Sihtricson in 943 and replaced him with Ragnald Guthfrithson. Both Olaf and Ragnald solicited Edmund's aid, visiting the English king in secret and accepting baptism – but this did not prevent Edmund from marching on York in 944 and driving them both out. On the surface, Edmund had re-established the kingdom of Athelstan.

But only on the surface. The old balance of English and Dane no longer existed: it had been complicated by a new element, the sturdy independence of the 'second generation' Norsemen, descendants of the adventurers who had followed the first Ragnald to York in Edward the Elder's time. Olaf Guthfrithson's invasion of 840–1 had given this Norse population new blood. The Norsemen and the Danes who had come to accept the English kings as their natural lords in Essex, East Anglia, and north-eastern Mercia, were natural rivals. To the latter, Edmund's come-back between Watling Street and the Humber was a deliverance, and this was emphasized by a special entry in the *Chronicle* for 942:

In this year King Edmund, lord of the English, protector of
men, the beloved performer of mighty deeds, overran Mercia,
as bounded by Dore, Whitwell gate, and the broad stream, the
River Humber; and five boroughs, Leicester and Lincoln,
Nottingham and likewise Stamford, and also Derby. The Danes
were previously subjected by force under the Norsemen, for
a long time in bonds of captivity to the heathens, until the de-
fender of warriors, the son of Edward, King Edmund, redeemed
them, to his glory.

This passage is an important one: it was composed as poetry and
deliberately stuck into the text of the *Chronicle* as a highlight. It
shows the effectiveness of the work of Edward and Athelstan in
that by 942 the descendants of Guthrum's army thought of themselves as Englishmen. And it is the earliest reference to a territorial
area beyond Watling Street which from now on would be given
capital letters: the Five Boroughs of the Danelaw.

The Britons of Strathclyde had aligned themselves with the
Norsemen of York, and Edmund's last campaign was a massive
expedition aimed at subduing Strathclyde and strengthening the
English alliance with Scotland. Edmund's army trampled its way
across Strathclyde, drove out King Dunmail, and left the battered
kingdom to Malcolm of Scotland.

In the last months of his reign, Edmund was caught up in the
toils of Athelstan's alliance with Louis of the West Franks. Once
again, the vikings of Normandy entered the English story. They
had captured King Louis in the summer of 945, and although the
hapless monarch was ransomed by the duke of the Franks he was
kept in custody by his redeemers. Edmund followed Athelstan's
approach and sent over a diplomatic mission to begin talks on
Louis' restoration. But in May 946 Edmund was killed, stabbed
to death – the first king of England to die violently. It was said
that his killer was a criminal who had returned from banishment,
and that Edmund died while preventing this thug from assaulting
his steward. Edmund's two sons were babies – they could not
succeed. The crown passed to the youngest son of Edward the
Elder: the atheling Eadred.

It took Eadred a year to secure the allegiance of Northumbria:
Archbishop Wulfstan of York and the Northumbrian earls swore
fealty to him at Tanshelf near Pontefract in 947. But, laments the

*Chronicle,* 'within a short space they were false to it all, both pledge and oaths as well'. The new spirit of restless independence north of the Humber caused Northumbria, once again, to break away from the English kingdom. The new leader in the north was the most famous viking of the age: Eric Blood-axe, once king of Norway, who had been driven out of his own kingdom in favour of his less violent brother Hákon.

Eric Blood-axe was something of an anachronism by the middle of the tenth century. A hundred years before, when the Danes and Norsemen followed leaders like Ivar the Boneless and Halfdan with avidity, he would have fitted in well. But with the crystallization of the more stable kingdoms of Denmark, Norway, and England, men like Eric became increasingly out of place as legitimate rulers. Nevertheless, they remained very dangerous, for they could appeal to all the independent and restless fighting men who preferred to follow a colourful viking leader of their own stamp. Eric was welcomed with open arms by the Norsemen in Northumbria, and attracted many recruits from the vikings of Ireland. He landed in Northumbria in 947 and was immediately hailed as the new king of York.

The most famous picture of Eric Blood-axe was painted by one of his enemies, Egil Skalla-grímsson. Egil, captured by Eric and faced with imminent death, saved his neck by composing a poem in praise of Eric called *Head-ransom*, which flattered Eric into merely banishing his victim. Egil's poem does not translate properly into modern English; the stress and metre is lost. But it remains one of the most vivid memorials of the viking age, with its clanging images drawn from Norse mythology and its praise of the warlord mighty in battle:

. . . I offered myself to the king as guest. It is my duty to sing his praise. I bore Othin's mead to the land of the English. I have composed a poem about the king, truly I praise him. I ask him for a hearing, since I have composed a poem of praise.

Pay heed, king – it becomes you well – how I utter my song, if I get a hearing. Most men have heard what battles the king fought, but the Storm-ruler saw where lay the slain.

There arose the crash of swords against the shield's rim; battle grew fierce round the king; the prince pressed on. Then could be heard there the fateful song of the storm of battle; the stream of swords roared as it flowed on mightily.

The weaving of spears did not miss its mark before the king's gay shield-ranks; the seals' plain roared in fury under the banners, where it wallowed in blood.

Men sank to the ground through the clash of javelins. From that Eric won renown.

. . . The prince bent the yew, arrows flew. Eric offered corpses to the wolves from his fight at sea.

Still do I wish to declare before men the disposition of the generous ruler. I shall hasten with my praise. He scatters the fire of the river and the prince holds lands in his grip. He is most deserving of praise.

The giver of gold armlets deals out gold; the distributor of rings will not endure niggardliness. Freely is spent by him the gravel of the hawk's land; he gladdens many seamen with Frothi's meal.

The inciter of sword-play throws the shield with his arm. He is a generous giver of rings. Both here and everywhere Eric's deeds grow greater, I speak advisedly, it is known east across the sea.

Pay heed, prince, how I have succeeded in my poem. I am glad that I received a hearing. With my mouth I have drawn Othin's sea from the bottom of my heart concerning this maker of battle.

I have brought the prince's praise to the end of the poem. I know the true measure in the company of men. I have brought praise of the king from the abode of laughter. It has come about that all have heard it.*

---

* For those not well versed in Norse mythology: 'Othin's sea' and 'Othin's mead' both mean poetry, the art bestowed by the magic mead which Othin, chief god of the Norse pantheon, stole from the dwarfs. 'Seals' plain' is one of many Scandinavian poetic names for the sea. 'Fire of the river', 'gravel of the hawk's land', and 'Frothi's meal' all mean gold. The 'hawk's land' is a man's hand, with reference to falconry. Frothi ordered gold to be ground in a magic mill, hence 'Frothi's meal'. The 'abode of laughter' is the poet's heart. In this translation 'arrows' renders the vivid poetic phrase 'wound-bees.'

Despite his formidable reputation – not to mention his energetic efforts to live up to his sanguinary nickname – Eric's career as king of York was short and stormy. This is about the only clear fact which emerges from the scanty information on these years. Eadred invaded Northumbria and his army was roughly handled by Eric's host, but he was nevertheless able to terrorize the Northumbrian leaders into abandoning Eric. But the return of Northumbria to English rule was ended (probably in 949) by the return of Olaf Sihtricson from Dublin and his acceptance as king in York. Olaf, in turn, was then expelled by Eric in about 952, and once again there was a Norse kingdom of York.

How it ended we do not know, but in 954 Eric, according to Roger of Wendover, 'was treacherously killed by Earl Maccus in a certain lonely place which is called Stainmore, with his son Haeric and his brother Ragnald, betrayed by Earl Oswulf; and then afterwards King Eadred ruled in these districts.' Stainmore is indeed a lonely place – up in the high Pennines between the head-waters of the Tees and Edendale. 'Earl Oswulf' was certainly the leader of English Northumbria; he may have started by accepting Eric's kingship only to become the last hope Eric had when the Northumbrians staged another of their uprisings. Eric's end has a lonely and heroic ring. He and all he stood for had outlived their time and the land he had thought to conquer and rule had rejected him. But all the scanty references to his death have a faintly respectful air, as if in homage to the passing of an age. It was no longer possible for a viking adventurer to carve out his own kingdom in England, and Eric was the last viking leader who tried to do so in the good old style and died in the attempt.

King Eadred died in November 955. He had shakily re-established Athelstan's English kingdom, but once again the line of succession was precarious. The next athelings in line to the throne were perilously young: Eadwig, the elder of Edmund's two sons, was barely sixteen, and Edgar only twelve. Eadwig was chosen as the new king. It was not a happy reign, nor did it last long. It saw the Mercian and Northumbrian earls renounce their allegiance to Eadwig and recognize the authority of his brother Edgar, which happened in 957; England was not formally reunited until Edgar replaced Eadwig in October 959. But in its own way this four-year reign of the unpopular boy king was an important one. For a start, England had no trouble from abroad in this period. Much more important was the rise to prominence of the councillors and churchmen who would make the reign of Edgar live for centuries in men's memory as a golden age of English history.

These included men like Byrthnoth, ealdorman of Essex, Æthelwold, ealdorman of East Anglia, and Ælfhere, ealdorman of Mercia, whose brother Ælfheah became ealdorman of Hampshire. But the most important in the long run proved to be the man whom Eadwig detested and forced into exile while he ruled: Dunstan, the brilliant abbot of Glastonbury, later archbishop of Canterbury.

Dunstan figured prominently in the scandal surrounding Eadwig's coronation. During the solemn feast after the crowning of the new king, Eadwig slipped away from the hall. It was Dunstan who found him in a nearby chamber with his crown set aside, fooling about with a lady and her daughter, both of whom were setting their caps at the young king with marriage in mind. Dunstan dragged Eadwig away after a fierce shouting-match and forced him back into the hall. Eadwig in fact married the daughter, Ælfgifu, who as queen won a reputation for herself as a model of piety. But Eadwig never forgave Dunstan and exiled him. So the story ran. Certainly the Church had little cause to complain about Eadwig: he was lavish with gifts of land to monasteries. Yet Eadwig's effective rule was limited to Wessex, thanks to the secession of Mercia and Northumbria; and there was a relieved sense of starting with a clean sheet when Eadwig died and Edgar was accepted as king by Wessex.

One of Edgar's first acts was to recall Dunstan, whom he soon promoted to the sees of Worcester and London. When Archbishop Oda died in 961, Edgar immediately advanced Dunstan to the see of Canterbury. It was the beginning of a remarkable partnership, in which the general reform of the English Church saw the great encouragement of monasticism for which Alfred the Great had longed. In this reform movement, Dunstan's 'lieutenants' were his old pupil from Glastonbury, Æthelwold, who became bishop of Winchester in 963; and Oswald, who had taken his vows at the 'model' reformed monastery of Fleury on the Continent and became archbishop of York in 972. The first decade of Edgar's reign saw a great purge of the monasteries of England, spearheaded by Dunstan, Oswald, and Æthelwold with the king's approval. This was not limited to clearing out unqualified clerks and replacing them with monks who had taken proper vows, but extended to the selection and appointment of bishops who were monks themselves – a procedure which had become normal by the end of the century. The reform movement was closely linked with similar trends across the Channel, and was highlighted around 970 by the publication of Bishop Æthelwold's *Regularis Concordia* – 'Agreement about the Rule'* – to be followed by the Church in England.

Certainly one of Dunstan's many great achievements was the splendid coronation of King Edgar – which did not take place until he had been ruling for over thirteen years. The ceremony was master-minded by Dunstan and was a highly important milestone in the history of the English monarchy. Dunstan insisted that the ceremony of the royal coronation must be a mirror-image of the consecration of a priest. This was why it did not take place while Edgar was under thirty years old, the lowest age at which a man could be ordained priest. It was said that Dunstan, an expert goldsmith and artist, made the crown himself: four-square for the City of God, blazing with the gems mentioned in the Book of Revelation – and that he insisted that Edgar shave off his beard for the ceremony in the manner of a priest undergoing ordination. The coronation took place at Bath in 973, and the careful reverence surrounding the ceremonial left its mark on the *Chronicle*'s entry:

> In this year Edgar, ruler of the English, with a great company, was consecrated king in the ancient borough, *Acemannesceaster* – the men who dwell in this island also call it by another name, Bath. There great joy had come to all on that blessed day which the children of men call and name the day of Pentecost. There was assembled a crowd of priests, a great throng of learned monks, as I have heard tell. And then had passed from the birth of the glorious King, the Guardian of Light, ten hundred years reckoned in numbers, except that there yet remained, by what documents say, seven and twenty of the number of years, so nearly had passed away a thousand years of the Lord of Victories, when this took place. And Edmund's son, bold in battle, had spent 29 years in the world when this came about, and then in the thirtieth was consecrated king.

* The Benedictine Rule.

1 ABOVE Offa's frontier with Wales: the famous Dyke, at Llanfair, Shropshire.

2 RIGHT
Sophisticated
coinage: a silver
penny of Offa's
reign (757–96).

3 ABOVE Viking raiders on a Lindisfarne tombstone (eighth to ninth century).

4 BELOW The superb lines of a Viking long-ship from Gokstad, Norway.

5 ABOVE War-
cruise and battle:
a Saga illustrated
on a carved stone
from Stora
Hammars,
Sweden.

6 RIGHT A Viking
sword from
Lincoln in the
Danelaw, with
typical 'cocked
hat' pommel.
Compare Cnut's
sword in Fig. 15.

7 ABOVE A gold and niello ring, decorated with two birds and a plant motif; the ring belonged to King Alfred's father, Ethelwulf.

8 LEFT A silver penny minted in the reign of Alfred's brother, Ethelred (865–71).

9 OPPOSITE A battle scene from a contemporary manuscript.

Et reuertentes uenerunt ad fontes iudicii. hec ē cades. p anticipatione dr. qd postea sic uocatū est. Significat aūt locū apud petrā. qui fons iudicii nominat. quia d̄s ibi populū iudicauit:

þa namon ða naman þa sige fæstan cyningas. sona on þā burgum sodoma ⁊ gomorra. ða god þe hi ðær fundon. ⁊ eac læddon aƿeg loth mid his æhtum. abrahames broðor sunu. ðe on þam burgum eardode:

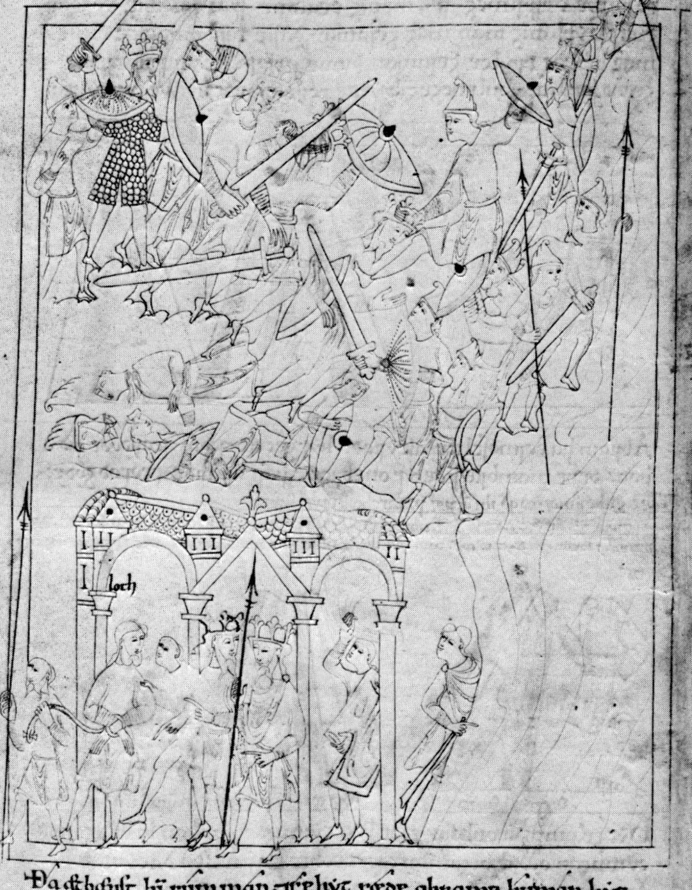


Ða cō þe berst hī sum man. ⁊ þæt he hyt sæde abrame hu man hys broðor sunu. onbethdum aƿeg lædde:

Damasc. nobilis urbs fenicis. Eodē aūt uocabulo ē masech ancille abrahā filius appellatus ē. porro masech qd sibi uelit in libris hebraicarū questionū plenius disputauimus. hic tantū in epistis sum funct officio: ut q ancillā abrahe masech nuncupatā pbemus:

10 ABOVE A coin of Alfred's reign (871–99).

11 BELOW The Alfred Jewel: made of gold, *cloisonné* enamel and rock crystal, it bears the inscription AELFRED MEC HEHT GEWYRGAN – Alfred had me made.

12 ABOVE King Athelstan presents a copy of Bede's works to
St Cuthbert.

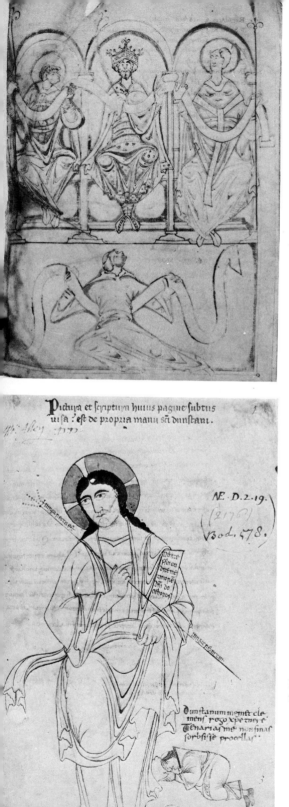

13 LEFT King Edgar, flanked by St Dunstan and St Ethelwold.

14 LEFT St Dunstan at the feet of Christ, from a tenth-century manuscript.

15 OPPOSITE Cnut and Queen Emma present a gold cross to the Church.

16 ABOVE
Edward the
Confessor on
his throne, a
scene from the
Bayeux
Tapestry.

17 RIGHT
William of
Normandy
knights Earl
Harold.

...ROLO DVX: ANGLORVM

18 BELOW A coin of Edward the Confessor's reign (1042–66).

...LAVES:POR REXIT: hIC:WILLELM:
DEDIT: HAROLDO:
ARMA

REVERSVS : EST

19 ABOVE Harold swears his oath to William.

20 LEFT In depicting Harold's return to Edward, the Tapestry emphasizes the Earl's apologetic gestures and bearing.

REGE M:

**21 RIGHT** Harold's coronation as shown in the Tapestry. More Norman propaganda, this scene stresses that Harold was a usurper crowned by a corrupt archbishop – the notorious Stigand, here shown in full regalia.

**22 BELOW** William's knights charge the English shield-wall at Hastings. These are Harold's housecarls, equipped with mailshirt and helmet, and their principal weapon is the spear, not the battle-axe. An unarmoured archer is shown at the right of the group.

**23 OVERLEAF** The death of Harold, who is hacked down by a mounted knight's sword at right – he is *not* the standing housecarl pulling an arrow from his helmet. The artist has given the Englishmen primitive heraldic devices for their shields. Weapons and armour are stripped from the dead in the lower margin.

HAROLD REX INTERFECTVS EST

'Bold in battle' was a conventional way of praising a good king, but in Edgar's case it only applied figuratively. The immunity from foreign attack which had carried England through Eadwig's brief reign lasted throughout that of Edgar's, and he never had to lead his people out to battle in the style of Alfred, Edward, Athelstan, Edmund, or Eadred. This happy chance earned Edgar the title by which he is usually remembered: 'the Peaceable'.

The second famous event of Edgar's reign was the unprecedented formal submission to him of every other king in all Britain. This was the natural sequel to his coronation and it took place at Chester in the same year, 973. It was no less of a prearranged ceremony than the coronation had been, and almost certainly Dunstan's Church had played a key role in assembling the cast. How many kings actually did homage to Edgar is in doubt; the *Chronicle* says six, but Florence of Worcester, writing under the Norman regime at the turn of the eleventh century, names eight: Kenneth of Scotland, Malcolm of Strathclyde, Maccus ('king of many islands'), and five Welsh sub-kings: Dunmail, Siferth, Hywel, Iago, and Juchil. These, according to Florence:

> . . . swore that they would be faithful to him and be his allies by land and sea. And on a certain day he went on board a boat with them, and, with them at the oars and himself seizing the helm, he steered it skilfully on the course of the River Dee, proceeding from the palace to the monastery of St John the Baptist, attended by all the crowd of ealdormen and nobles also by boat. And when he had completed his prayers he returned with the same pomp to the palace. As he entered he is reported to have said to his nobles that any of his successors might indeed pride himself in being king of the English, when he might have the glory of such honours, with so many kings subservient to him.

Edgar and his boatload of subservient royal oarsmen have passed into history together with Alfred and his overdone cakes. In both cases, however, the charm of the parable does not obstruct the underlying truth. Alfred had lived as a hunted fugitive: Edgar, his great-grandson, was the unchallenged overlord of all Britain.

As well as relishing all this peaceful magnificence, Edgar issued important laws which did much to aid the consolidation of the English kingdom. One basic measure had already been taken.

E

This was the Hundred Ordinance, a law defining the duties of the basic territorial unit of the kingdom: the hundred, building-block of the shire. Scholarly dispute seems likely to rage on over whether or not Edgar was in fact the king who issued it, but there is a considerable amount of evidence to point to Edmund, Eadred, or Eadwig as well. The law laid it down that the hundred-moot or court was to convene every four weeks and see to it that the king's law was generally enforced – 'each man is to do justice to another'. It was essentially a rural measure and livestock-rustling is the main offence mentioned: '. . . the value of the stolen property is to be given to him who owns the cattle, and the rest is to be divided into two, half for the hundred and half for the lord. . . .' The Ordinance ends on a grisly note, establishing the weight of the block of red-hot iron to be held by the man attempting to establish his innocence by the holy ordeal: three pounds.*

The Hundred Ordinance was a highly important measure for the tightening-up of local government on a national basis, for the Danelaw, too, had its basic hundreds, under the name of *wapentake*. With the Ordinance already at hand, Edgar's laws, 'to be common to all the nation, whether Englishmen, Danes or Britons, in every province of my dominion', added another layer of national bonding to the laws of the English kingdom. And the basic application-point of the law was the borough or hundred or *wapentake*:

. . . it is my will that every man is to be under surety both within the boroughs and outside the boroughs.

And witness is to be appointed for each borough and each hundred.

Thirty-six are to be chosen as witness for each borough; twelve for small boroughs and for each hundred, unless you wish for more.

And every man is with their witness to buy and sell all goods that he buys and sells, in either a borough or a wapentake.

And each of them, when he is first chosen as a witness, is to take an oath that never, for money or love or fear, will he deny any of the things for which he was a witness, and will never declare

* Athelstan had already passed a law for the ordeal of iron. The victim's hand was to be unbound after three days. If it were found unscarred, the man's innocence was proven.

anything in his testimony but that alone which he saw and heard. And two or three of the men thus sworn in are to be witness at every transaction.

Here we have the king of England ordering that his people should provide their own legal chaperones to provide for honest trading throughout the land. But Edgar's laws also reveal the considerable amount of 'home rule' which he permitted to the Danelaw:

Further, it is my will that there should be in force among the Danes such good laws as they best decide on, and I have ever allowed them this and will allow it as long as my life lasts, because of your loyalty, which you have always shown me. . . . If then my reeve or any other man, in high or low position, refuses it, and offers indignity either to the villagers or their herdsmen, the Danes are to decide by law what punishment they wish to apply in that matter.

This official recognition of 'home rule for the Danelaw' was nothing more than a written acknowledgment of the give-and-take relationship which had made the Anglo-Danish partnership work down to Edgar's time. But the concluding paragraphs of this code, issued at *Wihtbordesstan* some time in 962–3, show a similar recognition of provincial independence elsewhere in the kingdom:

Among the English, I and my councillors have decided what the punishment shall be, if any man offers resistance or goes to the length of slaying any one of those who are concerned in this investigation and who inform about concealed cattle, or any of those who give true witness and by their truthfulness save the innocent and lawfully bring destruction upon the guilty.
It is, then, my will that what you have decided on for the improvement of public order, with great wisdom and in a way very pleasing to me, shall ever be observed among you.
And this addition is to be common to all of us who inhabit these islands.
Now Earl Oslac and all the host who dwell in his aldermanry are to give their support that this may be enforced, for the praise of God and the benefit of the souls of all of us and the security of all people.

And many documents are to be written concerning this, and sent both to Ealdorman Ælfhere and Ealdorman Æthelwine, and they are to send them in all directions, that this measure may be known to both the poor and the rich.*

Edgar's *Wihtbordesstan* code ends with a sentence which suggests that, consciously or unconsciously, the royal clerk was trying to add to the king's reputation as 'the Peaceable': 'I will be a very gracious lord to you as long as my life lasts, and I am very well pleased with you all, because you are so zealous about the maintenance of the peace.'

That other yardstick of Saxon royal administration, official charters, shows a significant shift from the over-written blowsiness of Athelstan's time. Edgar's charters are short, crisp, and to the point. They retain all the traditional features of earlier charters – a pious statement of the king's intentions, a description of the property being handed over, and a curse on any man who dare break the deed. But they are usually a third the length of Athelstan's and the legal descriptions of the property are far more detailed. It is possible to trace this to the overhaul of clerkly posts carried out by Edgar and his zealous monastic bishops, especially Dunstan. These were not unworldly saints living in the Scriptures, but shrewd and capable officials who had dedicated themselves to the rooting-out of abuse in any form – whether it was a monastery full of loose-living monks or a slovenly office of bureaucratic clerks who preferred to show off their fancy Latin.

It would not be unfair to call this the watchword of Edgar's reign, in which the multi-national inhabitants of the English kingdom were certainly the most fortunate subjects in Western Europe. Free from foreign alarms and excursions, they were ruled by a popular king who made sensible laws with his able councillors, and asked no more of his people than that they should co-operate in keeping the law and the peace. Truly the fifteen years of Edgar's reign still seemed a golden age to the historians of later, troubled centuries. As the *Chronicle* saw it:

> . . . in his days things improved greatly, and God granted him that he lived in peace as long as he lived; and, as was necessary for him, he laboured zealously for this; he exalted God's praise

* Oslac, Ælfhere, and Æthelwine were the rulers of Northumbria, Mercia, and East Anglia respectively.

far and wide, and loved God's law; and he improved the peace of the people more than the kings who were before him in the memory of man. And God also supported him so that kings and earls willingly submitted to him and were subjected to whatever he wished. And without battle he brought under his sway all that he wished.

But this splendid reign was cut short with shocking speed on 8 July 975, with Edgar's sudden death – barely two years after his coronation and the water-pageant at Chester. Edgar was only thirty-two years old. 'His son then succeeded to the kingdom, a child ungrown, a prince of nobles, whose name was Edward.' Once again, a hoard of the fairest prospects for England had been placed in the hands of a boy king.

## Chapter 8

(D) In this year King Edward was killed at the gap of Corfe on 18 March in the evening, and he was buried at Wareham without any royal honours. And no worse deed than this for the English people was committed since first they came to Britain.

(C) In this year Ethelred was consecrated king on Sunday, a fortnight after Easter, at Kingston, and at his consecration were two archbishops and ten diocesan bishops. That same year a bloody cloud was often seen in the likeness of fire, and especially it was revealed at midnight. . . .

*Anglo-Saxon Chronicle:* 978 and [?] 979.

# Portents of disaster

Despite the over-all serenity of Edgar's reign, there had been signs before his death that there were plenty of forces only waiting for the absence of a firm hand on the tiller to make their presence felt. The following two examples, casually mentioned in the old histories of the reign, may be taken as straws in the wind. They certainly do not suggest a country steeped in flawless harmony.

The first is dated 962 in the *Chronicle*: 'And King Sigeferth killed himself, and his body is buried at Wimborne.' Who was this sub-king who was held in such respect that, despite his suicide, he was granted burial in one of the most venerated abbeys of Wessex? He is surrounded with total obscurity, but he was obviously a highly important figure who had found it impossible to accept Edgar's power-balance in England.

Far more important was a grim sequence of events in 969: 'In this year King Edgar ordered all Thanet to be ravaged.' This was an odd move on the part of 'the Peaceable', to say the least. Fuller details are provided by Roger of Wendover (who gives the date as 974). Roger's version gives a vivid picture of how even under Edgar the old hatreds between north and south could reach explosion-point: 'Merchants coming from York landed in the Isle of Thanet, and were at once taken prisoner by the islanders and robbed of all their goods.' This again hardly fits in with Edgar's honeyed words in praise of his peace-loving subjects at the end of the *Wihtbordesstan* law-code. Certainly Edgar reacted with a brutality which was something more than a just king punishing wrongdoers. Roger says that the king, 'moved by anger, was so furious with these pillagers that he despoiled all of them of their possessions and even deprived some of life'. The *Chronicle* put it more bluntly: he ordered the island to be ravaged.

Although Edgar could punish his own subjects with a heavy

hand, even he could do nothing to prevent the odd viking adventurer from setting up pirate bases on distant and uninhabited sectors of the English coast. This happened shortly after 965 when Thorgils Skarthi ('Hare-lip') and his brother Kormak Fleinn ('Arrow') built a fortress on the Yorkshire coast. Tradition has it that their nicknames led to the naming of Scarborough and Flamborough. They seem to have caused the local Northumbrians no trouble and there was no recorded attempt to oust them – but the fact that these adventurers could successfully build a fortress for themselves and their band on English soil was another indication that Edgar's peace was not all that it should have been.

Another source of internal dissension in England had a twofold root. The extensive land-grants to the Church had certainly brought about a pro-monastic and anti-monastic rivalry. Dunstan and Æthelwold, the leading lights of the Witan, were the obvious leaders of the pro-monastic party and were loyally supported by Byrhtnoth of Essex, Oslac of Northumbria and Æthelwine of East Anglia. But the man who really mattered was Ælfhere of Mercia. Although for a while he was out-voted in the Witan by Dunstan and the king's party, there was nothing to prevent Ælfhere from doing virtually as he pleased in Mercia after Edgar's death. Certainly the young King Edward could do little to keep Ælfhere in check:

> In his days because of his youth, the adversaries of God, Ealdorman Ælfhere and many others, broke God's law and hindered the monastic life, and destroyed monasteries and dispersed the monks and put to flight the servants of God, whom King Edgar had ordered the holy Bishop Æthelwold to institute; and they plundered widows time and again. And many wrongs and evil lawless acts rose up afterwards, and ever after that it grew much worse.

It was the inevitable back-lash of too many years of peace under an effective king, the strongest provincial lords feeling free to take an independent line and feather their own nests. Clearly Ælfhere was not alone in kicking over the traces, and he won much support in depicting Dunstan and the monastic reformers as a pack of greedy land-grabbers. What made this reaction really serious was that in Edgar's second son, the atheling Ethelred (ten years old when Edgar died, and even more suited to be a puppet king than the dutiful Edward), they had a potentially rival king. Edgar had married twice; Edward was the son of the first marriage and Ethelred of the second. Edgar's widow, Queen Ælfthryth, was now relegated to dowager status with the respectful title of 'Old Lady', and seems to have been involved with Ælfhere and the pro-Ethelred party.

England had wretched luck during Edward's brief reign. It was heralded by the appearance of a comet – a terrifying portent in medieval times – in the year of Edgar's death. In 976 England was blasted by an appalling famine and its inevitable sequel, disease. The depredations of the opposition party increased, and from the anonymous history of the life of Oswald, Dunstan's colleague as archbishop of York, we are told that it led to stormy scenes in the Witan:

The illustrious king died on 8 July, and by his death the state of the whole kingdom was thrown into confusion, the bishops were agitated, the noblemen stirred up, the monks shaken with fear, the people terrified. . . . Thus also the ealdorman of the Mercian people, Ælfhere by name, appropriating enormous revenues, which blind the eyes of many, ejected, as we have said, with the advice of the people and the outcry of the crowd, not only the sheep but the shepherds also. . . .

In those days, if the common crowd descried a man of our habit, an outcry was raised as if it saw a wolf among the sheep, for they put their trust in the above-mentioned ealdorman, being unmindful of the words of the psalmist who says: 'Put no trust in princes, nor in the children of men, in whom there is no salvation.' . . . When the fickle opinion and hostile madness of the enemy wished to reach with its pollution the eastern peoples of the Mercians, and to root out the glory of the people and the monasteries, God-fearing men stood firm against the blast of the mad wind which came from the western territories, driven from its proper course by the pleasures which withdraw the hearts of many from the right way and incite their minds to evil desires. The warlike thegn Ælfwold* opposed the iniquity which the will of Ælfhere, prospering according to the world's

---

* Brother of Æthelwine, ealdorman of East Anglia.

grandeur, was supporting, along with the people gathered to him. The wicked said among themselves, not rightly considering: 'Let us encompass the monks and oppress them, "and the inheritance shall be ours". May there be none to pity them, but let them be expelled, hurled down, derided, suppressed, bound, beaten, that not one may remain in all the land of the Mercians.' . . . But the holy mind of the righteous man Æthelwine was by no means ready to tolerate this, but assembling a noble army he, whom the prince of angels protected and strengthened, himself became the leader of the forces. After the death of the glorious King Edgar all the more noble thegns and the illustrious sons of leading men came to him with devoted heart, knowing for certain that in him was 'wisdom to do judgment'. In synod, he said he could in nowise suffer, while he lived, that the monks, who by the help of God maintained all the Christianity in the kingdom, should be expelled from the kingdom. And when the unworthy crowd wished to oppose him, there arose the intrepid thegn Ælfwold, his brother, tall of stature, pleasant in speech, dignified in aspect, but his face then burning with anger, and, like another Judas incited to war, said to all who could hear: 'If my life is preserved unharmed by Christ, I wish to preserve the things that are mine, and give them willingly to whoever pleases me and is obedient to my authority. If indeed Christ is prince of all things, shall he not have the portion which religious men gave to him for the redemption of their souls, but be driven far from us? How', he said, 'can we guard our own without his great help? By him who caused me to be re-born, I may not tolerate that such men be ejected from our territories, by whose prayers we can be snatched from our enemies. Then Ealdorman Brihtnoth* got up, 'a religious man and fearing God', and demanded silence and said to the army: 'Listen to me, veterans and young men, we all wish and desire that you should desire what the excellent thegn has now said.'

Some historians have argued that the anti-monastic reaction was not as black as it was painted by later religious chroniclers, and that there was a very sound political basis for halting the extension of land-grants to the Church. They have also expressed

---

* i.e. Byrhtnoth, ealdorman of Essex.

doubts about the development of the conspiracy to kill Edward and replace him with Ethelred, saying that there is really no proof that Queen Ælfthryth was involved. But the man who wrote the *Life of St Oswald* lived in Ethelred's reign, within twenty years of the event. Although it is certainly necessary to set aside the pious propaganda of his story, it gives us the unsavoury facts of one of the most notorious political murders in English history.

The plotters struck in March 978, when Edward had reigned for two years. Ælfhere of the Mercians and Queen Ælfthryth were party to it, and the actual murderers were the thegns of the young Ethelred, now rising thirteen years old.

Ælfthryth's household was a remote one: Corfe Castle on the Dorset coast. It was a lonely but dramatic place, where the castle knoll still plugs the gap in the Purbeck hills like a stone tooth. Here, on 18 March 978, Queen Ælfthryth and Ethelred awaited King Edward. He was paying his mother and brother a flying visit and he was alone, without the royal bodyguard of sword-thegn which would normally have attended him. But a group of Ælfthryth's thegns was waiting for Edward as he reined up his horse before the castle gate. One stepped forward with a welcome-cup for the king; another took the bridle of Edward's horse. As the king, sitting his horse, reached down to take the cup, the group of thegns closed round him. Edward was seized by the arm and pulled sideways in his saddle. He was heard to cry: 'What are you doing – breaking my right arm?' before he was stabbed in the back. What happened next is not clear, but he probably tried to break through the ring of assailants. It has been suggested that one of the thegns twisted the king's stirrup before stampeding the horse. Edward certainly fell from his saddle and was caught by one foot, mercilessly dragged by the maddened beast as it bolted. Even if the stab wound had not been fatal, Edward would have been battered to death before his horse was finally caught.

By the middle of the tenth century, acts such as this were nothing new. The whole history of the Anglo-Saxon kingdoms in England had been redolent with blood, violence, treachery, and sudden death. But the murder of the young King Edward was totally different, an utterly shocking act. For centuries it was remembered with shame. Edward himself earned the posthumous title of 'the Martyr'. He was unofficially canonized and miracles were attributed to him. It was said that when his mangled body was given proper burial it was found to be uncorrupted. His epitaph and the popular mood was written in the *Chronicle*:

Men murdered him, but God honoured him. In life he was an earthly king; he is now after death a heavenly saint. His earthly kinsmen would not avenge him, but his heavenly Father has greatly avenged him. The earthly slayers wished to blot out his memory on earth, but the heavenly Avenger has spread abroad his memory in heaven and in earth. Those who would not bow to his living body, now bend humbly on their knees to his dead bones. Now we can perceive that the wisdom and contrivance of men and their plans are worthless against God's purpose.

No pious interpretation of the facts in later years could deny that the plot had been a total success. There was no other choice left to the Witan but to elect Ethelred king of England. It was done with speed: the coronation took place at Kingston two weeks after Easter. Archbishops Dunstan and Oswald officiated. Politically, their hands were tied. There could be no question of launching a witch-hunt against Edward's killers. Despite the awesome nature of the crime, Ethelred's accession was popular. He looked the part – 'he was young in years,' says Oswald's biographer, 'graceful in manners, beautiful in face and comely in appearance.' He was popularly absolved from any personal implication in his brother's murder. This could never be forgotten, but in the year of Ethelred's coronation there was general hope that the erupting hatreds which had raged since Edgar's death would evaporate.

When Ethelred became king, he was only thirteen years old. The dominant members of the Witan remained Dunstan and Æthelwold; Ælfhere seems to have toned down his energetic anti-clerical policy in deference to the shock caused by the murder of Edward. The *Chronicle* has Ælfhere, in 979, presiding over the transfer of Edward's body from Wareham, where it had first been hastily buried, 'with great honour', to Shaftesbury. Presumably Queen Ælfthryth also took a prominent part in the ceremonial re-burial of her stepson, but there is no record of it. Cynics at the time must have muttered at the blasphemous farce, but it would have suited Ælfhere well as a political move – and would certainly not have been discouraged by Dunstan and Æthelwold. Ælfhere died in 983, being succeeded as ealdorman of

Mercia by his son Ælfric, but Queen Ælfthryth was certainly still alive in 996, when Ethelred made an extensive land-grant to his mother. There is a particular irony surrounding this grant: Ethelred had gained possession of the territory as a result of the crime of one of his subjects. In transferring it to his mother, who had been an instrument of his promotion to the throne, Ethelred must have felt that he was paying off an old debt – but also that he was taking the chance to buy a measure of absolution for himself. The prologue to his grant reads:

> Truly, these aforesaid lands a certain man, by name Wulfbald, is known to have held, and they were awarded to the control of my right by the most just judgment of all my chief men, on account of the guilt of his crime, as is found written in what follows in an account in English. And I concede to her these territories in exchange for the land which she previously gave to me, i.e. Cholsey, requiting a gift with a gift, desiring to obtain the divine promise: 'Give, and it shall be given unto you.'

There is a note of painstaking self-justification about nearly all of Ethelred's charters and grants, and it is possible to imagine him getting trapped by the wording of his grant to Ælfthryth. Eighteen years had passed since his brother's murder had brought him to the throne, but even so the dark implications which men could still read into 'the land which she previously gave to me' prompted the insertion of 'i.e. Cholsey'.

The gloomy omen of the bloody cloud which had ushered in the reign of Ethelred soon became hideous reality. One hundred years of English history were rolled back as once again viking raids began to hammer the English coast and find it a rich and vulnerable prey. The patient build-up of England's military resources by Alfred and his successors, the splendid fleet maintained by Edgar – all might never have existed. Southampton was the first victim, sacked by the crews of seven viking ships in 980. Later in the year, the Isle of Thanet was plundered by a viking force, while in the north-west a fleet from Ireland ravaged Cheshire. Cornwall and Devon were the chief sufferers in 981, the most notable viking raid sacking St Petroc's monastery at Padstow. Three crews hit the Dorset coast in 982, ravaging Portland – a raid which must have caused much pious head-shaking, for this was the neighbourhood of Corfe Castle, where King Edward had been murdered four years before. The *Chronicle* also states that London was burned down in 982, but gives no mention of the sizeable viking force which would have been needed to do this. The fire may well have been accidental. Certainly, even in later centuries, Englishmen were quick to point to acts of God in these ill-starred years.

What had happened to the English? Back in the ninth century even the earliest viking raids had been promptly tackled by the local *fyrd*, led either by the ealdorman or by the king himself. While Ethelred was still in his teens and firmly under the control of Dunstan and Æthelwold, he could be excused for not providing any energetic leadership for his people. But in fact it went much deeper than that. Ethelred was totally unwarlike. Alfred the Great, Edward the Elder, and Edmund may have won glory on the battlefield as teenagers – it was not for Ethelred. This put the onus on the ealdormen. As we have seen, Ælfhere of Mercia had other fish to fry in these years – there is not the slightest indication that he did anything to check the viking foray in Cheshire. But even in the other shires, where courageous ealdormen and thegns like Æthelwine and Ælfwold held sway, no energetic counter-measures seem to have been taken against this new wave of raids.

We are left with the obvious deduction: that England had had too many years of peace. The coastal shires in particular had got out of the habit of raising instant armies to see off chance raids from overseas. They were quick to re-learn the old lessons of vigilance; but the old victories were not to be repeated.

Against this ominous background of renewed viking raids, the first ten years of Ethelred's reign slipped by. One by one, the great men who had been the pillars of the kingdom for decades died – Ælfhere and Æthelwold in 983 and 984 respectively, and Dunstan himself in 988. Against this melancholy background, the *Chronicle* lists provoking events without explaining them. Ælfhere's son Ælfric was 'driven out of the land' in 985. There is no hint of formal exile; we are left to conclude that Ælfric tried to apply his father's heavy hand without being favoured with his father's political acumen, and that the Mercians decided that he had gone too far. Certainly there is no mention that the king or his councillors were involved. In 986, however, we are told that 'the king laid waste the diocese of Rochester'. As we have seen, Edgar had not hesitated to send a punitive expedition against his own people when he thought it necessary, but in the case of Ethelred's plundering of Rochester we do not know whether it was for common or garden law-breaking or, perhaps for co-operating with viking raiders. That same year, the English suffered another disaster comparable with the failure of the annual crop: '... the great murrain first occurred in England.' This would have made for a cruel winter, for in times of a national livestock epidemic it would be impossible to lay in the customary stocks of salted meat for the winter months.

Then, in 988, the year of Dunstan's death, came the first of two bloody clashes with viking raiders that made history. They occurred at opposite ends of the island – in Somerset and in Essex. They were both crushing defeats for the English. But both were remembered with a queer, inverse pride bordering on fatalism – a sad, defiant pride that would not be aroused again until Hastings in 1066.

The 988 defeat happened when a viking fleet from the west swept down on Watchet on the Somersetshire coast and razed it. This time, however, the English fought back in the old style. An energetic local leader, a thegn named Streonwold, called out the local *fyrd* and gave battle. It seems to have been a brave but premature piece of interception. The fight itself was a killing-match in classic style, with the victory going to the Danes, and Streonwold and the other English leaders falling in battle. He may well have made the fatal error which others had made before him and would do in later years: that of attacking before the full muster had been raised.

The whole story of the viking attack at Watchet could have been lifted direct from the period of the early viking raids in the ninth century. The viking leader was not named and his English opponent was a comparatively minor character, remembered only for his futile gallantry. But the next campaign was a very different matter. It was another dead loss to the English, giving them nothing more than the memory of one more epic defeat. And it opened a new chapter in the history of Saxon England: the humiliating period of repeated Danegeld, of yielding to incessant demands for more and more protection-money rather than defiance and resistance. It ushered in a period of shameful and unrelieved decline which ended only with the crown of England passing to a viking warrior-king.

In 991 a large viking fleet began to punish the south-eastern coast. The Watchet raiders had almost certainly been Irish-based Danes; these were Norwegians, led by the remarkable leader Olaf Tryggvason, afterwards king of Norway and a militant, convert-or-die Christian. Olaf's fleet started with Kent, pulverizing the Folkestone and Sandwich regions. The raiders then sailed north across the Thames estuary to Harwich harbour, pushed up the River Orwell and plundered the Ipswich region. Then they fell back along the coast to the Blackwater estuary and the site of the old *burh* of Edward the Elder at Maldon. But here their string of easy victories ended. Waiting for them was the host of Essex, raised and led in person by one of the 'grand old men' of Saxon England: Ealdorman Byrhtnoth, veteran statesman, former councillor of Edgar the Peaceable. Sensing that the raiding fleet was almost bound to try for a raid in the Blackwater estuary, he had positioned his army brilliantly.

The English host was not only sufficiently well positioned to attack the viking force, but to prevent the latter from landing at all. Olaf's ships were forced to make landfall on a tidal island in the estuary, separated from the mainland by a causeway covered at first by the high tide but commanded by Byrhtnoth's men. The old ealdorman had won the trick without a blow being struck, simply by occupying the right terrain in time. But a fatal decision to bring about a stand-up fight where both armies could bring their full strengths to bear resulted in disaster for the English – and inspired one of the most famous works of Anglo-Saxon literature, *The Battle of Maldon*.

All that survives of this epic poem (composer unknown) is the latter section describing the fight. It opens dramatically enough, with a formal summons from the leader of the invaders for the English to yield and pay tribute for peace. Shakespeare himself, even with the visits of Mountjoy to Henry v on the eve of Agincourt, never did better than the reply attributed to Byrhtnoth:

'Hear you, searover, what this folk says? For tribute they will give you spears, poisoned point and ancient sword, such war gear as will profit you little in the battle. Messenger of the seamen, take back a message, say to your people a far less pleasing tale, how that there stands here with his troop an earl of unstained renown, who is ready to guard this realm, the home of Ethelred my lord, people and land; it is the heathen that shall fall in the battle. It seems to me too poor a thing that you should go with our treasure unfought to your ships, now that you have made your way thus far into our land. Not so easily shall you win tribute; peace must be made with point and edge, with grim battle-play, before we give tribute.'

Holding the tidal causeway, waist-deep in the water, stood the warriors Wulstan, Ælfhere, and Maccus. They had a far easier task than Horatius and his two colleagues holding the Tiber bridge in the early days of Rome, for their slow-wading enemies could be shot down before they ever came to grips. The three were well supplied with javelins and easily coped with the first, tentative, viking attempt to win a beach-head on the mainland. Then the raiders changed their tune, 'betook themselves to guile, craved leave to land, to pass over the ford and lead their men across'.

Why Byrhtnoth listened to them has been debated ever since, but he did. A definite note of criticism tinges the poem as it proceeds:

> Then the earl, in his pride, began to give ground all too much to the hateful folk; Brihthelm's son called over the cold water (the warriors gave ear): 'Now is the way open before you; come quickly, men, to meet us in battle. God alone knows to whom it shall fall to hold the field.'
>
> The wolves of slaughter pressed forward, they recked not for the water, that viking host; west over Pante, over the gleaming water they came with their bucklers, the seamen came to land with their linden shields.
>
> There, ready to meet the foe, stood Brihtnoth\* and his men. He bade them form the war-hedge with their shields, and hold their ranks stoutly against the foe. The battle was now at hand, and the glory that comes in strife. Now was the time when those who were doomed should fall. Clamour arose; ravens went circling, the eagle greedy for carrion. There was a cry upon earth.

The poem proceeds like a Teutonic version of the *Iliad*: who did the mightiest deeds, who was wounded how – liberally interspersed with grim little speeches of encouragement and

\* i.e. Byrhtnoth.

defiance. Two points stand out: Byrhtnoth was killed fairly early on in the fight, and there were some panic-stricken desertions. But the hard core of the English force at Maldon fought to the death. These were close relatives of Byrhtnoth and his loyal thanes, men who could see no honourable life for them if they survived their lord. The principle was nothing new. What obviously startled the England of the late tenth century was the fact that such loyalty was still to be found – a grim consolation.

In practical terms there was no other satisfaction to be drawn from the disaster at Maldon. Byrhtnoth's East Saxon host seems to have been the only fighting army in the field in 991. Olaf's army was mauled by the carnage but there was nothing left to stand up to the survivors, and Sigeric, Archbishop of Canterbury, was the prime mover in advising Ethelred to make peace with Olaf. The latter was bought off with a massive Danegeld. He accepted Christianity and the *Chronicle* affirms that Ethelred stood godfather to him.

This uneasy peace was intended to be formalized by a remarkable treaty the text of which still survives. Extensive clauses were drawn up to safeguard English merchant shipping. Fair dealing for quarrels between Englishmen and Danes was reaffirmed. A general amnesty on all damage and feuds incurred during the period before the treaty was proclaimed. It was the first ever written English agreement to deal with unspecified 'seamen' – random vikings: 'And if anyone charges a man of our country that he stole cattle or slew a man, and the charge is brought by one viking and one man of this country, he is then to be entitled to no denial.' It is a frightened treaty, with the English bending over backwards to show how reasonable they were prepared to be in the face of brute force. But the real shock comes with the concluding sentence: 'Twenty-two thousand pounds in gold and silver were paid from England to the army for this truce.' Here was the shameful aftermath, the unanswerable proof of how much the heroism at Maldon had been wasted. Dressed up as a treaty providing for future mutual assistance between Olaf's army and the English, it was a confession of national insolvency.

Byrhtnoth's legacy to his people was the memory of a legendary fight – but that fight had been, when all is said and done, a foolish sacrifice. It was remembered because of that strange quirk in human nature which likes to remember lost battles caused by foolishness – Sir Richard Grenville and the *Revenge*, Custer's Seventh Cavalry and the Little Big Horn. At the time, it was easy to compare Byrhtnoth's gallant if unavailing end with that of the legendary hero Beowulf, who finally met his death at a ripe old age in a battle with a dragon. Fabulous attributes clustered around Byrhtnoth's memory; it was said that he was a six-foot-nine giant, and great excitement was caused when a mighty decapitated skeleton of similar dimensions was unearthed at Ely in 1769. He was one of the last of the long-serving councillors of Edgar the Peaceable to quit the scene; the last two, Archbishop Oswald of York and Ealdorman Æthelwine of East Anglia, died the following year.

To all intents and purposes, King Ethelred was now on his own, free from all the legacies of the past as far as his advisers were concerned – although his treasury officials were wincing from the appalling financial cost of buying a precarious peace. Prospects were not bright, yet the English had certainly faced worse ones before.

In the year 992, when Oswald and Æthelwine were laid to rest, the impact of Maldon still dominated the scene. The unknown poet who immortalized the battle put these words into the mouth of one of Byrhtnoth's companions as he faced the end on the battlefield: 'Thoughts must be the braver, heart more valiant, courage the greater as our strength grows less.' Here was a simple prescription for the survival of the English in the terrible twenty-five years that lay ahead. Winston Churchill, with his grim diagnosis of 'blood, toil, sweat, and tears', was to offer no less in 1940. The real difference lay in the quality of the country's leadership.

## Chapter 9

'Upon the king! Let us our lives, our souls,
Our debts, our careful wives, our children, and
Our sins, lay on the king! We must bear all.'

Shakespeare, *Henry V*, IV. i.

Then after midsummer the great fleet came to Sandwich, and did just as they were accustomed, ravaged, burnt and slew as they went. Then the king ordered the whole nation from Wessex and Mercia to be called out, and they were out on military service against the Danish army the whole autumn, yet it availed no whit more than it had often done before; for in spite of it all, the Danish army went about as it pleased, and the English levy caused the people of the country every sort of harm, so that they profited neither from the native army nor the foreign army.

*Anglo-Saxon Chronicle*: 1006.

# The nightmare returns

The unmitigated disasters of King Ethelred's reign have earned him the deathless title of 'the Unready' – a man synonymous with incompetence and failure. But the title is not completely fair. It is in fact a corruption of 'Rede-less' – evil-counselled, ill-advised – and this description is at the same time both accurate and well-deserved. As we have seen, the early years of Ethelred's reign had proved that he was no fighting king in the tradition of his fore-fathers. Ethelred certainly cannot be blamed for being unable to delegate responsibility: he was pathetically willing to delegate the lot. But he was as disastrous at picking honest and competent subordinates as he was at ruling effectively. Ethelred simply did not inspire respect or confidence, and he and his people suffered accordingly.

The immediate aftermath of Maldon and the treaty with Olaf in 991 proved this to the hilt. Ethelred and his councillors clearly had no confidence at all that Olaf would stick to the terms of the treaty, and in 992 they decided to take the precaution of concentrating what was left of King Edgar's splendid fleet at London. Clearly, the raiding fleet of 991, despite the treaty, was still at large on the east coast, and this was a wise move. It was only to be expected that the English fleet would have a split command, for it was supplied and manned by English and Danish contingents. But at no other time has an English fleet ever put to sea under the command of two bishops, a Danish earl, and an English nobleman!

The latter was none other than Ælfric, who had been driven out of England in 985. Ethelred had a pathetic trust in Ælfric, son of Ealdorman Ælfhere through whose machinations he had succeeded to the kingdom. By 992 Ælfric was back in England and ealdorman of Mercia again, and Ethelred gave him command of the English division of the fleet, with Earl Thored commanding the ships from the Danelaw. What happened next suggests that Ælfric had spent his exile intriguing with viking leaders across the North Sea. When the English fleet sailed to intercept the viking fleet in 992, Ælfric not only sent warning to the enemy but defected from the fleet on the eve of the battle, enabling the viking fleet to escape with the loss of only one ship. Battle was eventually joined, but the English fleet had lost the initiative and the division from East Anglia and London suffered a punishing reverse.

King Ethelred reacted viciously. In the following year he hunted down the young son of the defecting Ælfric and had him blinded. That was about the king's only contribution to the year 993 and it may well have had a decisive influence on the campaign of that year. A viking fleet sacked Bamburgh in the far north of Northumbria and captured rich spoils. The raiders then started to work their way south down the Yorkshire coast, past the Humber estuary into Lincolnshire. This was Danelaw territory, and the Danish earls reacted by raising 'a very large English army' to guard the coast. But when it seemed that the raiding army was on the point of being brought to decisive action, the three commanding Danish earls – Fræna, Godwine, and Frythegyst – refused battle and retreated. Bearing in mind the very simple but deep Danish belief in the duties of lordship, this could quite easily have been a gesture of defiance and protest against Ethelred's cowardly and spiteful treatment of Ælfric's son.

The next year any hopes which may have lingered for the survival of the peace with Olaf after Maldon were shattered. Olaf returned with another big fleet of ninety-four ships. This time he was acting in partnership with Swein 'Forkbeard' of Denmark, and the viking leaders headed straight for the Thames estuary and London. There they met with a severe shock. London held out stoutly, and the viking army lost heavily in trying to storm it. The Londoners proved that given a fair chance Alfred the Great's *burh*-system was still very much a match for any viking force; as the *Chronicle* puts it, 'they suffered more harm and injury than they ever thought any citizens would do to them'.

London survived with well-earned battle honours, but the victory went for nothing. Olaf and Swein cut their losses before the walls of London and proceeded to terrorize the entire south-east. 'Horsing' their army in the time-honoured style of Ivar the Boneless and Halfdan in the previous century, they rode at will through

Essex, Kent, Sussex, and Hampshire, with their ships keeping in close touch by following round the coast. The damage was immense, and there is no record that any attempt was made to raise an army and bring the invaders to battle. Ethelred and his councillors saw no other way out. They sent messengers to Olaf and Swein asking for peace, offering not only a paid tribute but even the supply of provisions if only they would stop the raiding. Not surprisingly, 'they accepted that'. The viking army marched insolently to Southampton and pegged out its winter quarters there. The whole of Wessex was scoured for provisions to keep the vikings comfortably through the winter, and suffered the additional indignity of putting up another big Danegeld of 16,000 pounds.

Pathetically, Ethelred tried to glean some shred of dignity from such a sorry capitulation by asking Olaf to come and meet him at Andover. The English had to hand over hostages which were kept in the viking camp during Olaf's trip. Ethelred showered gifts on Olaf and stood sponsor to him at his confirmation. 'And then Olaf promised – as also he performed – that he would never come back to England in hostility.' Not that he had any intention of doing so. Olaf had already set his sights on becoming king of Norway, which he managed the following year.

Swein of Denmark was pointedly omitted from the meaningless junket at Andover. England had not seen the last of him. And after the campaign of 994, Swein had abundant memories of the basic defencelessness of the kingdom of the English, and the readiness of its rulers to reach for their purses and pay vast sums of cash rather than fight.

Nevertheless, Swein and his forces left England with those of Olaf, and the island got a respite of two years. Spirits in the island were definitely not cheered by the visitation of a comet in the year 995, but there were no more viking raids until 997. The next raiders are identified in the *Chronicle* as 'Danes', but Swein is not mentioned by name. A powerful fleet came right down the Channel and rounded Land's End. It pushed up into the Severn estuary and raided in Wales, but concentrated on Cornwall and Devon. The vikings' last target on the north coast was Watchet, where memories of the last raid nine years before were still vivid. The vikings then headed back round Land's End and penetrated the estuary of the River Tamar. Using the river as a highway, they left a belt of devastation behind them as far as the town of Lydford. As they withdrew down-river to the sea, they found the richest prey of the raid. This was the splendid new abbey at Tavistock, a lay foundation, patronized by the ruling family of Devon. Glutted with the loot of Tavistock, they 'took with them to their ships indescribable booty'; but we have no way of knowing where they spent the winter of 997–8. All that is certain is that they did not quit English soil, for the following year saw them raiding 'as widely as they pleased' in Dorset.

Such a prolonged raid gave the English, even under Ethelred's half-hearted regime, time to raise forces against the enemy. But even in the bald account of the *Chronicle* it can be sensed that the English did not have their hearts in the task of smashing the invaders. The old fire had gone; they were morally beaten before a blow was struck. The *Chronicle* says that 'the English army was often assembled against them, but as soon as they were to have joined battle, a flight was always instigated by some means, and always the enemy had the victory in the end'. Nothing prevented the raiding army from setting up camp for another winter on the Isle of Wight, and getting its provisions from Hampshire and Sussex.

After over eighteen months of ominous reports from the west country, the eastern shires should have been fully prepared for the campaign of 999. Rounding the North Foreland into the Thames estuary, the viking fleet entered the Medway. But only the men of Kent were ready. They marched out to tackle the invaders, confident that they were only the spearhead of a massed force – but Ethelred left the Kentishmen on their own, and they were routed in battle. Kent was left to the Danes, who promptly 'horsed' themselves and set about the devastation of West Kent with gusto.

After wasting all the advance warnings he must have received from the west, and cravenly leaving the Kentishmen to their fate, Ethelred finally brought himself to order the collection of a large-scale army and fleet. Despite the king's procrastination, the fleet and army were rapidly mobilized – suggesting that the ealdormen had already issued preliminary orders for mobilization and that they had had no trouble in getting volunteers. The sense of total frustration and depression at the uselessness of what happened next is best expressed by the *Chronicle* itself:

But when the ships were ready, one delayed from day to day, and oppressed the wretched people who were on the ships. And ever, as things should have been moving, they were the more delayed from one hour to the next, and ever they let their enemies' force increase and ever the English retreated inland and the Danes continually followed; and then in the end it effected nothing – the naval expedition or the land expedition – except the oppression of the people and the waste of money and the encouragement of their enemies.

The utter inability of the English to prevent the Danes from coming and going as they chose was proved the following year, 1000, when the entire viking fleet embarked and crossed the Channel to spend the summer in Normandy. This viking province by now had a history of about seventy-five years behind it. Although it was rapidly absorbing French influences – its rulers had adopted the French title of 'duke' – it was still an open haven for viking fleets from overseas and blood ties with Scandinavia were strong. Back in England, Ethelred was left with an expensive fleet and army on his hands, but with the strong probability that the raiders would be back – almost certainly with Norman reinforcements. Now was the time to keep his forces in being and tighten the defences for another trial of strength. Instead he did the one thing that has left historians baffled ever since: he took the entire fleet and army and set off on a combined expedition to the Solway Firth and the Isle of Man, leaving the south defenceless.

It must be remembered that only scraps of the history of the north have survived for the over-all period of Anglo-Saxon England. What threat could have been posed form the north we simply do not know. But it is hard to imagine any danger more pressing than that of renewed viking trouble in the south. Ethelred's reputation, it is safe to say, was more than usually at rock-bottom after the fiasco of 999. There is a good case that he seized the chance of putting on a combined land and naval show of strength in the style of his grandfather Athelstan. But the expedition was only a moderate success, and came nowhere near cancelling the humiliations of previous years. Ethelred's troops pushed north into Strathclyde and were set to plundering there, 'and his ships went out round Chester and should have come to meet him, but they could not'. One concrete achievement was a descent on the Isle of Man, a long overdue show of strength as the island had been used as a viking base for over a century. In the middle tenth century, the Isle of Man had given little or no trouble – indeed, Maccus, its ruler, had been one of the minor kings who helped row Edgar on the Dee in 973. In the overview, however, Ethelred picked up little or no easy glory in his abortive northern expedition of the year 1000. The venture only revealed serious flaws in the English fleet – and was of no use at all in resisting the next viking assault, which came in the spring of 1001.

Once again it was the west country that suffered, A viking fleet entered the mouth of the Exe and laid siege to Exeter, but as at London in 994 the city held out defiantly. Refusing to bleed themselves white against this bastion of resistance, the raiders by-passed Exeter and set off eastwards on a march that rivalled the performance of the old Great Army of 866, plundering enthusiastically as they went. The *fyrd* of Hampshire was called out and led in pursuit by two of Ethelred's high-reeves, Æthelweard and Leofwine, and the English host finally caught up with the Danes in the region of East and West Dean, in western Sussex. A spirited fight gave the Danes the technical victory – 'they had control of the field' – although they lost far more heavily than the English. Nevertheless, the battle halted the Danish lunge to the east; their army withdrew to Devon. There it received a reinforcement which did much to lower the spirits of the English. The important Danish earl, Pallig, whom Ethelred had showered with gifts of cash and land, went over to the invaders with a small fleet of ships. The Danes in Devon embarked on an orgy of estate-burning. They were brought to battle at Pinhoe but managed to rout the English force, and withdrew to establish themselves on the Isle of Wight. Once again, Ethelred fell back on suing for peace.

This was part of a tortuous flight of diplomacy which ended, needless to say, in lowering his stock still further. Negotiations were already in train for the king's marriage to Emma, daughter of Duke Richard II of Normandy. By this marriage Ethelred hoped to win a powerful ally and deny Normandy as a convenient replenishment-base to future viking raiders of England. The events of 1001 had overtaken him, however, and he could not escape another crushing Danegeld (this time of 24,000 pounds in cash) and the agreement to provision the Danish army in the Isle of Wight until it felt like leaving.

The year 1002 came in with a faint breath of hope. The Danish army accepted the terms as offered, and the marriage settlement with Richard of Normandy was agreed. The lady Emma arrived in England and became Ethelred's new queen under the clumsy but venerated English name of Ælfgifu. But these hopes were dashed by a stroke of the king's which was darkly compared to the murder of his brother Edward for its baseness and treachery, and suicidal folly: the St Brice's Day Massacre of 13 November.

Almost certainly, it had been the defection of Earl Pallig which provoked Ethelred into his plan to end the danger of a Danish 'fifth column' in England by a wholesale massacre of the Danes. It was treacherous, because it meant a Gestapo-like pounce on the persons and families of Danish men who had served him well. It was stupid, because at best Ethelred could rely on only a small number of loyal murderers, and in any case England needed the Danelaw to cope with any future trouble in the Midlands and the north. And when Ethelred's killers disposed of the most important Danish hostage of all – Swein's sister Gunnhild – it created a merciless blood-feud on Swein's side which the Danish ruler could never forget.

An act of such stupendous folly could only have been justified if England and Normandy had just concluded a binding alliance against the Danes – and they had not. What makes the St Brice's Day Massacre really sickening is the hypocritical note of self-justification in a charter of the king to St Frideswide's monastery at Oxford two years later. This document gives a vivid picture of what the massacre had been like, and at the same time is a good example of Ethelred's propaganda in defence of his own misrule:

... I have restored the territories which belong to that monastery of Christ with the renewal of a new title-deed; and I will relate in a few words to all who look upon this document for what reason it was done. For it is fully agreed that to all dwelling in this country it will be well known that, since a decree was sent out by me with the counsel of my leading men and magnates, to the effect that all the Danes who had sprung up in this island, sprouting like cockle amongst the wheat, were to be destroyed by a most just extermination, and this decree was to be put into effect even as far as death, those Danes who dwelt in the

aforementioned town,* striving to escape death, entered this
sanctuary of Christ, having broken by force the doors and bolts,
and resolved to make a refuge and defence for themselves therein
against the people of the town and the suburbs; but when all the
people in pursuit strove, forced by necessity, to drive them out,
and could not, they set fire to the planks and burnt, as it seems,
this church with its ornaments and its books. Afterwards, with
God's aid, it was renewed by me and my subjects, and, as I have
said above, strengthened in Christ's name with the honour of a
fresh privilege, along with the territories belonging to it, and
endowed with every liberty, regarding royal exactions as well as
ecclesiastical dues.

This bland statement of how desperate men and women were
burned alive in a church to which they had fled for sanctuary
is as callous and repellent as Cromwell's letter to Parliament
describing how the Irishmen of Drogheda were burned alive in
*their* churches. In Ireland, the slaughter of Drogheda is still
vividly remembered today, after three centuries and more. The
impact of the St Brice's Day Massacre on the viking world can
only be imagined. It was the cardinal error of Ethelred's reign.

The immediate aftermath of the massacre suggests that Ethelred
may even have been so stupid as to embark on his mass-murder
programme before the last of the Danish fleet had left the Isle of
Wight. The first recorded event for the year 1003 is a Danish
attack on Exeter. That a strong Norman influence had been absorbed by the government thanks to Ethelred's marriage to
Ælfgifu-Emma is proved by the fact that the reeve charged with the
day-to-day government of Exeter was a Norman, Count Hugh
– the *Chronicle* crushingly calls him a 'French *ceorl*'. Hugh handed
Exeter over to the Danes, thus, we can only presume, removing
all faith in the value of the Norman alliance. The Danes sacked
the city and looted it bare, then marched north-eastwards into
Wiltshire.

Unbelievably, Ethelred had still not accepted that Ælfric of
Mercia was a professional self-seeker and turncoat. He had given
Ælfric command of the English forces which were now mustered
against the Danes – the *fyrds* of Wiltshire and Hampshire. Ælfric
then disgraced himself by a nursery-school trick on the eve of

* Oxford.

battle: he began to retch and say that he was sick as soon as he came in sight of Swein's army. The English force broke up in confusion, and Swein was left to his own devices in 1003. He stormed the *burh* at Wilton and razed it to the ground, plundered Salisbury, and fell back to meet his ships on the coast. It was the mildest foretaste of what he had in mind for the English and their land.

The following year, 1004, Swein's fleet landed in Norfolk. The Danes marched on Norwich and burned it down. Their opponent was the Danish-born Ulfcetel, said by Florence of Worcester to be 'ealdorman of the East Angles'. Ulfcetel had clearly not had time to muster the *fyrd* and like King Edmund of East Anglia back in 866, when faced with the invasion of the Great Army, he decided to buy time with a truce. Swein had no intention of giving the English anything, let alone time. His army broke the truce and pushed inland to Thetford. Ulfcetel's reaction was shrewd: he sent a detachment to burn the beached Danish long-ships, but his men let him down. Swein's fleet survived, but the march to Thetford gave Ulfcetel three weeks in which to muster his forces. The East Anglians positioned themselves between Thetford and the coast, and gave battle as soon as the Danes set out on their march back to the coast. It was a sad repetition of Maldon; Ulfcetel's incomplete army was wiped out on the battlefield, but for the first time King Swein was forced to modify his opinions about the weakness of the English. The tragedy was remembered with pride in the *Chronicle*: 'There the flower of the East Anglian people was killed. But if their full strength had been there, the Danes would never have got back to their ships; as they themselves said that they never met worse fighting in England than Ulfcetel dealt to them.'

An act of God enabled Swein to inflict another humiliation on the English in 1005 by doing nothing but sailing home to Denmark. Another terrible famine hit England. Swein could afford to wait; he certainly did not want to embark on a long campaign in a starving country, where there would be no supplies at all to keep his men fit. He merely took them home, leaving the English to their famine. He planned to return in the following year, timing the peak of his campaign, as always with large-scale viking armies, for the harvest-season when mobilization would put the greatest stress on the English.

The first half of 1006 saw another of Ethelred's vicious purges, this time in the ranks of his own nobility. The king had a new evil genius, an unprincipled thug named Eadric Streona. Four victims are mentioned by name in the *Chronicle*: '. . . Wulfgeat was deprived of all his property, and Wulfheah and Ufegeat were blinded and Ealdorman Ælfhelm killed.'* Details supplied by the later historian, Florence of Worcester, make it clear that Eadric Streona was the man behind the king's order.

July saw the return of Swein's fleet. It landed at Sandwich, and set off on a march that was more of a parade than a military campaign.

Once again the south-east burned as Ethelred called out the full muster of Wessex and Mercia. A totally abortive autumn campaign followed, with the English army trailing apprehensively behind Swein's host and doing no damage to anyone apart from the Englishmen of the shires. Ethelred's army broke up and its men went home for Christmas; the Danes returned to the Isle of Wight, provisioning themselves royally as they went. They then put on an insolent show of their total supremacy:

> . . . and then towards Christmas they betook themselves to the entertainment waiting them, out through Hampshire into Berkshire to Reading; and always they observed their ancient custom, lighting their beacons as they went. They then turned to Wallingford and burnt it all, and were one night at Cholsey, and then turned along Ashdown to Cuckhamsley Barrow, and waited there for what had been proudly threatened, for it had often been said that if they went to Cuckhamsley, they would never get to the sea. They then went home another way.

While this gesture of contempt was being made, Ethelred was far in the west, in Shropshire, collecting his Christmas food-rents. No wonder a total sense of defeatism swept England that winter. Not even a glimmer of satisfaction was won by a gallant English force which tried to block the Danish route-march on the River Kennet. The Danes swept the Englishmen aside and carried on to the sea. 'There the people of Winchester', comments the *Chronicle* bitterly, 'could see that army, proud and undaunted, when they went past their gate to the sea, and fetched themselves food and treasures from more than 50 miles from the sea.'

---

* Ælfhelm was ealdorman of southern Northumbria, and Wulfheah and Ufegeat were his sons.

Spring saw what the English were beginning to accept as inevitable: their king offering another Danegeld (36,000 pounds this time, the highest yet) to get rid of his enemies. Fully provisioned by the already-despoiled English, Swein took his triumphant army back to Denmark.

The next twenty-four months of uneasy freedom from Danish attack saw the king and his council take two measures for the defence of England in the future. The first was the appointment of Eadric Streona as ealdorman of Mercia. It was essential that the Midland shires should be entrusted to an energetic viceroy, and Ethelred had come to trust Eadric. The second, in 1008, was a royal proclamation that a new national fleet was to be built. This fleet was the greatest single national achievement in the entire history of England as far as the production of military hardware was concerned. Using a twentieth-century comparison, it certainly eclipsed such dubious feats as the factory output during 'Tanks For Russia' week in the Second World War. Every 310 hides of land was to contribute to the building of a new warship. Nor was this all. Every eight hides had to provide a mail corselet and a helmet to equip the crews. Considering the unheard-of sacrifices which the English had had to make ever since the death of Edgar in 975, it was incredible that the fleet was manned and ready by the campaigning season of 1009. How many ships it comprised we do not know; it is hard to believe that the quota was entirely met. Suffice it to say that it gave Ethelred the best fleet England had ever had. The decision was taken to concentrate the lot at Sandwich, at the toe of Kent, a landfall for which viking raiders had shown a marked liking, and tackle any future sea-borne assault from there. But the prospects of the new fleet were weakened by an instant outbreak of combined mutiny and piracy which showed that, although England could build the ships, it was completely lacking in loyal or competent admirals.

The trouble started while the ships of the fleet were still mustering. Brihtric, a brother of Eadric Streona, brought a charge of treachery against one of Ethelred's fleet commanders, a South Saxon thane by the name of Wulfnoth. What happened next gives a vivid glimpse of the low opinion to which royal justice had slumped in Ethelred's reign. Wulfnoth would have had plenty of opportunities to come to know Ethelred's favourite punishment: the cruel ignominy of blinding. He did not bother to plead his case to the king, but escaped to the fleet and won over the crews of twenty ships, with which he sailed away and turned pirate. This was a serious threat not only to Wulfnoth's hapless victims but to the strength of the new fleet; swift counter-measures were essential. Brihtric (who had presumably argued that his case against Wulfnoth had been proved) took it upon himself to bring Wulfnoth to book.

We do not know whether or not this was the culmination of a private power-struggle between Brihtric and Wulfnoth for the supreme command of the fleet. It may very well have been. Eadric Streona, now virtually the ranking commander of land forces, may have been trying to get his brother the plum position of fleet commander, and failed by orthodox channels. It is interesting that the *Chronicle* states clearly that Brihtric was motivated by the desire 'to make a big reputation for himself'. He certainly took a big enough force after Wulfnoth – eighty ships, bigger than many viking raiding forces – but he made a total mess of the assignment. Brihtric's fleet was caught on a lee shore by a surprise gale and wrecked, whereupon Wulfnoth swooped down and burned the surviving ships. The results were catastrophic:

> When it became known to the other ships, where the king was, how the others had fared, it was as if everything was in con- fusion, and the king betook himself home, as did the ealdormen and chief councillors, and deserted the ships thus lightly. And the people who were on the ships took [the ships] back to Lon- don, and let the toil of all the nation thus lightly come to naught; and no better than this was the victory which all the English people had expected.

Inexorably, the Danes came – immediately after the English summer festival of Lammas on 1 August. They came in two huge fleets, one under Thorkel the Tall, which landed as the English had foreseen at Sandwich, and the other under Earls Heming and Eilaf, landing at Thanet. Joining forces after securing their beach-head in Kent, the Danes lunged inland. It was the end of an era for the English, for the invaders would not quit English soil until the crown of England had passed to their own ruler.

Kent fell without a struggle, even before the Danes had laid so much as a finger on Canterbury – the terrified people bought off the invaders with 3,000 pounds. On that, the entire fleet re- embarked and coasted west to their old base, the Isle of Wight, commencing terror-raids not only on Sussex and Hampshire but as far inland as Berkshire. Ethelred proclaimed the full muster of England, but – as usual – the Danes had timed their stroke for harvest-time and there was not even the palest shadow of resistance. The incredible happened, and King Ethelred actually took command of the English army. Not only that, but he managed to get it between the Danes and their ships – but a decisive battle was prevented by the shilly-shallying of Eadric Streona.

In mid-November, Thorkel and the other two earls broke their camp on the Isle of Wight and shifted back to Kent. Establishing winter quarters on the Thames, they drew a tightening net of fire and terror around London, and launched repeated attacks on the town, which reaped yet more laurels in a superb defence. This was a splendid chapter in the long history of the city, and the *Chronicle*'s account glows with pride and affection as it mentions the siege: 'But, praise be to God, it still stands untouched, and they always suffered loss there.'

After Christmas 1009, the Danes gave up their attempt to storm London and drove up the Thames to Oxford, which they burned. On their return march down-river, they heard that an English army had formed at London ready to intercept them. The Danish leaders declined an engagement, making an early crossing of the Thames at Staines and swinging eastward back into Kent. As winter passed and the spring of 1010 began to stir, the Danes were hard at work strengthening their camp and overhauling their fleet.

In April 1010, the Danes swarmed up the East Coast and landed at Ipswich. It is clear that there were many among the leaders of the Danish host who still had vivid memories of the rough handling they had had at the hands of the East Anglian army during the last Danish foray there. The Danish objective was Ulfcetel's army and a decisive battle. This was fought at Ringmere on 5 May, against a coalition army from East Anglia and Cambridgeshire. It was a sad affair for the English. The tremendous size of the Danish army panicked the East Anglians into instant retreat, but the Cambridgeshire men stood their ground and went down fighting. It was as pointless as Maldon. The English defeat at Ringmere left the whole of East Anglia wide open to the Danes – but it soon became obvious that the invaders had decided to abandon the methodical pace of their assault.

Massed, raging, invincible, the Danes set off on a breath-taking march the like of which had not been seen in England since 877. After the ravaging of Cambridgeshire the army went down the Thames into Oxfordshire, Buckinghamshire, up the Ouse to Bedford and Tempsford, finally staggering back to the ships with its booty. The careful defence system built up by Alfred the Great and Edward the Elder vanished in chaos and panic. Resistance melted as the men of the English armies began to stream home and national morale collapsed again:

> And when they were in the east, the English army was kept in the west, and when they were in the south, our army was in the north. Then all the councillors were summoned to the king, and it was then to be decided how this country should be defended. But even if anything was then decided, it did not last even a month. Finally there was no leader who would collect an army, but each fled as best he could, and in the end no shire would even help the next.

Thus did the *Chronicle* write the anguished and bitter account of the collapse of the English kingdom in 1010. It was rammed home by a final searing march by the Danes up to Northampton and far south into Wiltshire, returning to base at Christmas. For the cowering English, winter passed in utter hopelessness.

The spring of 1011 brought home to Ethelred and his councillors the full horror of their position. North of the Thames, the Danes held all East Anglia, Essex, Middlesex, Oxfordshire, Cambridgeshire, Hertfordshire, Buckinghamshire, and Bedfordshire, and they had a stranglehold on Huntingdonshire and Northamptonshire. In the south, they controlled the eastern half of the old kingdom of Wessex: Kent, Surrey, Sussex, Berkshire, Hampshire, and much of Wiltshire.* Not even in the darkest days of Alfred's reign had the English lain so completely helpless before their enemies. There was no alternative. Ethelred and the Witan began negotiations for another exhausting pay-off; and the *Chronicle*, evoking the bitterness of the national mood, positively rages:

> All those disasters befell us through bad policy, in that they were never offered tribute in time nor fought against; but when

---

* It is interesting that the *Chronicle*, in the melancholy list of conquered shires, includes the old territory of the *Hæstingas*, still recognized as distinct from the rest of Sussex (see p. 14).

they had done most to our injury, peace and truce were made with them; and for all this truce and tribute they journeyed none the less in bands everywhere, and harried our wretched people, and plundered and killed them.

This concluding statement suggests that the Danes, glutted with victory, were certainly not being reined in by their king, but were beginning to launch minor operations of their own. This was proved in September 1011, when a section of the Danish army fell upon Canterbury. Their objective was the rich archbishopric and monastery, and they made a rich haul of hostages, most important of them being Archbishop Ælfheah himself. The Danes – who had gained entry into Canterbury thanks to the treachery of Archdeacon Ælfmær – plundered the town bare and took the archbishop back to their ships. The capture of the archbishop while the Danegeld negotiations were still in progress strengthened Swein's bargaining-power to an impossible degree. Ælfheah was a *ne plus ultra* in hostages and as long as he remained in Danish custody Swein could safely have done what he liked with the English.

The threat to the archbishop's safety must have been a pressing reason for the speedy collection of the tribute-money – a record-breaking 48,000 pounds, handed over shortly after Easter in April. But Ælfheah's gaolers saw no reason why they should not increase their share of the loot by putting pressure on their captive. They ordered him to ask Ethelred for an additional 3,000 pounds' personal ransom. Ælfheah refused. Nothing could shake him. Had he been in Swein's personal charge matters might have turned out differently; but his courage earned him a brutal death.

Saturday, 19 April 1012, closed with a drunken feast in the Danish camp where Ælfheah lay prisoner. Tumult and disorder began to sweep the hall as the Danish victors drank themselves crazy on looted wine. Finally Alfheah was dragged into the hall. Blood-lust erupted. Ælfheah was pelted unconscious with ox-heads and greasy bones and finished off by having his head split with a battle-axe.

Neither then nor in later centuries did the horrified English forget their martyred archbishop, who became invested with the respect due to a saint. The shock caused by the murder can be imagined. It had appeared that no further degradation could possibly be imposed on the English; that was abundantly disproved by this new atrocity.

Deep down, all unseen and obscured by the chaotic situation into which Ethelred had contrived to bring his kingdom, a new spirit began to stir – new, that is, to the beaten generation of 1012. It was the spirit which had brought the last muster of Wessex to Edington in 878. Further defeats lay ahead. But there were still enough sparks to kindle a last and glorious blaze of English resistance – if and when another Alfred could be found.

# Chapter 10

Destroyer of the chariot of the sea, you were of no great age when you pushed off your ships. Never, younger than you, did prince set out to take his part in war. Chief, you made ready your armoured ships, and were daring beyond measure. In your rage, Cnut, you mustered the red ships at sea.

From *Knútsdrápa*, a poem in praise of King Cnut, by Ottar the Black.

Then the atheling Edmund began to gather the English army.

*Anglo-Saxon Chronicle*: 1016.

# Last ditch

After Ælfheah's battered corpse had been retrieved by the English and reverently laid to rest in St Paul's minster in London, the final payments of the Danegeld were made. There had been no mention that the Danes were to leave England, but after the cash had been handed over their army began to disperse through the conquered shires – an army, now, of occupation. But almost at once it became apparent that Swein's army, powerful as it was, had its flaws at the top. Thorkel the Tall deserted Swein and accepted service with Ethelred, bringing over forty-five Danish ships on the understanding that the English would feed and equip them.

It had always been a fact of life that the larger a viking army was, the more independent leaders it had able to command loyalty of their own. This had not escaped the English, but it was typical of Ethelred that no effective effort was made to exploit this weakness until two-thirds of southern England had been occupied by the invaders. Nevertheless, Thorkel's change of coat offered a long overdue gleam of hope to the English. Thorkel and his mercenaries provided Ethelred with a hard core of professional fighting men who would not be affected by the seasonal tug of getting the harvest in at the crucial moment of a campaign. If the partnership proved a success, there was every reason to hope that more Danes would desert Swein. But there were obvious dangers. England's new allies would have to be made to feel that they could keep their self-respect as warriors, that their oaths to their new king had been justified – in short, that the king of the English was a lord worthy of them. Needless to say, Ethelred's record as king caused the gravest doubts on that score. Above all, he was not the man to prove the worth of the new alliance in a swift and decisive action when Swein made his inevitable next move in the year of 1013.

Thorkel and his fleet joined Ethelred in London, the strength of whose fortifications was known only too well to the Danes. Swein did not, therefore, waste time in sacrificing more men in an attempt to wipe Ethelred and Thorkel off the face of the earth. Instead he made the shrewd move of making sure that his enemies would get no help from Northumbria and the Danelaw – provinces which Swein had not yet touched.

Launching the 1013 campaign earlier than normal – before August and harvest-time – Swein took his fleet up the east coast to the Humber. He was not intending to take the traditional objective of York, but to make another unanswerable show of strength, and he did this by sailing up the Trent as far as Gainsborough with his full force. It was enough. Earl Uhtred of Northumbria accepted that resistance would be futile and submitted to Swein, together with the men of coastal Lincolnshire (Lindsey), the Danes of the Five Boroughs, 'and quickly afterwards all the Danish settlers north of Watling Street'. The king of Denmark was now master not only of the south and east, but also of the Danelaw and Northumbria – in short, of all England as far north as the Tyne apart from western Wessex.

Swein plainly thought that this was enough. He took abundant hostages from his new subjects, ordered them to provision his army and fit it out with horses, and prepared for a decisive march to the south to pressure Ethelred into final submission. The fleet was left on the Trent. Guarding the ships – and the English hostages – was a man Swein knew he could trust: his own heir, Cnut, a respected warrior at the age of eighteen.

Swein's hope that Ethelred would cave in when he heard that the north had gone was dashed. The Danish army swept south across Watling Street with maximum 'frightfulness', although the *Chronicle* notes that Swein kept his men in check until they had left the territory of his new subjects of the Danelaw. Once across Watling Street into English Mercia, the ordeal of the English began again. Oxford submitted with hostages rather than fight; so did Winchester, the ancient capital and coronation-town of the kings of Wessex. Swinging round to the north, Swein prepared to close in on London. A note of over-confidence and carelessness creeps in here for 'many of his host were drowned in the Thames because they did not trouble to find a bridge'. This is certainly an interesting comment on the all-round professionalism of the most successful viking army which had ever campaigned in England. When the Danes closed up to London, they got another shock. Ethelred and Thorkel had stayed in the town to lead the defence, and another fighting siege began. Once again, the Londoners managed to beat off the attackers and the defences held.

Not for the first time, the Danes abandoned London. There was good reason for this, for Swein still had to settle accounts with the west. He took his army across England to Bath, crossing the Thames at Wallingford, and showed the mailed fist again. The results were equally gratifying. Ealdorman Æthelmær of Devon accepted that Ethelred's cause was lost and came to Bath with all the western thegns to swear allegiance. Swein was now the un-challenged master of all England, and the last pocket of resistance in London collapsed. The Londoners at last sent a deputation to deliver hostages to the Danish king and swear allegiance to him. The *Chronicle* records how a last merciless squeeze was put on the English: 'Then Swein demanded full payment and provisions for his army that winter, and Thorkel demanded the same for the army which lay at Greenwich, and in spite of it all they ravaged as often as they pleased. Nothing therefore was of benefit to this nation, neither from the south nor from the north.'

Meanwhile, what of Ethelred? He now had to cope not only with the loss of his kingdom but with the break-up of the royal family, the latter apparently on the advice of the churchmen in the Witan. Accompanied by Abbot Ælfsige of Peterborough, Ælfgifu-Emma left England for Normandy, where her brother Richard was now duke. Her two sons, Edward and Alfred, also went overseas in the care of Bishop Ælfhun. Ethelred himself stayed with Thorkel's restless fleet until Christmas, which he spent on the Isle of Wight, before sailing to join Emma in Normandy.

In all of this, carefully described in the *Chronicle*, there is no mention of the senior atheling, Edmund, son of Ethelred by his first wife, Ælfgifu, who was by now an enigmatic young man of twenty-two. Edmund, as heir-apparent to the throne of England, had had an appalling youth as far as psychological influences were concerned. Not only had he lost his own mother while still a boy: he had grown up as the most susceptible eye-witness to the disastrous incompetence of his father. In an era when men were thrust to greatness at impossibly early ages by modern stan-dards, Edmund seems to have been denied any opportunity to show what he was made of. It is to be presumed that he went to Normandy with Ethelred – and it is a safe bet that he reflected with bitterness on the different fortune of his younger rival, Swein's heir, Cnut.

Then the entire scene was turned upside-down by the sudden death of King Swein on 3 February 1014. England's conqueror, the top warrior of the viking world, was gone. The incredible news was flashed to Normandy – to the exiled Ethelred it must have come like a bolt from the blue. The Danes in England reacted by a unanimous election of Cnut as their new king; the English Witan did not hesitate. They summoned Ethelred to return to his people; 'and they said', comments the *Chronicle* pointedly, 'that no lord was dearer to them than their natural lord if he would govern them more justly than he did before'. Ethelred was cautious. He sent his young son Edward back to England as his messenger to the Witan. He greeted his people. He said he would be a gracious lord to them, and reform all the things that they hated. All the things that had been said or done against him would be forgiven. Bygones were bygones. The Witan accepted his one condition: that they must all turn to him without treachery. Reconciliation seemed complete: '. . . friendship was then established with oath and pledge on both sides, and they pronounced every Danish king an outlaw from England for ever.' Ethelred returned to England in the spring and was welcomed with hysteria which seems to have rivalled that which greeted the return of Charles II in 1660.

Ethelred was thus swept back on to his throne on a wave of relief and general goodwill, and what he did next was without precedent. He actually led an English army on a successful expedition. The young Danish king, Cnut, had not lost his nerve when he got the news of his father's death and the English reaction, but had hung on at Gainsborough with the fleet. He had terrorized the people of Lindsey into agreeing that 'they would provide him with horses and then go out and ravage all together'. But Ethelred, of all people, proved too quick for Cnut. He led an English army north into Lincolnshire and established the upper hand in Lindsey with great brutality. Cnut accepted reality and put to sea with the fleet. He would have had to return to Denmark in any case to make sure of his accession at home, but his departure left the hapless folk of Lindsey at Ethelred's mercy. Cnut's parting gesture was to touch at Sandwich and disembark the English hostages which had been handed over to Swein – minus their hands, ears, and noses.

The heavy-handed punishment dealt out to the people of Lindsey, and this last atrocity, were not the only prices England had to pay for getting Ethelred back and ousting the Danes. Thorkel's fleet still lay in the Thames, and it had to be paid off. This cost the English 21,000 pounds – and the year ended with another of the natural disasters which plagued the entire reign. On 28 September, England was hit by terrible sea-floods which inundated many coastal villages and drowned thousands of helpless victims.

For all that, unbelievably, the English were their own masters once more. Two obvious worries stood out. The first was the reality behind the clean sheet which had been granted to and guaranteed by Ethelred on his return; the second was the problem of a return invasion by Cnut of Denmark. Neither issue was left in doubt for long. The most serious of 'all the things which they all hated' was that crafty character, Eadric of Mercia, a proven traitor and intriguer, whom Ethelred maintained as ealdorman of Mercia. When the Witan convened at Oxford in the spring or early summer of 1015, Eadric carried out another of his criminal intrigues. This time his victims were the chief thegns of the 'Seven Boroughs' (the Five plus York and Torksey), Sigeferth and Morcar. After poisoning Ethelred's mind against the two men, Eadric 'enticed them into his chamber, and they were basely killed inside it'. Ethelred not only approved but confiscated all the property of the murdered thegns' and ordered Aldgyth, the widow of Sigeferth, to be taken to Malmesbury.

With this event the short but momentous public career of the atheling Edmund began. Until then he had played a negative role. (His brother Athelstan, whose existence we know of only by his will, is an even more shadowy figure, and seems to have died shortly after this time.) Edmund's violent reaction to his father's order to seize Aldgyth suggests all the mystery of a lost love affair. He himself headed north, made off with Aldgyth, and married her at once. In addition to defying his father's will, he went still further, seizing possession of all the former estates of Sigeferth and Morcar. He was accepted by the people of the Five Boroughs, but it would be unwise to read too much into this.

Any new lord must have been preferable to the unscrupulous Eadric, who now became Edmund's most bitter enemy.

With the English divided so early, Cnut returned with a fleet before Ethelred could take any action against his recalcitrant son. He landed in Somerset and commenced a large-scale terror-raid against Somersetshire, Dorset, and Wiltshire. Ethelred chose this moment to fall ill and remained *hors de combat* at Cosham in Hampshire. Meanwhile, two English armies were being formed: by Edmund in the north and by Eadric in Mercia. The two joined up with neither leader trusting the other an inch. Edmund knew it was only a matter of time before Eadric betrayed him and the armies soon parted, leaving the wretched Wessex men to face Cnut alone. Edmund's caution had been justified. Eadric promptly went over to Cnut with forty ships, and Wessex succumbed. Fed and horsed at the expense of the West Saxons, Cnut's army passed the winter in the south-west.

The English were prodded into action by another Christmas-time march by the Danes, north-west across the Thames at Cricklade and deep into Warwickshire. Ethelred was by now in London. The only leader the English had who was doing something was the atheling Edmund, who began to raise a new army. Recruits streamed in. The mood of the hour was a desire to re-create the enthusiasm which had hailed Ethelred's return. The men gave Edmund a good deal of trouble, the main demand being that the king must lead them in person. When the king stayed in London, the Mercian contingent took the lead in going home and the army dispersed.

As soon as the Christmas festivities were over, the full muster of England was proclaimed again, to be ignored on pain of death. The army took shape once more; and once more Edmund sent word to his father in London, begging him to take command with all the men he could bring with him – and so he did. But Ethelred had a lifetime of deception and guilt behind him, and he was prey to a whirl of fears and doubts. It was whispered to him that a double-cross was afoot, and the whisper was enough to induce him to desert the army and return to London.

Dramatically let down by his father, Edmund set off for the north. This made sense to most Englishmen: 'every one thought' that he and Uhtred of Northumbria would muster a reserve army to throw into the coming struggle with Cnut. Instead, the atheling and the earl led their forces through Staffordshire and Shropshire on a punitive expedition against the English, ending up at Chester. This insane-sounding move is, however, given a motive by Florence of Worcester: he says that this expedition was carried out because the locals refused to enlist to fight the Danes. Unfortunately for Edmund and Uhtred, Cnut moved faster than they did, and he launched the campaign of 1016 while the English commanders were still punishing their own people.

Cnut's route from the west country sliced through Buckinghamshire, across the Thames, and north into Lincolnshire. He was making for the north, for York and Northumbria, and his strategy was sound. 'When Uhtred learned this, he left his ravaging and hastened northwards, and submitted then out of necessity, and with him all the Northumbrians.' It was a desperate attempt to save his earldom, but it failed even to save his own skin. Cnut, apparently, was prepared to overlook the fact that Uhtred had broken his earlier oath of allegiance to Swein – but Eadric Streona was with him, and it was on Eadric's advice that Uhtred was killed. Cnut appointed a Norwegian, Eric of Hlathir, to be his new viceroy in the north, and headed south with his fleet. He was determined to take London at last and finish with Ethelred once and for all.

But Ethelred did not live to see their coming. His illness the previous year had been an ominous symptom. He died at last on 23 April 1016, one of the worst rulers, it is safe to say, that England has ever suffered from. He was buried in St Paul's with due ceremony, but the English had little time to reflect on the deliverance of his death. News had come of Cnut's approach. The Witan was split down the middle. One faction was prepared to swear allegiance to Cnut. The Londoners and the councillors who stayed with them hailed Edmund as king. When Edmund himself heard the news of his father's death, he wasted no time in going down to Wessex with his army and receiving its submission.

Meanwhile, Cnut's fleet had reached Greenwich at the beginning of the second week in May. He had a new plan to reduce this bastion of English resistance: the digging of a ship-canal round the south side of London's defences. An outer ring of Danish earthworks was dug round the whole *burh* complex, sealing off the Londoners from any relief. But even with the Danish fleet pressing them hard from upstream and downstream, the Londoners held out as stoutly as ever. While the Danes continued to besiege London, King Edmund at last began to move.

The first clashes of the campaign occurred in Dorset and Wiltshire as Edmund moved east. They were not stand-up fights; Edmund did not want to squander his strength in unimportant engagements, and his opponent, none other than the renegade Eadric, was not exactly noted for his keenness on the battlefield. At this stage the pivot of operations was the siege of London. Edmund kept coming, attracting more recruits as his armies traversed the Home Counties. The English burst in on the Danish siege lines around London and broke them. As the Danes, confused, made for their ships, Edmund led the English army across the Thames at Brentford and forced a battle on Cnut's army. The Danes could do nothing against the new-found fury of their opponents and were routed – the first English victory since the time of Edmund's namesake, Athelstan's brother. So keen were the English to get to grips with their enemy after decades of humiliation that many were killed in doing so: '. . . a great number of the English people who went ahead of the main force,' says the *Chronicle*, 'wishing to get booty, were drowned there through their own carelessness.' Their loss did not jeopardize Edmund's first, vital achievement as king of the English: proving to his disillusioned people that the Danes were not in fact invincible in a straight fight. What is more, he seems to have done it with an incomplete muster, for immediately after the fight he pulled back into Wessex for more recruits.

Despite this disconcerting setback, Cnut did not give up. He rallied his army after the fight at Brentford and flung it yet again at London, the third great siege of the wars, and no more successful than the other two. Cnut resorted to a terror-march through England, a tactic which had produced abundant results in past years. He took the army by sea up the east coast to the Orwell estuary and upstream, then deep into Mercia, then south and east back to Kent. On this march the Danes rounded up vast herds of livestock which they drove back to their camp – the only living things they spared on their march. But this time they did not cause abject collapse and an instant mass payment of protection-money. All that happened was that Edmund had enough time to proclaim the full muster of England, and raise a full-dress army which he promptly led into Kent via Brentford.

Cnut was taken completely by surprise and had to quit the English mainland, pulling back his shaken forces on to the Isle of Sheppey.

The aftermath of this second English victory, at the mouth of the Medway, proved a mixed blessing for the English. Eadric Streona abandoned Cnut and came in to Edmund at Aylesford. This traitor had proved himself to be utterly unreliable but, with Cnut's army still in being, Edmund decided that he could not do without him. This was a decision that Edmund had to take alone and it was sadly adrift: 'No greater folly was ever agreed to than that was,' comments the *Chronicle* dolefully.

Two consecutive defeats made no difference to Cnut's determination to keep up the pressure on the English. Once again he crossed the Thames estuary, landed in Essex, and set off on a route-march through Mercia. It seemed that there could be no rapid end to the cycle.

Edmund, however, promptly showed his people that he had just as much determination as his rival, and set off with the English army on Cnut's trail. This pursuit was not the abject, jackal-like lurking which had characterized Ethelred's campaign: it was pressed hard with another battle in view. Edmund finally ran the Danish host to earth at Ashingdon, in Essex, in mid-October 1016. This was to be no ordinary fight, but the clincher. Edmund had with him the full Witan of England, united, and a rich crop of leading churchmen. They wanted another Edington. But they also had Eadric Streona.

Battle was finally joined at Ashington on 18 October. No quarter was given or taken – but Eadric, as men had feared, showed his true colours yet again by retreating with his men, the *Magonsæte* of Herefordshire, which completely unseamed the English battle-line. Cnut had a hard fight of it, but his Danes were the victors. They had beaten a truly national army which had fought as no English army had fought since Athelstan's day. This was proved by the abnormally high list of leading men killed in action. These included Bishop Eadnoth of Dorchester and Abbot Wulfsige of Ramsey. The English ealdormen who died at Ashingdon consisted of Ælfric of Hampshire, Godwine of Lindsey, and Ulfcetel of East Anglia – the Ulfcetel who back in 1004 had given Swein's veterans such a fight as they had never known before. The final leading casualty listed in the *Chronicle* is Æthelweard, son of Æthelwine of East Anglia, Edgar the Peaceable's old councillor. But a general epitaph had to do for the rest: 'and all the nobility of England was there destroyed'. This could have been the aftermath for Alfred's host at Edington in 878, but Edmund's defeat at Ashington in 1016 had been the defeat of the army of *all* England, not merely of three Wessex shires.

Edmund escaped from the battle; he was not a man to indulge in any out-dated heroics and die in a useless battle. He was in fact like Alfred in that he was, to all intents and purposes, the last of his line: the two young athelings, his half-brothers, were overseas, and if he died the English would be utterly leaderless. He had hoped for a decisive victory at Ashingdon but had got a shattering defeat instead. But this was not the end. As long as he continued to survive as a focus for resistance, Cnut could never become England's new king but would remain an alien destroyer to be fought to the death. Edmund fled far to the west into Gloucester to raise yet another army from the western shires.

What happened next is a classic proof of the historical fact that a lost battle does not inevitably mean a lost war. It was Cnut who accepted that he could never conquer England, certainly as long as Edmund lived. The *Chronicle* says that Cnut's decision to negotiate with Edmund was made on the advice of Eadric Streona, but as both Cnut and Edmund had been double-crossed by Eadric it is hard to imagine his advice being taken seriously after Ashingdon. The wonder is that Cnut did not have him killed at once, but for the moment he was spared; and the pattern of the Wedmore negotiations of 878 was repeated.

The two kings finally met at Alney, near Deerhurst in Gloucestershire. Hostages were exchanged and the talks began. The crucial point at issue was the partition of England – virtually a freezing of the *status quo*. Alfred's old frontier with Guthrum seems to have been the line which was finally accepted by both sides. Cnut would take the old Danelaw, Edmund Wessex, the old kingdom of his line. There was to be one important exception. London would form part of the Danish sphere of influence. Moreover, another cash payment must be made to the Danish army. That, too, was agreed. Cnut and Edmund clinched the treaty 'with pledge and with oath', and parted.

In many ways it was a hard peace for the English, particularly for the Londoners, who had had the hardest consistent fighting in the wars. They had to buy a peace for themselves from Cnut's fleet, which based itself in the town for the winter of 1016. But a mere three years before, all England had been helpless before Swein of Denmark. King Edmund had changed all that. Without his error of judgment with regard to Eadric Streona, he might indeed have won more; but, like Alfred the Great, his efforts had prevented the total destruction of English independence.

So it was that the Alney conference of 1016 turned the clock back 134 years to the situation after the partition of England. A diagonal barrier ran once more across the island. The eastern sector reverted to the Danes under Cnut: the south and west remained English under Edmund. But the situation was only superficially the same. Too much had happened during those 134 years. In 878 there had not been a powerful aristocracy with extensive holdings on both sides of the frontier: in 1016 there was, and by no stretch of the imagination could the situation be described as stable. There were too many divided loyalties. It was only a question of whether Cnut or Edmund would be first off the mark when hostilities resumed.

It remains fascinating to weigh up the characters and resources of the two kings and wonder what really would have happened. They were so alike. Edmund (who earned the nickname 'Ironside' for his achievements) was no more of a quitter than Cnut. Nor were the English, now they had the right kind of leader to follow. But the whole question remains an academic one. On 30 November 1016, Edmund Ironside died. His son by Aldgyth was a baby. The other two athelings were still overseas. There was nothing the Witan of England could do but offer the crown to Cnut.

The last resurgence of the fighting spirit of Saxon England had succeeded only in preserving the independence of a fraction of the kingdom. Now it had all gone for nothing. An era ended with the death of Edmund Ironside – the era of the post-Alfred years. The accession of Cnut and the course of his remarkable reign was to haul England closer to the orbit of Denmark and Norway, as the marriage of Ethelred to Emma had exposed the country to the fateful influence of Normandy. For fifty tense years, these two forces impinging on Saxon England were to rest in an uneasy balance.

## Chapter 11

Cnut, king of all England, and of Denmark, and of the Norwegians, and of part of the Swedes, sends greeting to Æthelnoth the metropolitan, and to Ælfric, archbishop of York, and to all the bishops and leading men, and to the whole race of the English, whether nobles or *ceorls*.

I make known to you that I have recently been to Rome, to pray for the remission of my sins and for the safety of the kingdoms and of the peoples which are subjected to my rule. . . .

From Cnut's letter to the English of 1027.

# England under Cnut

Cnut of Denmark was England's new king. At last it seemed that Saxon England's long fight against the viking invasions had been lost, and that the inevitable extinction of the traditions of the English was at hand. In fact, Cnut soon played the remarkable part of a conquering viking ruler turning into one of the best kings England ever had. He kept the peace; he enforced the laws – traditional English laws; he was a generous patron of the Church; and he raised the country's prestige on the international scale to unprecedented heights. It was a unique and thoroughly splendid reign which was vividly remembered with acute regret for generations. By the time Cnut died in 1035, England was only one of his three subject kingdoms, but it was his favourite realm – a land in which he had been a figure of dread in his youth, but which he had come to love and honour. In return, Cnut was honoured by the English, who paid him the supreme honour of inventing an affectionate parable about him – the Alfred-and-the-cakes tale of how he curbed the flattery of his courtiers by standing on the shore and vainly forbidding the tide to come in. Cnut, in short, became part of the national heritage of England – no mean feat for a foreign conqueror, by any standards – and has always remained one.

It is easier to understand how this came about if we look at the considerable advantages which Cnut enjoyed when he became king of all England by default at the end of 1016. As we have seen, Edmund Ironside had been Cnut's only effective rival, and when he died Cnut had the field to himself. There was, however, one fly in the ointment, a character who had played no part whatsoever in the previous dramatic years. This was the atheling Eadwig, a hitherto-unmentioned brother of Edmund, who suddenly found himself pitchforked into a position of fatal prominence because he was the only son of Ethelred still in England. Cnut also had to remember the other two young athelings overseas, Edward and Alfred. These boys were out of his reach in Normandy. In addition there were the two baby sons of Edmund himself, Edmund and Edward, the latter of whom was born in early 1017. The essential point at the end of November 1016, however, was that all five of them were only long-term threats: none of them was in a position to challenge Cnut's assumption of the crown. Nothing mattered but the massed Danish army, ready to resume hostilities as soon as Cnut gave the word. With no opposition, and with the big battalions at his back, Cnut was therefore well placed to take over supreme power by the technical consent of his new subjects. And a mixture of tacit intimidation on his side and perjury on the English side won him the crown in formal negotiation.

Every modern dictator knows that by far the best way to seize supreme power is to do it 'constitutionally'. Although this may ease his new subjects' consciences at the time, it generally fools nobody; and Cnut's take-over in 1016–17 certainly did not fool the medieval English historian Florence of Worcester, whose account of the proceedings is an extremely indignant one.

On hearing of Edmund's death, Cnut invited the worthies of the English Witan to meet him in London forthwith. What he did then makes us think of Cæsar ostentatiously putting aside the crown on the feast of Lupercal. He concentrated on the men who had been present during the negotiations with Edmund at Alney, and, feigning ignorance, fed them with loaded questions about whether or not the late king had stipulated who was to succeed to the crown of England if Edmund died while Cnut was still alive:

> And they said that they knew beyond doubt that King Edmund had entrusted no portion of his kingdom to his brothers, either in his life or at his death; and they said that they knew that Edmund wished Cnut to be the supporter and protector of his sons, until they were old enough to reign. In truth, God is to witness, they gave false testimony, and lied deceitfully, imagining both that he would be more gracious to them because of their lying, and that they would receive a big reward from him. Some of these false witnesses were put to death not long afterwards by that same king.

Cnut was then able to proceed smoothly to his own acceptance as king, complete with oaths of fealty and a formal renunciation of the sons and brothers of Edmund as claimants to the crown. The next item on the agenda was the atheling Eadwig. Florence must have been stretching the bow more than somewhat when he referred to Eadwig as 'the illustrious and much honoured brother of King Edmund', for no other source so much as mentions Eadwig before Edmund's death. Nevertheless, the appeasement-minded Witan voted for Eadwig's exile.

A sordid tangle of double-crossing ensued. Cnut was more than satisfied with the subservience of the Witan but he wanted to make certain of Eadwig. The new king thereupon summoned Eadric Streona and put his cards on the table: 'he enquired of him how he might entrap Eadwig, to endanger his life'. Master intriguer that he was, Eadric seized the chance to grind his own axe and advised Cnut to give the job to Æthelweard. Æthelweard was in fact a member of the old royal family himself: he was descended from Alfred the Great's elder brother, Ethelred, and Eadric wanted him out of the way. Cnut then summoned Æthelweard who agreed to co-operate in the murder of Eadwig. 'Nevertheless, he did not intend to kill him, but promised this by way of pretence; for he was sprung from a most noble English family.' There matters rested for the moment.

The year 1017 began with Cnut formally taking up the reins of power in England. This took the form of an emphatic partition. East Anglia went to Thorkel the Tall, Mercia to Eadric Streona; Earl Eric, installed in early 1016, retained Northumbria. Significantly, Cnut took Wessex for himself. Cnut then issued a formal amnesty: 'he made a treaty with the leading men and all the people, and they with him, and they established a firm friendship between them with oaths, and laid aside and put an end to all ancient enmities'.

Then the previous double-crossing broke out in a brisk purge. On Eadric Streona's advice, Eadwig (now sneeringly referred to as 'king of the *ceorls*') was exiled. The sentence was never carried out, and Eadwig, 'deceived by the treachery of those whom he had considered hitherto his closest friends', was killed soon after. True to his character, Eadric also advised Cnut to do away with Edmund Ironside's baby sons, but the king balked at that 'because it would be a great disgrace for them to perish in England'. The odyssey of the two athelings began; it was later embroidered with decided flights of fancy, but we know they escaped their would-be murderers and ended up in Hungary. There the elder son, Edmund, died; but his brother Edward married the Hungarian princess Agatha and produced a future queen of Scotland (Margaret), a nun (Christina), and yet another claimant to the English throne (Edgar the Atheling).

Cnut then played his first definite card in the reconstruction of a lasting peace by marrying Ælfgifu-Emma, Ethelred's widow, in July 1017. This not only gave the English proof that Cnut's promises of continuity were not empty, but restored the alliance with Normandy on which Ethelred had pinned such vain hopes. He rounded out the year 1017 by finally settling accounts with Eadric Streona at Christmastime. He had Eadric killed in the palace at London 'because he feared to be at some time deceived by his treachery, as his former lords Ethelred and Edmund had frequently been deceived'. As an added touch, Eadric's body was thrown over the city wall and left to rot. No tears were shed for Eadric. He had been living on borrowed time anyway, and his only hope must have been that he and Cnut could talk the same language as far as back-stabbing was concerned. Eadric must have hoped that his re-appointment as ealdorman of Mercia meant that Cnut needed him, but he was in fact supremely expendable. In an age where power politics at the top were habitually carried out at the point of the assassin's dagger, Eadric died as he had lived if ever a man did. Cnut also did away with three prominent noblemen: Æthelweard, Northman, and Brihtric. Although a master of the game himself, he had emphatically proved that he stood alone when it came to double-dealing. His final settlement of accounts with Eadric did his image as much good as his marriage to Queen Emma.

Back in the ninth century, the leaders of the Great Army had saved themselves a good deal of trouble by using the existing structure of government in their newly conquered territories instead of rooting it out. Cnut was wise enough to do the same, and in any case he had an excellent reason for doing so. By the end of Ethelred's reign, England, thanks to her ordeal by Danegeld, was by far the best-equipped country in the Christian West for raising large sums of money quickly, and this was precisely what Cnut wanted. He had no intention of keeping a large and dangerous army and fleet in England, and both had to be paid off. This was the main item of business in the year 1018. Including the sum paid by the people of London (10,500 pounds), the amount raised came to 82,500 pounds. It was the worst Danegeld of them all, but Cnut intended it to be the last. He kept a fleet of forty ships under his own control and packed off the rest home to Denmark. The next task was tackled in a great council at Oxford: a formal settlement of relations between the Danelaw and the rest of England, and the framework of law on which Cnut's reign was to rest.

This was a decisive event, one which showed Cnut's sense of realism and political tact. Version 'D' of the *Chronicle* summed up the work of the Oxford council with admirable economy, saying that 'the Danes and the English reached an agreement at Oxford according to Edgar's law'. It was a decisive statement, putting it on record that the political ideal for both Englishman and Dane was the *status quo* of Edgar the Peaceable's day, and that Cnut, ruling as a Christian king, pledged himself to honour and observe those customs. A re-hashed law-code was issued with a preamble which may be taken, to use a modern political term, as Cnut's 'election manifesto':

This is the ordinance which the councillors determined and devised according to many good precedents; and that took place as soon as King Cnut with the advice of his councillors completely established peace and friendship between the Danes and the English and put an end to all their former strife. In the first place, the councillors determined that above all things they would ever honour one God and steadfastly hold one Christian faith, and would love King Cnut with due loyalty and zealously observe Edgar's laws. And they agreed that they would, with God's help, investigate further at leisure what was necessary for the nation, as best they could. Now we wish to make clear what can benefit us in religious and secular concerns, let him pay heed who will. Let us very resolutely turn from sins and eagerly atone for our misdeeds and duly love and honour one God and steadfastly hold one Christian faith and diligently avoid every heathen practice.

Here was the viking conqueror, having cleared the ground of all possible rivals and bled the country white with another huge war-tax, solemnly announcing that from now on it would be, quite literally, 'back to the good old days' for the English kingdom. The terrible army of the Danes, paid off by its own master, had gone home at last. And it soon became apparent that Cnut really did intend to practise what he had preached at Oxford.

The English were extremely lucky in that Cnut had important reasons for not wanting them to be unhappy while he was engaged in urgent business elsewhere. In the first five years after the Oxford assembly of 1018, Cnut had to make two expeditions to Denmark to secure his interests there, and on neither occasion did the English cause him any trouble while he was away. His first visit, in 1019, had a particularly urgent motive. The throne was vacant and Cnut had to move in before any rival had a chance to supplant him.

This was the penalty for Cnut's remaining in England after the death of Swein, for the Danish kingdom had passed to Cnut's brother Harold. But Harold died soon after Cnut's formal accession in England – in 1018 or 1019 – by which time England was secure enough for Cnut to cross the North Sea with a small fleet of nine ships. He left England to the effective rule of the earl of East Anglia, Thorkel the Tall.

Cnut stayed in Denmark throughout the winter of 1019–20. While he was away he sent a remarkable letter to the magnates of England, one which was clearly intended to be communicated to the Witan by Thorkel as effective viceroy. It is an amazing document – virtually a miniature law-code and bulletin-briefing rolled into one. It is a clear statement that the king, though overseas, was keeping very much in touch and intended the fact to be known. It also shows considerable political sensitivity, in making the English feel that their Danegeld had in fact been put to excellent use:

King Cnut greets in friendship his archbishops and his diocesan bishops, and Earl Thorkel and all his earls, and all his people, whether men of a twelve hundred wergild or a two hundred, ecclesiastic and lay, in England. . . .

Since I did not spare my money as long as hostility was threatening you, I have now with God's help put an end to it with my money.

Then I was informed that greater danger was approaching us than we liked at all; and then I went myself with the men who accompanied me to Denmark, where the greatest injury had come to you, and with God's help I have taken measures so that never henceforth shall hostility reach you from there as long as you support me rightly and my life lasts.

Now I thank Almighty God for his help and his mercy, that I have so settled the great dangers which were approaching us that we need fear no danger to us from there; but [we may reckon] on full help and deliverance, if we need it.

Now it is my will, that we all thank Almighty God humbly for the mercy which he has shown for our help. . . .

If anyone, ecclesiastic or layman, Dane or Englishman, is so presumptuous as to defy God's law and my royal authority or the secular law, and he will not make amends and desist according to the direction of my bishops, I then pray, and also command, Earl Thorkel, if he can, to cause the evil-doer to do right.

And if he cannot, then it is my will that with the power of us both he shall destroy him in the land or drive him out of the land, whether he be of high or low rank.

Cnut then charges the reeves of England, the local law-officials of the shires, to do their duty justly 'with the witness of the bishops of the dioceses' – but he sternly reminds them who is the supreme peace-keeper and fount of justice:

And if anyone gives asylum to a thief, or interferes on his behalf, he is to be liable to the same penalty to me as the thief, unless he can clear himself of liability to me with the full process of exculpation.

And it is my will that all the nation, ecclesiastical and lay, shall steadfastly observe Edgar's laws, which all men have chosen and sworn to at Oxford.

The letter concludes with a re-emphasis of the partnership between Church and State and the duties to the Church which Cnut wanted to be observed: oath-keeping, the taboo against abducting nuns, the keeping of feasts, and regular church-going – 'so that all together through the mercy of the eternal God and the intercession of his saints we can and may come to the bliss of the heavenly kingdom and dwell with him who liveth and reigneth ever without end. Amen.'

This letter was something quite new in the entire history of Saxon England. It is easy to pick cynical holes in it and call it a piece of smooth propaganda, but the whole document was beautifully and most carefully composed – Dunstan himself could not have done better. Cnut had clearly taken a skeleton clerical staff with him back to Denmark – professionals who had learned their trade under Ethelred's regime. Above all, it broke new ground in identifying Cnut with his English subjects in a common fight against any future trouble from viking raiders – the one threat which even Cnut's supremacy in the Scandinavian world could not dispel. Very soon that threat became a reality in the person of Thorkel the Tall, Cnut's own viceroy.

Thorkel's record is an interesting one. As the most powerful warlord in Swein's great army, he had already changed sides once and had served Ethelred for a spell, and he clearly found Cnut's regime too restricting for him. Trouble between them boiled up in November 1021 when Cnut proclaimed Thorkel an outlaw. Cnut obviously knew very well that Thorkel would have no trouble in raising a fleet and army of his own, and had no intention of being caught napping. In 1022 Cnut took command of the fleet and based himself on the Isle of Wight: danger was clearly in the air. But in 1023 the king sailed to Denmark and a reconciliation with Thorkel was agreed. Thorkel stayed in Denmark as regent, guardian of Cnut's son; Cnut returned to England, with Thorkel's son.

Cnut did not have to boast of bringing 'peace with honour' with him – peace was enough .But when he came back he made a ceremonial gesture which aroused even more respect from his English subjects. After Cnut's first trip to Denmark, he and Thorkel had gone to Ashingdon, site of the last great battle with Edmund Ironside, and dedicated a church 'for the souls of the men who had been slain there'. Now, in 1023, he honoured the memory of the martyred Archbishop Ælfheah as he had honoured that of Edmund. Ælfheah's remains were taken from London for a sumptuous re-burial at Canterbury in a solemn, week-long journey which the *Chronicle* records in full:

In this year in St Paul's minster in London, King Cnut gave full permission to Archbishop Æthelnoth and Bishop Brihtwine and to all the servants of God who were with them to take up the archbishop St Ælfheah from the tomb, and they did so on 8 June. And the illustrious king, and the archbishop and the diocesan bishops, and the earls, and very many ecclesiastics and also lay-folk, conveyed his holy body on a ship across the Thames to Southwark, and there entrusted the holy martyr to the archbishop and his companions. And they then bore him with a distinguished company and happy jubilation to Rochester. Then on the third day Queen Emma came with her royal child Hardacnut, and they then all conveyed the holy archbishop with much glory and joy and songs of praise into Canterbury, and thus brought him with due ceremony into Christ Church on 11 June. Afterwards on the eighth day, on 15 June, Archbishop Æthelnoth and Bishop Ælfsige and Bishop Brihtwine and all who were with them placed St Ælfheah's holy body on the north side of Christ's altar, to the praise of God and the honour of the holy archbishop, and to the eternal salvation of all those who daily visit his holy body there with devout hearts and with all humility.

Glory and joy and songs of praise – there had been little of that eleven years before, when Ælfheah had been battered to death by drunken Danes. Now a Danish king had ruled in England for six years and had formally made atonement for the atrocities of the past. The solemnity and rejoicing of the ceremony really set the seal on Cnut's compact with his people. And it is worth pointing out that the account quoted above is the longest entry in the *Chronicle*'s coverage of Cnut's eighteen-year reign. Like a Geiger counter, which only crackles when there is positive trouble to record, the *Chronicle* falls silent for the period, emitting sporadic flickers of data. Half of the facts it does provide refer to the deaths of leading churchmen or highlights in Church history; the other half refer to events far from home. Those events represented Cnut's efforts to extend his authority over the entire Scandinavian world: over Norway and Sweden as well as Denmark. They could have resulted in years of fruitless wars with England footing the bill both in money and manpower. But this did not happen.

The tortuous histories of Sweden and Denmark in this period may be briefly summarized here. Suffice it to say that, in 1026, Cnut's power was menaced by a triple coalition. His enemies consisted of Anund, king of Sweden; Olaf, king of Norway; and two brothers, Ulf and Eilaf. The latter two men had deserted Cnut's cause: Ulf had married Cnut's sister, Estrith, and had replaced Thorkel the Tall as regent of Denmark, while his brother Eilaf had been made an earl in England by Cnut. Cnut met the coalition head-on, crossing to Denmark, raising a fleet, and heading through the Kattegat to force a decisive battle. This was fought at the Holy River in eastern Scania, and Cnut was beaten. After the battle, however, he did get the limited satisfaction of arranging Ulf's murder.

Before Cnut tried again, he took the precaution of sounding out the disaffected leaders in Norway who were unhappy with Olaf's rule. He finally made his second attempt in 1028, and this time he took help from England – but it was not a national expeditionary force. He took the entire professional fleet, plus ten ships fitted out and manned by 'English thegns'. With this fleet he crossed to Denmark and made rendezvous with a large Danish fleet. Cnut then coasted north into Norwegian waters, pausing at intervals to pick up the allegiance of Norwegian leaders who had decided to desert Olaf. There was no battle at all this time. Cnut's fleet reached its 'furthest north' at Nidaros, and, when the warlords of Thrandheim came over to him, Olaf's cause was lost. Cnut was the new master of Norway. The problem now was to find a deputy who could rule it in such a way that both Cnut and the Norwegians would be satisfied.

Cnut held a 'summit conference' of the northern warlords at Nidaros in 1028. At this meeting, his son Hardacnut was proclaimed king of Denmark. Norway's viceroy was to be Hákon, son of Eric of Hlathir. Hákon had served Cnut well in England and was now proclaimed earl of Norway.

The course of events in the north was soon affected by the complexities of Cnut's own family life. While the wars in England were still blazing, Cnut had taken a 'common-law' wife: Ælfgifu, daughter of a former earl of Northumbria, who became generally known as 'Ælfgifu of Northampton' and bore him a son, named Swein. This relationship was never recognized by the Church and became a positive embarrassment when Cnut decided to marry Ethelred's widow, Emma. Nevertheless, he did not dismiss Ælfgifu of Northampton. She must have been a most extraordinary woman, for he developed a deep respect for her political qualities. The Nidaros settlement was soon jeopardized by the death of Earl Hákon in the winter of 1029–30 – he was drowned at sea. Cnut decided to send his illegitimate son Swein over to Norway under the supervision of his mother. Olaf of Norway, hastening back on hearing of the news of Hákon's death, was killed in a battle near Thrandheim in July 1030, leaving the field to Ælfgifu and Swein.

It would be pleasant to say that Cnut's mistress turned out to be as good a ruler as her lover, but in fact she was a disastrous failure. It was not completely her fault, for the Norwegians were a people possessed by the demon of individual freedom – the restless independence which had already driven them 'west over seas' from their native land to colonize Iceland, Greenland, and even to make the first European landings in North America. The Norwegians found Ælfgifu's policy of more taxes, heavier penalties for crimes of violence, and increased state service utterly intolerable. The dead Olaf became one of the most rapidly honoured popular saints of all time. His son, Magnus, was looked to as a deliverer. By the time Cnut died, in November 1035, Ælfgifu and Swein had been driven out of Norway; and for generations afterwards good Norwegians shuddered at the memory of 'Ælfgifu's time'.

Much has been made of Cnut's 'empire of the north', but his power was clearly not as absolute as he would have liked. For all that, Cnut's image as a sort of viking Charlemagne is a true one, certainly as far as his international reputation was concerned. For over two centuries, the Northmen had been the bogeymen of the civilized world; now, thanks to Cnut, they had gained respectability. It was possible for a Danish king to talk on equal terms with every monarch in Europe – not only that, but hold top-level talks with the pope and the emperor themselves. Of all the English monarchs who came after Cnut, only one, Henry II, enjoyed such eminence. Cnut was intensely proud of his own importance, which was officially recognized by his famous journey to Rome in 1027.

The basic reason for the trip was for Cnut to attend the coronation of the new Holy Roman Emperor, Conrad, by Pope John XIX. For Cnut personally, it was also a pilgrimage, and at repeated visits to churches and shrines he gave gratifying displays of humility and devotion. But protocol and religion were not the only motives. He had hard business to discuss with Pope John and Emperor Conrad; and on his return journey he sent another of his remarkable letters to the leaders of the English people:

I make known to you that I have recently been to Rome, to pray for the remission of my sins and for the safety of the kingdoms and of the peoples which are subjected to my rule.

I had long ago vowed this journey to God, but I was not able to perform it until now because of the affairs of the kingdom and other causes of hindrance.

But now I give most humble thanks to my Almighty God, who has granted me in my lifetime to visit his holy Apostles, Peter and Paul, and every sacred place which I could learn of within the city of Rome and outside it, and in person to worship and adore there according to my desire. . . .

Be it known to you, that there was there a great assembly of nobles at the celebration of Easter, with the lord Pope John and the Emperor Conrad, namely all the princes of the nations from Mount Garganus to the sea nearest [to us];* and they all both received me with honour and honoured me with precious gifts; and especially was I honoured by the emperor with various gifts and costly presents, with vessels of gold and silver and silk robes and very costly garments.

I therefore spoke with the emperor and the lord pope and the princes who were present, concerning the needs of all the peoples of my whole kingdom, whether English or Danes, that they might be granted more equitable law and greater security on their way to Rome, and that they should not be hindered by so many barriers on the way and so oppressed by unjust tolls; and the emperor and King Rodulf,† who chiefly had dominion over those barriers, consented to my demands; and all the princes confirmed by edicts that my men, whether merchants or others travelling for the sake of prayer, should go to and return from Rome in safety with firm peace and just law, free from hindrances by barriers and tolls.

Again, I complained before the lord pope and said that it displeased me greatly that my archbishops were so much oppressed by the immensity of the sums of money which were exacted from them when according to custom they came to the apostolic see to receive the *pallium*. It was decided that this should not be done in future.

Indeed, all the things which I demanded for the benefit of my people from the lord pope and the emperor and from King Rodulf and the other princes through whose lands our way to Rome lies, they most willingly granted, and also confirmed what they had conceded with an oath, with the witness of four

* From Foggia to the North Sea.
† Of Burgundy.

archbishops and twenty bishops and an innumerable multitude of dukes and nobles who were present.

Therefore I give most hearty thanks to Almighty God, that I have successfully accomplished all that I had desired, just as I had designed, and have carried out my vows to my satisfaction....

But I send ahead this letter, in order that all the people of my kingdom may be gladdened at my success, because, as you yourselves know, I have never spared – nor will I spare in the future – to devote myself and my toil for the need and benefit of all my people.

The Rome conference of 1027 was, in short, a resounding personal success for Cnut and for England. His new *entente* with the pope and the emperor was a unique achievement, won face to face, and not by the second-hand negotiations of Athelstan and Offa of Mercia before him. Moreover, the close understanding between Denmark and the empire lasted; right at the end of Cnut's reign, Schleswig passed to Denmark under the terms of a marriage agreement between Cnut's daughter Gunnhild and Henry, son of the Emperor Conrad.

Apart from the failure in Norway there was one serious flaw in Cnut's foreign policy: Normandy. As long as Emma's brother, Duke Richard II, was alive, Cnut's relations with Normandy were good. But Richard died, and in 1027 the duchy passed to his younger son Robert, an arrogant and independent man who could see no good reason to keep the alliance in being. He continued to give asylum to his cousins, the athelings Edward and Alfred. Cnut tried to revive the alliance by giving Robert his widowed sister Estrith (relict of the rebel earl, Ulf) in marriage, but the Norman duke rejected her. (He was at this time already the father of an illegitimate son by Arlette, daughter of a tanner from Falaise. The baby was called William.) Relations with Robert of Normandy remained cool, and Edward and Alfred were still there when Cnut died.

In his eighteen years as king of England, Cnut only had to fight one campaign there. This was just after his return from home, when he marched against Scotland. He had no trouble in securing the nominal submission of the king of the Scots, Malcolm, and two sub-kings (named in the *Chronicle* as Mælbæth and Iehmarc) but, as in Norway, it was only a temporary peace. The eleventh century was a particularly unstable period of Scottish history, the period of Duncan, Macbeth, and Malcolm III. The brunt of the fighting had to be borne by the earls of Northumbria; and this brings us to the one big innovation made by Cnut in England: the great earldoms.

For centuries, the English had been used to the rule of the ealdormen in the shires, and the hereditary descent of the office through respected English ruling families. Ethelred's wars changed all that. Cnut's rule was exercised by earls whom he appointed – Danes more often than not. This was something the English found hard to get used to. An English earldom was a mark of favour and new ones were carved ruthlessly out of the old ealdormanries. It is impossible to draw a map of England at the close of Cnut's reign showing the precise frontiers of the new earldoms: they were still 'first-generation' honours, and flexible. But, after the king himself, the earls were the men who mattered: Siward of Northumbria, Leofric of Mercia, Godwine of Wessex.

Cnut's earls were the traditional English ealdormen writ large; the same applied to the new military caste in English society, the housecarls, professional fighting men and the hard core of Cnut's army. Their parallel in English society was the thegn; but under Cnut the housecarls became practically a class apart. They were expensive to maintain. England may have had no more crippling wars under Cnut, but her people had to pay an annual *heregeld* or 'army-tax' for the upkeep of the armed services. The price for peace under Cnut was therefore a yearly tax, the grievance of which was underlined by the uneasy awareness of an alien aristocracy which could rely on professional military power.

As a lawgiver, Cnut imitated Edgar and Alfred, issuing a massive compilation of traditional law, updated to provide for the larger Danish population in the island. Its lasting virtue was its size and scope, which made it a textbook of English law until the sweeping reforms of the twelfth century.

Cnut's attitude to the Church has often been debated. By no stretch of the imagination can he be described as a model Christian. If he could not get what he wanted by an honest war, he was quite unscrupulous, as we have seen, in using a convenient assassin to get rid of a rival. He never lost the viking hardness of his youth; he could be cruel and petty. But none of this prevented him from startling his contemporaries by his obvious respect for the life of the

Christian Church. As a lay patron in traditional style, he was unusually lavish.

One testimonial to Cnut's generosity to the Church has given us the only portrait of Cnut we have. It shows the king and queen presenting a gold cross. Cnut's hair and beard are emphasized; they are untrimmed, Danish-style. His left hand grasps the hilt of a viking-pattern longsword with the typical 'cocked-hat' pommel. Ælfgifu-Emma's coronet peeps out from beneath her wimple, the folds of which are adjusted by an angel. It is a charming picture, executed in flowing line – but the artist has taken pains to depict what is unmistakably a forceful warrior in his own right.

Cnut died on 12 November 1035, at Shaftesbury. He was buried in the traditional resting-place of the kings of Saxon England: Winchester. His reign had ended a long nightmare for England, and made the country great as never before. But England could never be the same again. Like Offa of Mercia in the late eighth century, he had created a mould of kingship that could fit no one but himself.

He was a puzzle, an enigma – a usurper, yet an unprecedented success with his conquered people. While he lived, England was safe. But he left no clear successor. The confusion felt across the Channel is well expressed in a letter to Cnut from the bishop of Chartres in thanks for a generous donation. The letter pulls no punches, but admits to a gratified surprise:

> When we saw the gift you conferred on us, we were amazed at your wisdom, and equally at your piety; wisdom, indeed, that you, a man ignorant of our language, separated from us by a long stretch of land and sea, not only vigorously administer the concerns which are round about you, but also diligently inquire into those round about us; piety, truly, when we perceive that you, whom I had heard to be a ruler of pagans, not only of Christians, are also a most generous benefactor to the churches and servants of God. Giving thanks therefore to the King of Kings, from whose dispensation such things descend, we ask that he may cause your kingdom to be prosperous under you, and may absolve your soul from sins. . . .

## Chapter 12

All that the cold sea waves encompass
Young and loyal yielded allegiance,
With all their heart to King Edward the noble.
Ever gay was the courage of the guiltless king
Though long ago, of his land bereft
He wandered in exile, over earth's far ways,
After Cnut overcame Ethelred's kin. . . .
At length he came forth in lordly array,
Noble in goodness, pure and upright,
Edward the glorious, guarding his homeland,
Country and subjects – till on a sudden came
Death in his bitterness, bearing so dear
A lord from the earth.

*Anglo-Saxon Chronicle*: 1065.

# Edward the Confessor

Chaos and confusion were Cnut's immediate legacies to England when he died. It was largely his own fault. He had two illegitimate sons, Swein and Harold, by Ælfgifu of Northampton, and one legitimate son, Hardacnut, by Ælfgifu-Emma, and he had tried to leave Swein and Hardacnut a slice of power on both sides of the North Sea. Cnut's original idea had been that Hardacnut should succeed him in Denmark and England and Swein in Norway. Harold, as the youngest bastard, was not immediately provided for.

It was widely rumoured that Harold and Swein were not Ælfgifu's sons, but changelings whom she had procured to satisfy Cnut's demands for sons – the gossip had it that Swein's father had been a priest, while Harold had been a shoemaker's son. Eight centuries ago, Florence of Worcester had to admit that 'since the matter is in doubt, we cannot settle what is certain about the birth of either', and it is hardly more profitable to continue the debate now. The trouble in November 1035 was that Hardacnut could not possibly come straight over to England from Denmark without leaving Magnus of Norway a free hand in Scandinavia. And the magnates of England, faced by this power-vacuum, were deeply divided as to the best course to take.

Godwine and Queen Emma headed the southern faction. The widowed queen naturally held out for the accession of Hardacnut and she was backed by the most powerful earl in the south. The queen had taken up residence at Winchester, presiding over the treasury of England. Leofric of Mercia, however, wanted to wait and see what happened in Denmark before making up his mind for or against Hardacnut, and in this he was backed by the Londoners and the majority of the thegns north of the Thames. They wanted a regency, with Harold officiating.

An emergency Witan was held at Oxford to thrash the matter out, and Harold's supporters prevailed. A compromise solution partitioned the kingdom. As the *Chronicle* has it: 'And it was then determined that Ælfgifu, Hardacnut's mother, should stay in Winchester with the housecarls of her son the king, and they should keep all Wessex in his possession; and Earl Godwine was their most loyal man.' Harold, however, had other ideas, and promptly sent a band of housecarls down to Winchester to seize the royal treasure. This decisive act, for all its immorality, did much to sway waverers to Harold's cause. 'And', Florence records, 'with the consent of very many of the nobility of England, he began to reign as the legitimate heir; not, however, as powerfully as Cnut, because the more rightful heir, Hardacnut, was expected.' Florence adds an ominous fact as a postscript to the first year of the interregnum: 'Robert, duke of the Normans, died, and his son, William the Bastard, then a minor, succeeded him.'

By far the most important English magnate who embraced Harold's cause was Godwine of Wessex, and in 1036 he showed his true colours. Across the Channel, the exiled athelings Edward and Alfred had attracted a following of Norman soldiers and crossed to England to confer with their mother in Winchester. It was by no stretch of the imagination an invasion, and Alfred at least was prepared to go to London for a meeting with King Harold. Godwine, however, viewed the prospect of a *rapprochement* between the athelings and Harold with the greatest alarm. He had Alfred's party ambushed on the way to London and imprisoned the young man; 'and of his companions some he dispersed, some he put in fetters and afterwards blinded, some he tortured by scalping and punished by cutting off their hands and feet; many also he ordered to be sold. . . .' Apart from thus liquidating Alfred's Norman escort, Godwine also 'killed by various and miserable deaths 600 men at Guildford'. This additional fact is interesting and suggests that, despite the success of Cnut's reign, there was still considerable support for Ethelred's descendants, in Surrey at least – Saxon Jacobites, as it were – and Godwine was certainly not the man to tolerate such an influence in his earldom.

In Winchester, Queen Emma reacted promptly and packed Edward straight back to Normandy. But she could do nothing to save Alfred from a terrible fate. With the help of friends in the Danelaw, Godwine shipped Alfred, in chains, to the Isle of Ely.

As his boat touched the shore, the helpless Alfred had his eyes
ripped out and he was handed over to the care of the monks of
Ely. He did not survive this brutal treatment but died shortly
afterwards. They gave him a decent funeral – 'very honourably,
as he deserved, in the south chapel at the west end, full close to the
steeple'.

Godwine's brutality was firmly endorsed by Harold, who was
clearly pleased that the danger of a loyalist reaction in favour of
the athelings had been crushed in the bud. The year 1037 saw
Harold consolidate his power by being formally accepted as undisputed king of England. The last adherents of Hardacnut gave
up – 'and Hardacnut was deserted because he was too long in
Denmark' was the *Chronicle*'s verdict. He then turned on his
rival's mother, Ælfgifu-Emma, and expelled her from the land
'without any mercy to face the raging winter'. Emma did not return to Normandy; she found asylum with Count Baldwin of
Bruges, who 'received her well there and maintained her there as
long as she had need'.

An air of hardness and uneasiness surrounds what is known of
Harold's reign of four years and sixteen weeks. There was a brisk
war with the Welsh in 1039 in which an Anglo-Danish force from
Mercia was badly cut up and Earl Leofric's brother was killed.
Harold – who earned the unflattering name of 'Harefoot' – certainly seems to have ruled with ferocity, but without his father's
political touch. He kept up Cnut's war-tax; in his time sixteen
new warships were fitted out, 'at eight marks to each rowlock,
just as had been done in King Cnut's time'. But Harold never
inspired full confidence in his subjects. He seems never to have
married, and produced no heirs. Meanwhile, across the sea in
Denmark, there was Hardacnut; and when Harold died at Oxford
on 17 March 1040, the English magnates sent for him, 'thinking
that they were acting wisely'.

Hardacnut came over to England with a sizeable fleet of sixty
ships in the summer of 1040, and was at once accepted as king.
He then appalled his new subjects by levying the biggest war-tax
raised in peacetime in living memory: 21,099 pounds. On top of
that, 11,048 pounds were paid to build thirty-two new warships.
This was particularly hard on the people because it was a bad
year for wheat – and the men of Worcestershire revolted. When
Hardacnut's tax officials arrived, a mob turned on them and they

fled to the cathedral for sanctuary. That did not stop the mob, which swept into the church, dragged the tax-men from their hiding-place, 'in an upper room of a tower of the monastery,' according to Florence of Worcester, and lynched them.

Hardacnut's reaction was to call out a large army and send it west to make an example of Worcester. It was commanded by the earls of all England. Among them was Godwine, who had had no little trouble in making his peace with Hardacnut. The new king had been incensed at the murder of his half-brother Alfred, and Godwine only saved his neck by appeasing Hardacnut with the present of a magnificent warship and swearing on oath that he had had nothing to do with the murder.

Thanks to Florence of Worcester, who had an abundance of local information on which to draw, we have a succinct account of the great punitive expedition of 1041. The earls had a simple, brutal task: 'to kill, if they could, all the men, to plunder and burn the city and to lay waste the whole province'.

> When 12 November arrived, they began to lay waste both the city and the province, and did not cease to do so for four days; but they captured or killed few either of the citizens or of the men of the province, because, having notice of their coming, the people of the province had fled in all directions; a great number of the citizens, however, took refuge in a certain small island which is called Bevere, situated in the middle of the Severn, and having made a fortification, defended themselves manfully against their enemies until peace was restored and they were allowed to return home freely. Accordingly, on the fifth day, when the city had been burnt, everyone went off to his own parts with much booty, and the king's wrath was at once appeased.

The revolt of the Worcestershire men of 1041 is particularly important because it shows that, long after the end of Ethelred's wars, and after twenty-four years under Danish rule, local feeling could still blaze out in armed resistance if provoked too far. It is reasonable to guess that the earls called off the campaign in the west and patched up an armistice because of pressure from the western earls, who did not want to resume their rule over a mutinous people. Both sides had done enough for honour and it could safely be left at that. The revolt is the major recorded incident of Hardacnut's brief and thoroughly unpopular reign. He stands out as a completely unsympathetic autocrat who was determined to prove that he was Cnut's genuine son – he had Harold Harefoot's body dug up and thrown into a swamp. He also felt strong enough to summon the atheling Edward to join him at court.

Edward was therefore most probably with Hardacnut when the king attended a wedding feast at Lambeth in June 1042. The host was 'Osgod Clapa, a man of great power'; the bride was Osgod's daughter Gytha, and the groom was 'Tofi, surnamed the Proud, a Dane and an influential man'. In the midst of the cheerful babble and roaring of toasts stood King Hardacnut, 'cheerful, in health and high spirits, drinking with the aforesaid bride and certain men. . . .' Suddenly the king collapsed in convulsions 'in the midst of his drinking'. He was carried from the hall, rigid and unable to speak, and died shortly afterwards on 8 June. Nobody mourned for him. The *Chronicle* wrote this vicious epitaph: 'And also he did nothing worthy of a king as long as he ruled.' Like Harold Harefoot, Hardacnut, last Danish king of England, died childless. But the Witan had no difficulty in electing his successor: Edward the Atheling, restored at last to his inheritance after years of exile – the legitimate descendant of Alfred the Great.

Edward the Confessor has to be one of the most misunderstood kings in English history. He is commonly seen as an unworldly greybeard, surrounded by priests, helpless before the power of Earl Godwine and his sons, obsessed with getting the new West Minster finished before he died, and at the end faced with the agonizing choice of handing over England to Harold Godwine's son or accepting a take-over by William of Normandy. What happened during his extraordinary reign totally disproves this. Granted, Edward was in love with religion and would probably have made an excellent monk. Granted, Godwine and his sons wielded power such as no English subject had ever enjoyed. But for all that, Edward was the man who mattered: they could only go so far. For twenty-four years Edward was the lynch-pin on which Saxon England turned. Edward certainly cannot be blamed for what happened after his death: he had taken adequate steps to provide for a smooth succession to the throne of England.

Why, then, did matters end with 'William the Conqueror, 1066'? It is so easy to forget that, by the middle eleventh century,

Normandy was not a hostile power with its sights set on the conquest of Saxon England. England had been wide open to Norman influence ever since Edward's father had married Emma of Normandy back in 1002: William of Normandy's father was Edward's cousin, Edward himself had been reared in Normandy, and the place had contributed much to his own accession in 1042. The death of Hardacnut in that year switched off the dominant current of Danish power which had played on England since the wars of Ethelred and Swein. Edward the Atheling, Ethelred's son, was the natural choice to fill the power-vacuum in England – but from behind him radiated the renewed influence of Normandy, whence he had come. Edward himself came to accept that he was an invaluable stop-gap, as far as the succession to the throne was concerned. True, there were other athelings of England out there somewhere, but God alone knew where, and they had to be discounted as practicable successors. It was up to Edward to do the best he could to scotch the dangerous ambitions of Godwine and his sons, and arrange a smooth hand-over of power to the Norman ruling line of which he was a relative by blood.

In 1042, however, it was the ancient pedigree of his father's line – not that of his Norman mother – which mattered. Edward was the heir of the *Cerdicingas*, the ancient West Saxon line of Cerdic, and the *Cerdicingas* had something unique. It is hard to express properly in modern-day terms: 'divine right' is certainly an incomplete way of putting it. It was more of a hero-worship for a ruling family which had always produced law-giving hero-kings: Ine, and Egbert, and Alfred the Great, and Edward the Elder; Athelstan, Edmund, Edgar the Peaceable. Englishmen could gloss over the appalling inadequacies of Ethelred the Unready – honour had been more than satisfied by the deeds of Edmund Ironside. Edward the Confessor was almost a hero even before he had begun to rule. He was the people's choice, the man the country needed; and he began his reign with limitless reserves of goodwill and support.

One thing Edward lacked desperately in 1042, however, was cash; and his first act as king was to rob his mother. He rode down to Winchester in person, accompanied by the formidable Earls Siward of Northumbria, Leofric of Mercia, and Godwine of Wessex, and an army of their combined housecarls, and informed the dowager Queen Emma that his need was greater than hers.

Emma had clearly not been required to contribute to the exactions of her son Hardacnut, and the *Chronicle* gives Edward an interesting motive:

'And they . . . deprived her of all the treasures which she owned, and which were beyond counting, because she had formerly been very hard to the king, her son, in that she did less for him than he wished both before he became king and afterwards as well. And they allowed her to stay there afterwards.

Considering that Emma had certainly saved Edward's life in 1036, this seems a bit hard. But the *Translation of St Mildred* goes even further in approving Edward's action:

While he was reigning in peace like unto Solomon, his own mother was accused of inciting Magnus, king of Norway, to invade England, and it was said that she had given countless treasures to Magnus. Wherefore this traitor to the kingdom, this enemy of the country, this betrayer of her own son, was judged, and everything she possessed was forfeited to the king.

All in all, the general impression given is that of full marks for a decisive and justified action which was carried out in collaboration with the leading earls of England.

For the first five years of his reign, Edward relied heavily on these earls – all of them Cnut's creations. He also needed the powerful fleet which was one of the most important legacies of the Danish interregnum, for Magnus of Norway was a very real threat. Edward had to take the fleet to sea in 1045 as a precaution against invasion, and turn down repeated requests for help from Swein Estrithson, who had succeeded Hardacnut as king of Denmark. The danger passed in 1048 when Magnus died – but Swein Estrithson could not prevent the most renowned viking warrior of the age, Harold Hardrada, uncle of Magnus, from becoming Norway's new king.

For all the readiness of the fleet, however, Edward failed to intercept and destroy a viking fleet of twenty-five ships which carried out a neat and destructive raid in 1048. The raiders looted Sandwich and then attacked Thanet, but the local *fyrd* beat them off. Essex, however, where the raiders turned next, was not so lucky, and suffered heavily before the raiders re-embarked.

This was the only recorded trouble from overseas of the entire reign. After these dramatic events, Edward was free to concentrate on problems at home in England – and foremost among those problems was Earl Godwine.

Godwine, shrewd trimmer that he was, never forgot that, although he was the strongest individual in England after the king himself, he was nevertheless not strong enough to stand on his own. It was child's play for Godwine to abandon his role as Queen Emma's champion and ride to Winchester with King Edward to despoil her. But after the invasion scare was over, Godwine wasted no time in bringing his power to bear on Edward and doing his best to run the country the way he, Godwine, wanted. This entailed cornering all the plum appointments in Church and State for his friends and lackeys, and seeing to it that his own sons became earls over as much territory as possible. He had in fact been quick off the mark with a grass-roots beginning, successfully persuading Edward to marry his daughter, Edith.

Edward was by no means a free man when he agreed to the marriage. Godwine had done him an invaluable favour by backing him up over the seizure of Queen Emma's treasure and the favour must be returned. As long as an invasion seemed likely, it was vital to keep Godwine happy – neither Swein Forkbeard nor Cnut at the height of his power had ever been able to keep his earls at heel. Godwine was a creation of Cnut, memories of the notorious desertions of Thorkel the Tall under Cnut were still very much alive, and Edward did not want Godwine to emulate Thorkel and go over to Magnus. Hence the marriage to Godwine's daughter in 1045 – the marriage which played no little part in the creation and maintenance of Edward the Confessor's saintly image.

Edward was certainly not a doddering greybeard when he married Edith – he was about forty-two – but Edith was admittedly young enough to be his daughter. Nowadays such an 'age gap' in a marriage provokes little or no comment; nor does the fact that a married couple may or may not have children. But this is not the case with royalty, and certainly not nine hundred years ago. Edward and Edith were expected to produce an heir. When they did not, the rumours began to fly thick and fast, ranging from the sanctimonious to the vicious. The king, while a wandering exile in peril of his life, had taken a strict vow of chastity. The king had suffered an accident while hunting which had made him impotent. The king secretly preferred men to women. As we have seen in the case of Harold Harefoot (*vis-à-vis* the rumours that he was not even an honest bastard, but a changeling), this 'Sunday papers' mentality was acutely alive in the eleventh century. But what are the facts?

The easiest facts about the problem are the ones we simply do not know. The couple *may* have been naturally barren. Edward's one worldly weakness was his passion for hunting, and he *may* have done himself an injury on horseback. Certainly there is no proof at all that he was homosexual – there are no Piers Gavestons or dukes of Buckingham associated with Edward the Confessor. All in all, the whole argument reminds us of the mystery surrounding England's 'Virgin Queen', Elizabeth I. There was nothing to stop her from taking an innocuous prince consort. But note the parallel. Both Edward and Elizabeth, as conscientious rulers, were also born survivors in a murderous age. The fact that both of them had survived to wear the crown of England was astonishing. Both of them came under pressure to marry and produce heirs in traditional style. But they did not. And I believe that Edward anticipated Elizabeth's decision by five hundred years. Granted, he was the legitimate king by virtue of his family descent (as Elizabeth was the undoubted daughter of Henry VIII). But Edward decided to get England out of the whole dynastic mess she was in by arranging a change-over to the parallel, related dynasty on England's doorstep. Edward may not have become king with the firm intention that William of Normandy should be his heir. No more did Elizabeth take over from 'Bloody Mary' in 1558 with the intention of nominating the king of Scotland as her successor. But as the childless years went by, the idea of handing over power to a candidate who had a genuine claim, but who was at the same time a 'new broom', became increasingly attractive.

Edith was the only daughter of Godwine's remarkable family, which still stands out as unique in English history. There has never been such a powerful 'instant aristocracy', established by a foreign king, which has wielded such massive power for a generation and then vanished from the scene. The nearest equivalent is John of Gaunt and his sons (legitimate and illegitimate) at the close of the fourteenth century – and even John of Gaunt was the

son of Edward III, a direct descendant of the Plantagenet line
which had ruled England for two centuries.

Swein was Godwine's eldest son. He was an utterly ruthless,
treacherous, traditional soldier of fortune in a century when such
men thrived – but Swein lived his life at the extreme of unaccept-
ability and eventually died as he had lived, a self-seeking *condottiere*
exiled from England, in 1052.

Harold Godwineson proved himself the most able of the lot.
He was as hard as Swein and, for that matter, Godwine himself;
but he kept within the pale, he was a survivor, and his military
talents made him indispensable as the first soldier of England.
He was exactly like his father in that Edward could not do without
him, and he slipped naturally into Godwine's shoes.

Next came the most interesting character of the family: Tostig
Godwineson, all nerves and fire, one of those familiar historical
figures whose natural talents were obvious to everyone but who
had the fatal knack of making everyone distrust him. Tostig and
Harold were like oil and water. They were natural rivals, a situation which Edward did his best to exploit by fostering Tostig as
earl of Northumbria to counter Harold's influence in the south.
Tostig was certainly the most intelligent of Godwine's sons. As
an administrator, he was authoritative, effective, and far-seeing.
He was, needless to say, loathed by everyone from his subjects
upward. Tostig was the embodiment of frustrated ambition, a
self-destructive man because he lacked the more prosaic qualities
of patience and animal cunning.

Gyrth and Leofwine were the youngest Godwinesons who
counted for anything in these troubled years. They, too, were important enough to receive earldoms, but they were politically
inert, content to follow Harold's lead. The family was rounded
out by Godwine's youngest son, Wulfnoth, who was too young to
take an independent line of his own, and Beorn, Godwine's
nephew.

By the end of the year 1046, Godwine's family web was developing nicely. His daughter Edith was queen, Swein had an
earldom on the Welsh frontier, while Edward had appointed
Harold to be earl of East Anglia. Godwine, however, had not had
things his own way in the field of Church preferments. The see
of London had fallen vacant and Edward had insisted on the appointment of a Norman abbot, Robert of Jumièges. Godwine's

nominee, Stigand, was an outsider in the eyes of the Church; he had received his first appointment from Cnut, and had established himself as the chief confidant of Queen Emma. Godwine nevertheless managed to obtain Edward's approval for Stigand's appointment as bishop of the East Angles.

From 1046 to 1051 Edward was locked in a power-struggle with Godwine which ended in apparent victory. His main advantage over the formidable earl was that the young Godwinesons were not united; each had his own axe to grind. It was easy to outlaw Swein: he committed the unpardonable sin of abducting an abbess, and then took service with Baldwin of Bruges, whose chief claim to notoriety was harbouring viking raiders who wanted a handy base for raids in the Channel. Swein then blackened his name still further by murdering the young Earl Beorn. Exiled from England, Swein eventually died in the Levant – ostensibly on pilgrimage. But in 1051 Edward took the momentous step of exiling Godwine and all his sons. Godwine, with Tostig and Gyrth, joined Swein in Bruges; Harold and Leofwine went to join the vikings of Ireland. It was the pinnacle of Edward's power, for civil war had loomed before popular opinion melted away from Godwine. Edward had also managed to appoint Robert of Jumièges to Canterbury, Ulf to Dorchester, and William to London – all of them Norman bishops of his own making.

Twelve months later, however, Godwine was back. This time the tables were turned and civil war was averted at the price of restoring Godwine and his sons to their earldoms. There was also a brisk purge of Edward's Norman appointments: '. . . Archbishop Robert and Bishop William and Bishop Ulf escaped with difficulty with the Frenchmen who were with them and so got away overseas.' The official reason for the anti-Norman purge was 'because they were most responsible for the disagreement between Earl Godwine and the king'. The final touch to Edward's humiliation in 1052 was the appointment of the irregular Stigand to the vacant see of Canterbury.

Edward's attitude to Godwine was pretty clear: he hated him and refused to accept Godwine's oaths that he was not to blame for the death of Alfred the Atheling. But the king accepted that Godwine could only be brought to heel by an all-out civil war, and he shied away from the prospect on both moral and realistic grounds. In any case, Godwine did not remain long on the scene after his triumphant return. On Easter Monday, 1053, he collapsed in Edward's presence and died four days later. This sudden death also attracted gossip, and in particular the rumour that Godwine choked to death on a piece of bread while trying to prove to Edward, yet again, that he was innocent of Alfred's murder.

Harold became earl of Wessex (the news of Swein's death in the east had arrived the year before). This left the earldom of East Anglia vacant, but Tostig's ambitions were not satisfied. East Anglia went to Ælfgar, son of Leofric of Mercia.

Tostig did not have long to wait, however. In 1054 the tough old earl of Northumbria, Siward, led a Northumbrian expeditionary force into Scotland to assist Malcolm Canmore against the usurper Macbeth. The expedition was successful, but it was a personal tragedy for Siward. His housecarls suffered heavily in the fighting and his own son and nephew were killed. Shakespeare, in *Macbeth*, has Siward accepting the sad news with admirable phlegm:

SIWARD

'Had he his hurts before?'

ROSS

'Ay, on the front.'

SIWARD

'Why, then, God's soldier be he!
Had I as many sons as I have hairs,
I would not wish them to a fairer death:
And so, his knell is knoll'd.'

Siward of Northumbria died at York the following year. He typified the old England of Cnut, being the epitome of the civilized viking. Siward was buried in a church which he had had built and consecrated 'in the name of God and St Olaf'. His successor as earl of Northumbria was Tostig.

At the same time, Harold seems to have put pressure on Edward with a false accusation, for without apparent reason Ælfgar of East Anglia was outlawed. He did not take it lying down, but went to Wales and Ireland and raised an army, with which he did so much damage in Herefordshire that Edward gave in and reinstated him. It was a definite setback for Harold, who was

trying to install Gyrth or Leofwine in East Anglia as a counter-
balance to Tostig's accession in Northumbria. Harold had, however, continued his father's policy of promoting his own nominees
to leading Church appointments. And in November 1056, the
elderly Bishop Athelstan of Hereford died, giving Harold the
chance to insert one of his supporters. The appointment was made,
but it did not last long, as the *Chronicle* records with an air of
satisfaction:

> . . . Leofgar was appointed bishop. He was Earl Harold's priest,
> and he wore his moustaches during his priesthood until he
> became a bishop. He gave up his chrism and cross, his spiritual
> weapons, and took his spear and his sword after his consecra-
> tion as bishop, and so went campaigning against Griffith the
> Welsh king, and they killed him there and his priests with him,
> and Ælfnoth the sheriff and many good men with them; and
> the others fled.

Harold and Leofric of Mercia had to take over and clear up the
mess, forcing Griffith to renew his oath of allegiance to Edward.
Uneasy peace returned to the Welsh frontier for a while.

The greatest excitement was caused in 1057 by the return of
another wanderer – none other than Edward the Atheling, younger
son of Edmund Ironside. He had been born after his father's
death and smuggled out of England as a babe-in-arms to save
him from Cnut. By 1057 he was more of a Hungarian than an
English prince. But there is a maddening mystery surrounding the
way in which he came home and promptly died. The obvious
interpretation is not good enough, for contemporary writers were
as puzzled as we are. The *Chronicle*, for instance, laments: 'We
do not know for what reason it was brought about that he was
not allowed to see [the face?] of his kinsman King Edward. Alas,
that was a miserable fate and grievous to all this people that he
so speedily ended his life after he came to England, to the misfortune of this poor people.' It is impossible to imagine Edward
deliberately ordering the murder of anyone, let alone his half-
brother's son. Harold is the obvious candidate as the villain of the
piece – but, even if he had tried to poison the king's mind against
the atheling, it is just as hard to imagine Edward listening to such
obvious subterfuge from the ambitious head of the house of
Godwine. Edward the Atheling came home and died, and although

there was plenty of suspicion of foul play nothing was ever proved. But his death underlined the succession problem. Now the once-fruitful line of the *Cerdicingas* had dwindled to the king himself and the late atheling's children: Edgar the Atheling and his sister Margaret. Christina, who took the veil and became abbess of Romsey, was out of the running.

There was another important death in 1057: Leofric of Mercia, one of the very few English-born earls appointed by Cnut. Ælfgar succeeded his father, with Gyrth Godwineson sliding neatly into the vacant earldom of East Anglia. As Harold had granted Leofwine extensive holdings in Kent and Sussex, the sons of Godwine together formed the largest landholding party in Saxon England. Harold tried repeatedly to induce King Edward to exile Ælfgar – and succeeded for a very brief period; but the heirs of Leofric were still ruling Mercia as the Confessor's life moved into its last five years.

It seemed impossible that Harold could make any further addition to his own stature, but the Welsh campaign of 1063 was a godsend to him. Griffith of southern Wales had been a thorough nuisance throughout the reign, harbouring exiles, launching repeated raids into western England, and repeatedly breaking his duty of fealty to Edward. Harold – acting, for once, with help from Tostig – led a combined naval and land offensive against Griffith which ended with the Welsh king being murdered by his own people. Harold made the savage gesture of sending Griffith's head to Edward, together with the figurehead and ornaments from the Welsh flagship. Griffith's kingdom was parcelled up between his two half-brothers, Bleddyn and Rhiwallon, 'and they swore oaths and gave hostages to the king and the earl, promising that they would be faithful to him in everything, and be everywhere ready on water and on land, and likewise would pay such dues from that country as had been before given to any other king.' Harold had not only put a temporary end to the Welsh problem: he had established himself beyond a doubt as the top soldier in England.

It was probably in the following year, 1064, that there occurred one of the most controversial episodes of Edward's reign: Harold's visit to William of Normandy and the oath of allegiance he allegedly swore to the Norman duke. The documentary evidence is almost totally one-sided and gives the Norman version. It also exists in pictorial form in the splendid Bayeux Tapestry, woven after 1066.

This shows Harold receiving instructions from Edward and riding to Bosham, on the south coast, to take ship for Normandy. It shows Harold making landfall in the territory of Count Guy of Ponthieu, and being arrested and brought before the count. The news is brought to William, who promptly orders Harold to be handed over. We then see Harold, decked out as a Norman knight, riding with William on an expedition against Dinan castle. On the way, disaster threatens at a river crossing and Harold saves the day by dragging trapped knights from a quicksand. After the capture of Dinan, William knights Harold. Then Harold is shown between two altars, swearing an oath to William – after which he returns to England and makes his report to Edward. Next comes the death and burial of Edward, followed immediately by Harold's coronation, the uneasiness of the new king and his people at the appearance of a comet, and Duke William's invasion.

Whole books have been written over the correct interpretation of the Tapestry. We know that it contains several associated stories which were familiar in the eleventh century but which have since been lost.* But it also contains a vivid sense of expression, as well as a wealth of detail. Edward is shown giving Harold firm instructions. When Harold returns, he approaches the king in an atmosphere of unmistakable dejection, hands spread, head low. But there is absolutely no sign of concealment or deception about Harold's oath. The altars' relics are clearly shown and the oath is being properly witnessed. Why, then, did the story grow that Harold had been tricked by William into swearing an oath on concealed relics which was much more binding than he had intended?

Edward sent Harold over to Normandy with the formal promise that England would pass to William when Edward died – that is clear enough. This would involve Harold's promising to act as regent until William could come to claim his own, and, not unnaturally, Harold would not have been happy about this. But it

* One of the most famous is the panel with the legend 'Where a clerk and Ælfgifu'. This follows Harold's arrival at William's palace, and shows a tonsured man posturing before a veiled woman. A semi-obscene figure in the margin, holding a similar pose, suggests some now-forgotten scandal then associated firmly with Harold's trip to Normandy.

was a completely straightforward mission, and Harold could not wriggle out of it. When he came back to England he was certainly William's man by virtue of his oath in Normandy. Even assuming that William had seen to it that the oath Harold actually took was far more binding than Harold would otherwise have wished, it only meant that Harold had carried out Edward's wishes in a more sophisticated form.

It is quite possible that Harold came back to Edward, as the Tapestry depicts, downcast and angry that William had tricked him. But he would have been very foolish to make a fuss about it, as this would only emphasize his sworn obligations to William – and in any case Harold Godwineson, a true son of his father, is not remembered for his sense of duty to anything but his own career, let alone for mere oaths. In any case, any recriminations which may have raged at Westminster after Harold's return were soon cut short by the tumultuous events of the year 1065.

Earl Ælfgar of Mercia had died in 1063, and had been replaced by his young son Edwin. Two years later Earl Tostig of Northumbria, who had ruled the north in growing unpopularity for the last ten years, was faced with a general insurrection by the thegns of the north. It was a well-prepared coup. Tostig's housecarls were massacred. His few supporters, whether English or Danish, were also killed. Tostig's armoury and treasury were captured and taken to York; and the earl himself was outlawed. The Northumbrian thanes chose Morcar, brother of Edwin of Mercia, for their new earl, and Edwin supported him. A joint mission was sent to Edward for the royal approval, which was granted. Tostig and his family fled across the Channel and were granted asylum by Count Baldwin of Flanders.

As Christmas 1065 approached, Edward the Confessor was preparing for his death. He was ready to go. He had done his best, preventing a total seizure of power by Godwine and his equally ruthless sons, and making use of their best qualities. He also believed that he had done everything in his power to smooth the coming of Duke William as his successor. He now clung to life to see the realization of his dearest dream: the completion and consecration of the glorious new cathedral which he had built, the West Minster. The ceremony was held on 28 December 1065. Eight days later, Edward the Confessor was dead.

His people firmly believed him to be a saint. Many miracles

were attributed to him in his own lifetime. Edward was justly respected as being the only man who could hold the ambition of Godwine and his sons in check. He could not eradicate the evils created by that ambition, but he had made a passable job of harnessing it for the security of the kingdom. What he could not have bargained for was the genuine wave of nationalist feeling which greeted the act which made a mockery of all his policies: Harold Godwineson's successful bid for the English crown.

For there can be no doubt that in England Edward's attempts to inoculate the kingdom with Norman influences had met with growing resentment. The return of the Godwinesons in 1052 had been popular in that it brought about a purge of the 'Norman clerks' whom Edward had appointed. There was nothing unexpected about Harold's claim, when it came. Nor was it without precedent in the five centuries of Saxon England's turbulent history. Harold's accession was a popular one. Nothing proves this more clearly than the tone of the *Chronicle*, which had hitherto recorded the deeds of Godwine and his sons with unveiled criticism. But with whole-hearted enthusiasm, the *Chronicle* endorses the story which justified Harold's seizure of power – that Edward had entrusted the kingdom to him before he died:

> ... And angels led
> His righteous soul to heaven's radiance.
> Yet the wise ruler entrusted the realm
> To a man of high rank, to Harold himself,
> A noble earl who all the time
> Had loyally followed his lord's commands
> With words and deeds, and neglected nothing
> That met the need of the people's king.

Harold certainly wasted no time. On 6 January 1066, the newly consecrated West Minster began its long career with two splendid ceremonies: the funeral of King Edward and the coronation of King Harold. The note of indecent haste which underlay Harold's coronation could not be disguised, and was pointedly included in the Bayeux Tapestry. This shows the funeral procession of Edward *before* his death, as if to state that the Confessor was buried almost before he had died.

The abrupt end to the ruling dynasty of Cnut had plucked England out of the close association with Scandinavia which had been forced on the island since the death of Ethelred. Harold's accession in January 1066 was a deliberate attempt to defy Edward's move towards a peaceful Norman succession. By no stretch of the imagination could England be described as united as the year 1066 began. But nobody could doubt that, if any man could restore unity and safety to the land, it was Harold Godwineson. 'And Earl Harold was now consecrated king,' says the *Chronicle*, 'and he met little quiet in it as long as he ruled the realm.'

*Chapter 13*

The bloodstained battle-ground was covered with the flower of the youth and nobility of England. The two brothers of the king were found near him, and Harold himself stripped of all badges of honour could not be identified by his face, but only by certain marks on his body. His corpse was brought into the duke's camp, and William gave it for burial to William, surnamed Malet, and not to Harold's mother, who offered for the body of her beloved son its weight in gold. For the duke thought it unseemly to receive money for such merchandise, and equally he considered it wrong that Harold should be buried as his mother wished, since so many men lay unburied because of his avarice.

William of Poitiers, *The Deeds of William, duke of the Normans and king of the English.*

# Nemesis from Normandy

Harold Godwineson was king of the English, and from the outset of his reign the waging of a war of survival was inevitable. Harold was faced not merely with the challenge of William of Normandy but with the renewed threat of invasion from Norway by King Harold Hardrada and the additional problem of which of the two would receive the help and support of his own exiled brother, Earl Tostig. But before these problems resolved themselves he had an intensive stint of public-relations work to do in order to convince the English that he was a viable king. Harold, in short, had to try to wipe out all the traditional hostility which the house of Godwine had stirred up against itself; and by and large it is clear that he succeeded.

Harold made a significant start on the very first day of his reign, by insisting that he must be crowned not by Stigand, archbishop of Canterbury, but the more respectable Aldred of York. Stigand had attained the primacy of the English Church 'by the back stairs' – by private preferment – and he was an intense embarrassment to Harold now. The king's coronation gesture was well judged and it was not lost on the English. By taking the crown from Aldred and not from the dubious Stigand, Harold was showing that he was deliberately turning his back on the murky past of the Godwine family and its lackeys. It was also an embarrassment to the Norman artist who designed the Bayeux Tapestry, whose task it was to show Harold as a bare-faced usurper. The Tapestry, in fact, shows Harold on his throne with Archbishop Stigand proclaiming the new king to the people. But gestures were not enough. Harold had to show that he was an effective ruler and he had to do it fast. According to Florence of Worcester's account, he did just that:

On taking the helm of the kingdom Harold immediately began to abolish unjust laws and to make good ones; to patronize churches and monasteries; to pay particular reverence to bishops, abbots, monks, and clerks; and to show himself pious, humble, and affable to all good men. But he treated malefactors with great severity, and gave general orders to his earls, ealdormen, sheriffs and thegns to imprison all thieves, robbers, and disturbers of the kingdom. He laboured in his own person by sea and by land for the protection of his realm.

Harold was also shrewd enough to realize that, although he and his brothers held the upper hand in England, the country could see no lasting security without the reconciliation of the houses of Godwine and of Leofric. Another constructive gesture was called for in the form of a political marriage. Harold therefore repudiated his mistress, Edith Swannehals ('Swan-neck'), who had given him at least four illegitimate children. His new bride and queen was Edith, sister of Edwin and Morcar, earls of Mercia and Northumbria. As far as long-term interests were concerned, it was an even more constructive marriage than that of Cnut to the widow of King Ethelred.

Harold therefore made excellent use of the first four months of his reign to prove himself as an energetic and effective ruler worthy of his people's confidence. The inevitable effect of the Confessor's last years had been a tendency towards laxity and disorder in the shires, and Harold clearly put a stop to that with a heavy hand. But in May his troubles started in earnest. His exiled brother, Earl Tostig, had also not been wasting time. He had raised a fleet in Flanders and he brought it across the Channel in May 1066.

Tostig's first attempts to make an effective come-back were extremely ill-judged. All he succeeded in doing was acting like a traditional viking leader, not an earl of the land with a legitimate grievance, and this added considerably to the strength of Harold's position. Tostig started by landing in the Isle of Wight and exacting tribute from the islanders to pay his crews. He then set off along the south coast with a series of plunder-raids, pausing at Sandwich.

When Tostig arrived, Harold was at London, centrally placed to tackle trouble coming from the north or south. He immediately concentrated the English fleet and a land force, and set off for Sandwich to deal with Tostig. The latter did not wait for Harold's arrival but sailed off up the east coast and started plundering on the coast of Lindsey. This was his second mistake; far from even trying to make his peace with Edwin and Morcar, he only succeeded in pushing the northern earls into a closer alignment with Harold by plundering their territory. The brothers raised a combined army and and drove the raiders off. Tostig sailed north to Scotland and stayed with Malcolm of Scotland for the rest of the summer. He had done much to strengthen Harold's hand: he had put the English on their guard against foreign raiders of any description and had only worsened his own prospects by acting as he did. Certainly, the impression we get is that of an alert country, acting with energy against a foreign threat. It was encouraging start to Harold's reign – just what he needed, in fact, to bring over the last waverers to his side.

While Tostig fled north to Scottish waters, Harold stayed with his fleet at Sandwich. He was under no illusions that the greatest threat would come from Normandy. News had come across the Channel of the forces which Duke William was raising for the invasion, and Harold 'watched all the summer and autumn for his coming. In addition he distributed a land force at suitable points along the sea-coast'. At least, Harold could reflect that William would not be getting any help from Tostig. But the latter was not wasting his time in Scotland. He was putting the finishing touches to the arrangements which would make him a leading ally of Harold's other challenger: Harold Hardrada, king of Norway, who was raising a massive invasion fleet of over 500 ships.

The Norwegian menace of 1066 was the result of the violent reaction to Cnut's attempt to bring all Scandinavia under a single control. As we have seen, that reaction was most strongly marked in Norway, whose king, Magnus, had made persistent claims on the English throne and in the 1040s had been on the verge of invading the island. Harold Hardrada, uncle of Magnus, was a titanic figure. He was revered as the brother of St Olaf of Norway – but he was also the last and in many ways the greatest of the warrior-kings of the viking era. He had been at the battle of Stiklestad in 1030 when Olaf died, and was then only fifteen years old. Escaping to the eastern Baltic, he headed through Novgorod and took the long route down the great rivers of Russia to the Black Sea. There he joined the elite Varangian Guard, the hand-picked corps of English and Scandinavian warriors recruited

H

by the Eastern Empire, and served with distinction in the Mediterranean before returning to Norway as a wealthy hero. He was accepted as king of Norway in 1047 and his rule, though effective, was harsh – hence his nickname of Hardrada, 'Hard-Ruler'. Harold's unsuccessful efforts to conquer Denmark had not diminished his towering stature in the Scandinavian world; and he saw the situation in England in 1066 as a splendid chance to become the greatest Norse conqueror of all time.

Harold, meanwhile, remained at Sandwich, his attention riveted on the threat from Normandy. Duke William's invasion was imminent and time was on his side. Great commander and ruler though he was, Harold was facing the age-old problem of keeping a full-size English army and fleet in being. By the end of the first week in September he had to dismiss the *fyrd* and withdraw the fleet to London. The weather, however, seemed to be on the side of the English: screaming winds from the north, which kept the invasion fleet of William of Normandy penned in its ports across the Channel.

This was the moment Harold Hardrada picked to cross the North Sea with his huge fleet. He made a rendezvous with Tostig's small fleet off the Tyne and coasted down towards the Humber. The Norwegian fleet met little or no opposition and headed up the River Ouse, anchoring at Riccall, a mere ten miles from York itself. The news of the invasion was rushed south to King Harold, but for the moment the northern earls Edwin and Morcar were on their own.

From what happened it is clear that Edwin and Morcar made an excellent team. Despite the speed of the Norwegian descent on their lands, they were able to raise a powerful army and station it at Fulford, two miles south of York. On 20 September, battle was joined. The fight lasted all day, but at the end it was the English who broke and fled: 'More were drowned in the river than slain on the field.' York lay at the mercy of Harold Hardrada and Tostig, and its citizens sought peace. It was agreed that there would be an exchange of 150 hostages, and Harold withdrew his army seven miles east of York to Stamford Bridge on the River Derwent. There he waited for the hostages to arrive before heading south for the decisive trial of strength with Harold.

Harold, however, met him head-on. A scorching march with his *corps d'elite* of housecarls, plus as many of the *fyrd* who had the time to join up, brought Harold as far as Tadcaster by the evening of 24 September. The following day he pushed through York and caught Harold Hardrada's army completely by surprise. By nightfall on 25 September 1066, Harold Godwineson had won a total and crushing victory. Harold Hardrada and Tostig were killed in the fighting. The Norwegian casualties were so high that only twenty-four ships were needed to take the survivors home to Norway.

Harold's victory at Stamford Bridge was due in no little measure to the reputation of his opponent. It was a seed-bed for legend: Harold of Norway should be granted six feet of English soil – or, as he was a tall warrior, seven! Norse sagas exulted in the ferocity of the surprised Norwegians, undaunted although they were fighting without their armour. But it is the English *Chronicle* which pays admiring tribute to a nameless hero of the battle – and he was not an Englishman:

> There was one of the Norwegians there who withstood the English host so that they could not cross the bridge nor win victory. Then an Englishman shot an arrow, but it was no use, and then another came under the bridge and stabbed him under the corselet. Then Harold, king of the English, came over the bridge and his host with him, and there killed large numbers of both Norwegians and Flemings. . . .

Harold's triumph at Stamford Bridge ended a long story. This was the last set-piece battle between an English army and a Scandinavian invading army. It had been a long and hard road since 'three ships of the Northmen' had killed a king's reeve at Dorchester three centuries before. The England which rejoiced in the victory of Stamford Bridge owed what unity it had to the pressure of the long viking wars, and its very ruler was an Anglo-Dane. But there was no time for reflection after the victory. Harold's army, victorious but tired, was granted no respite. On 28 September, three days after Stamford Bridge, William of Normandy landed at Pevensey.

The famous clash between Harold of England and William of Normandy is given additional fascination when we remember that Harold had actually met William, been knighted by him, and had seen the way the duke led his men in battle. He fully appreciated William's iron discipline, his patience, and the will to survive, which had brought him through years of civil war to the undisputed control of Normandy, beating all comers. Much more important was the mobility of William's mounted knights and the method of his tactics. All these reasons were good enough to prompt Harold's decision to return to the south and tackle William as soon as possible. He had, however, two severe problems: Edwin and Morcar could give him no effective aid after the slaughter at Fulford; and there was no time at all to raise the full muster of the southern shires.

The extraordinary campaign of 1066 therefore moved to its climax at Hastings as Harold raced his tired housecarls back to the south. What reinforcements he was able to pick up came from the housecarls of his brothers, Gyrth and Leofwine, and casuals who were able to join up with the army. We are told that Harold left London with only half his army. It was at this point – the arrival on the Thames – that Harold made what proved to be a decisive mistake. He could have afforded two, or better still, three days in which to send out his gallopers and rake in new reinforcements. The rate at which the *fyrd* had been raised in the past shows that it could have been as high as 1,000 men per day. But Harold did not wait. He pressed on to the south. Nor did he surprise William. Norman mounted scouts spotted the tired English force as it paused on the high ground between Battle and Hastings for the night of 13 October.

There has been much pontificating on the theme that the destruction of Harold's army at Hastings was the victory of the mounted knight over the axe-wielding foot-soldier, the opening of a new chapter in the history of warfare. This is simply untrue. The best accounts of the battle are Norman, and they are frank in the repeated failure of the Norman knights to break the English shield-wall. We have the vivid picture of Duke William snatching off his helmet and galloping among his discouraged knights to show that he was still alive. Harold was defeated for three main reasons: William's grip on the battle and his skill in modifying his tactics; the lack of discipline of the *fyrd*; and the relentless erosion of the ranks of housecarls by the Norman arrow-fire.

It has been estimated that at the outset of the battle Harold's army numbered 7,000 at most and William's appreciably less. This balance swung in William's favour thanks to the ruse of the feigned retreat. Small bodies of Norman knights would pretend to panic, then wheel round and cut down the English *fyrd* as it swarmed out into the open in undisciplined pursuit. The housecarls never budged, and William used arrow-fire to whittle down their numbers. The famous tradition that Harold was hit in the eye by an arrow does not come from the Bayeux Tapestry. This shows Gyrth and Leofwine falling comparatively early in the fight, apparently the victims of lance-thrusts. Then comes a period of definite confusion, in which we get a glimpse of Odo, the fighting bishop of Bayeux, swinging his mace, and William raising his helmet, with his standard-bearer pointing to show that the duke is still alive. Finally, when the shields of the last housecarls are indeed bristling with arrows, we find the legend: HAROLD REX INTERFECTUS EST – 'Harold the king was killed' – above a knight cutting down a mailed axeman with his sword. We are told that the last stand of the housecarls was made in the deepening dusk, and that, after Harold died, the exhausted Normans still suffered heavily at the hands of a die-hard party of Englishmen who trapped many over-eager Normans in a hidden ravine.

William's victory at Hastings did *not* win him all England at one stroke. He had eliminated the only field army in England and had wiped out the house of Godwine – but all he had done was to force open the door. The English had by no means given up. In London, the teen-age Edgar the Atheling, last of the male *Cerdicingas*, was proclaimed king in Harold's place.

The Norman march on London reminds us of Cnut's favourite tactic during the wars with Ethelred: a calculated display of 'frightfulness'. It followed a clash at the southern gates of London with the supporters of Edgar. William burned his way west through Surrey, into northern Hampshire and Berkshire, to reach the Thames and cross it at Wallingford. As he closed in on London from the west, the defiance of the atheling's supporters began to crumble. Archbishop Stigand came in to William's camp and swore fealty to him. Twenty-five miles out from London, at Berkhamstead, the English leaders met William and negotiated for peace. He received the oaths of fealty from Edgar, Edwin and Morcar, Archbishop Aldred, and the bishops of Worcester and Hereford. Of most immediate importance was the submission of the Londoners, which permitted William to be crowned king of England in Edward the Confessor's West Minster on Christmas Day 1066.

After a frightened period of acquiescence, there was a violent English reaction. A heavy taxation levied by William was nothing new, but the new mound-and-palisade castles with their strong foreign garrisons were hated emblems of alien rule. Six months after Hastings, William returned to Normandy, leaving England under the government of his seneschel William fitz Osbern and his half-brother Odo of Bayeux. William's hopes that the English leaders would co-operate in the acceptance of the new regime came to nothing. It took time for the English resistance to gather momentum, and William had been very wise in taking Stigand, Edgar, Edwin, Morcar, and Earl Waltheof (youngest son of Siward of Northumbria) with him to Normandy. He came back to England with his hostages at the end of 1067, and the first task awaiting him was the suppression of an outbreak in the west. The men of Devon defied him and held out in Exeter for eighteen days before agreeing to terms. There was further trouble in the west when Harold Godwineson's illegitimate sons launched a raid from Ireland. But William was really faced with a crisis in the summer of 1068, when Edgar, Edwin, and Morcar slipped away from William's court and headed north. There the Northumbrians were preparing for open resistance under the leadership of their new earl, Cospatric. The inevitable storm broke in the following year.

William's reaction to the sullen hostility of the Northumbrians was to send Robert de Comines north to take over the earldom. But a terrible fate awaited him. On 28 January 1069, Robert and his men were trapped in Durham by an insurgent army. Robert himself was burned alive in the bishop's house while his forces were cut to pieces in the streets. The rebels then came to York and forced the men of the city to declare for Edgar. But William's new castle held out, and the king himself came north and relieved it. William fitz Osbern scattered the Northumbrian rebels and a brief peace settled on the north.

This was in turn broken by the decision of the English leaders to call in King Swein of Denmark as their champion against William. Swein, however, did not come himself; he sent a large enough fleet (240 ships), which emulated Tostig's mistake of May 1066. It attacked and was beaten off at Dover, Sandwich, Ipswich, and Norwich, before heading for the Humber. There it joined forces with a new Northumbrian army under Edgar, Cospatric, and Waltheof. Together they fell upon York and smashed the Norman garrisons there.

This time the Northumbrians were not alone. In the west, the men of Devon and Cornwall immolated themselves against the defences of Exeter. Somerset and Dorset broke out, and were smashed in turn. In Mercia there was a general revolt headed by a resistance leader from Herefordshire, a thane known as 'Edric the Wild'. He set Mercia ablaze, but was also pinned down by the baneful power of William's castles. William was forced to take the field in person, and he started with the Mercian rebels, smashing their host in pitched battle at Stafford. Then he turned north against York – and the last agony of Saxon England began.

William's army was not merely composed of Norman knights; it included a formidable percentage of mercenaries, both French and English. He started by sealing off York with a wide belt of 'scorched earth'. Next, he began negotiations with the Danish fleet and bought it off, leaving the English rebels on their own. The defection of the Danes was fatal to the rebels and William had no trouble in recovering York, where he spent the Christmas of 1069 amid widening desolation. He had decided not merely to punish the north, but to ruin it so thoroughly that never again would it be profitable for anyone to bring an army there. It was the most hideous winter the north was to know for centuries. By the spring of 1070 all Yorkshire was a blackened, deserted waste.

William's problems were not yet over. In May 1070 King Swein of Denmark crossed the North Sea and took command of the Danish fleet in the Humber. He headed down the east coast to the Wash in order to make contact with the last pocket of English resistance: the rebels of the Danelaw under Hereward of Bourne, a Lincolnshire thane, who had based themselves on the fen country surrounding Peterborough and the Isle of Ely.

Hereward the Wake has become one of England's folk heroes. He was blamed for the sack of the richest monastery in England – Peterborough, the 'Golden City', which was looted bare by an Anglo-Danish force. This was clearly to give the Danes their payment for supporting the rebels of Ely, but the immediate aftermath was the return of Swein to Denmark. Hereward and his die-hards held out in Ely. They were joined in 1071 by Earl Morcar. By this time Edwin was dead, killed by his own men.

William himself marched his army to Ely and took it, capturing Morcar and Bishop Æthelwine; but Hereward and a handful of his men slipped through the Norman lines and escaped. It was said that they took to the forests and led the life of outlaws, giving the later legends of Robin Hood their first tenuous form.

But with the capture of Ely in 1071, the last serious resistance of the English had been broken. It had failed because it had no unity. Once Harold Godwineson had died, they fell apart. The tragedy of all the rebellions between Hastings and the surrender of Ely was the waste of all that spirit and defiance on piecemeal and futile struggles against the greatest military strategist of the age.

# Chapter 14

Alas, how miserable and pitiable a time it was then. Then the wretched people lay driven very nearly to death, and afterwards there came the sharp famine and destroyed them utterly. Who cannot pity such a time? Or who is so hard-hearted that he cannot weep for such misfortune?

*Anglo-Saxon Chronicle*: 1087.

# Sad heritage

It is easy to sympathize with the great English rebellion of 1069–1070, but to do so obscures the fact that William had, after Hastings, made a genuine attempt to rule through the existing framework, maintaining in power as many of the magnates of Edward and Harold who were prepared to accept him as king. William always maintained that he was Edward the Confessor's legal heir, claiming no powers that Edward had not had at his disposal. He had never intended to wipe out the old ruling class of Saxon England and graft on a new one composed entirely of Normans. But the fact remained that the severe fighting of Fulford, Stamford Bridge, Hastings, and the Great Rebellion had largely accomplished this. After William had smashed his enemies, he resolved that England would never be given the chance of a second try. But he did not bring this about by wiping out every man and institution he considered dangerous.

Edgar the Atheling, for example, might be considered to have been an obvious candidate for execution or life imprisonment, but William allowed him to live. After William dislodged him from his initial exile at the Scottish court, Edgar went to Flanders but later returned to Scotland. William was caused not a little alarm in 1074 when Edgar accepted an offer from the king of France, Philip, to take over lands on the Norman border on condition that the French might use them as a base for raids on eastern Normandy. Edgar set out from Scotland but was ignominiously shipwrecked on the way, and William was relieved to have the chance of talking the atheling out of the idea.

Edgar stayed on at the Conqueror's court but left William in 1086 'because he did not have much honour from him'. The atheling appeared again in the reign of the Conqueror's successor, William Rufus. In 1097 Edgar actually led an army into Scotland on the orders of Rufus to instal his own nephew on the Scottish throne. Nine years later, when Rufus was dead and the Conqueror's other sons, Robert and Henry, were fighting for the control of both Normandy and England, Edgar picked the wrong side and was captured at the battle of Tinchebrai in Normandy; but Henry spared his life and let him go. Edgar finally ended his days in Scotland with his kinsfolk. Last of the *Cerdicingas*, he owed his life in 1106 to the fact that his sister Edith had married King Henry. He died in 1125, fifty-nine years after Hastings.

Earl Morcar, who gave up the struggle and surrendered to William after the siege of Ely, was also allowed to live – but in prison. He was briefly freed on the Conqueror's death in 1087 but William Rufus was prepared to take no chances. He arrested Morcar again and put him back behind bars, this time for ever. Cospatric, however, who had also fought with the rebels, was restored to his earldom in 1070; but three years later he defected and became the man of Malcolm of Scotland.

Stigand, archbishop of Canterbury, the veteran colleague of Earl Godwine and King Harold, was deposed from the primacy in 1070 – but not by William. A papal commission from Rome did the job at a special session at Winchester. Even when deposed, Stigand did not entirely vanish from the scene. He lived on at his huge manor at East Meon, near Winchester. He died about 1072.

Earl Waltheof was another English lord who had no cause to complain. But he undid himself by his own stupidity, joining a foolish plot against William in 1075, while the king was in Normandy. Waltheof was tempted into the plot by two discontented *Frenchmen*: Ralph, earl of Norfolk, and Roger, earl of Hereford. They were frustrated by William's garrisons and popular opposition: '. . . the castle garrisons which were in England and also the local people came against them and prevented them all from doing anything. . . .' The plot fizzled out. Waltheof threw himself on William's mercy by going to Normandy and giving himself up. 'But the king made light of it until he came to England and then had him captured.' William had an excellent reason for making sure of Waltheof, for the plotters had invited a Danish fleet to come to their aid. The Danes turned up too late to be of any use, but did a lot of damage in a raid on York. In the following year Waltheof was beheaded on William's orders.

In the same year as Waltheof's arrest, 1075, another great name from the past died: Edith, widow of Edward the Confessor. This gave William a splendid chance to pay homage to the memory of the old regime. Queen Edith was given a ceremonial funeral at Westminster and buried beside her husband. But it was typical of William that he used the occasion to make an example of all the disaffected Bretons whom he suspected of being involved with the plot. The *Chronicle* inserts a grim little poem to mark the event:

> Some of them were blinded
> And some banished from the land
> And some were put to shame.
> Thus were the traitors to the king
> Brought low.

The examples mentioned above help us to understand William's position by the year 1075, nine years after Hastings. He was generous with offers of patronage to leaders of the old order in England whom he believed might prove useful in his service. But if any man in whom he had reposed trust let him down he was merciless in revenge. Another significant point, underlined by the fate of Waltheof and his fellow-conspirators, was that by 1075 men were no longer prepared to turn out *en masse* to fight against their alien rulers. King William's genius for applied terror had taught them that it did not pay.

When Cnut conquered England, his innovations were few and can be boiled down to the establishment of the great earldoms and the extortion of an annual war-tax even in time of peace. The structure of English society was basically untouched. But by the end of the reign of William the Conqueror, English society had been totally changed. The English had been shut out from any position of political influence. From top to bottom of the social pyramid, foreigners ruled with an iron hand.

The first and most obvious change in the land was William's abolition of the old provincial layout of Saxon England by his splintering of the great earldoms. No longer would it be possible for a family like the house of Godwine to hold over half of England. William's earls were certainly great landowners, but their holdings were split up and parcelled out and separated from each other by the holdings of others. Wessex, Mercia, Northumbria, and the Danelaw vanished as political entities.

With the old English earldoms and ealdormanries, the great

English landowners quitted the scene. The basic reason for this was a simple one. William insisted that the prime duty of any man holding land from the king was to produce on demand a set quota of knights for the king's service. The emphasis was on *mounted knights*, not mere manpower, and mounted knights were totally alien to the English way of making war.

This might not have been the case had Harold Godwineson been permitted to live out his span as king – he was a great commander and while visiting William had seen what Norman knights could do. There were indeed some misty parallels between a Norman land-holding knight and a Saxon thegn, but very few. Basically, the only man who really knew about fitting out knights was a knight himself, trained from boyhood in the new warfare. No wonder the old English landowning families went to the wall. Knight service was applied to all landowners, moreover, and that included the Church. We can only wonder what on earth the abbot of Evesham did when he received this summons from William in 1072:

> William, king of the English, to Æthelwig, abbot of Evesham, greeting. I order you to summon all those who are subject to your administration and jurisdiction that they bring before me at Clarendon on the Octave of Pentecost all the knights they owe me duly equipped. You, also, on that day, shall come to me, and bring with you fully equipped those 5 knights which you owe me in respect of your abbacy.

– and this was as early as 1072, only six years after Hastings.

This was a total revolution. Think of a prosperous nation which has been beaten to its knees by an invader with totally different weapons. The victorious invader insists that anyone holding land under the new regime must produce a quota of those weapons. Of course, the first hand-outs of land go to those who can do it. Nobody completely unable to comply stays for long. And so the conquered country ends up with a new ruling class – and that is what happened after William became king of England. And the natural sequence was a spate of 'sub-letting' of land, with the top lords allowing smaller fry to purchase fees of land from them and grant tenure in their turn. The whole lengthening chain led to the king. There were no free landowners; everyone held from somebody else above him, and so on up to the king. In short, after

1066 you could not choose your lord and swap allegiances, retaining your landed possessions as you made the change.

Matters were far worse at the other end of the chain, with the men who lived and worked on the land. As we have seen (p. 60) the peasant was technically free before the Conquest. This was changed. There was a new and ruthless attitude. The knight who ended up in his possession had to pay his way to his social superior and he was encouraged to regard his peasantry as inanimate objects, to be reckoned up as assets of the property along with barns, acres of good ploughland, and livestock. William did not institute this new slavery himself, at a single stroke; it grew with the firm establishment of his new order in land ownership. By the end of the twelfth century it was virtually complete. The old villein, whose status had been recognized (and, it must be pointed out, whose duties were defined) in the Confessor's time was now a chattel, a serf. He could not appeal to the courts in matters which affected his social obligations to his lord. He and his family could be bought and sold. Slavery had always been known from the earliest days of the Saxon kingdoms, but not like this. When those who had been slaves in the Confessor's time died out, there was no need to replace them.

It was an increase of hardness on a par with William's formal abolition of the death penalty: 'I also forbid that anyone shall be slain or hanged for any fault, but let his eyes be put out and let him be castrated.' William's regime built a frightening new world in England.

Town life received a tremendous shot in the arm from the Norman Conquest, and so did trade. Naturally, Norman traders and craftsmen were offered favourable terms to set up in business and the new lords often tended to apply customs from back home. William, however, was careful to distinguish between Frenchmen settled in England in Edward's time and Frenchmen who settled after 1066. To start with, there was a tremendous increase in the power of the lord of the borough. He could gain complete control of smaller markets and demanded a much greater borough 'farm' – the sum paid to him for his financial rights. This was a period of *definition* for English society. It was essential for the new rulers of the land; for the English population it was a crushing imposition.

Both Englishmen and Normans, however, were outraged and

frightened by William's most audacious achievement: the great Domesday Survey, so called because judgments made on its information were as unalterable as Doomsday itself, which reckoned the wealth of England down to the last pig. Never before had the sources of wealth been subjected to such a pitiless scrutiny. The objective was basically to provide the king with every penny to which he was legally entitled, but it gave him a vast dossier on all his subjects as well.

The *Chronicle* records the Survey, which began in 1086, with indignation:

> . . . the king had much thought and very deep discussion with his council about this country – how it was occupied or with what sort of people. Then he sent his men over all England into every shire and had them find out how many hundred hides there were in the shire, or what land and cattle the king himself had in the country, or what dues he ought to have in twelve months from the shire. Also he had a record made of how much land his archbishops had, and his bishops and his abbots and his earls – and though I relate it at too great length – what or how much everybody had who was occupying land in England, in land or cattle, and how much money it was worth. So very narrowly did he have it investigated, that there was no single hide nor virgate of land, nor indeed (it is a shame to relate but it seemed no shame to him to do) one ox nor one cow nor one pig which was there left out, and not put down in his record; and all these records were brought to him afterwards.

Bishop Robert of Hereford wrote an account of his own, and this adds the really sinister note of the Survey:

> A second group of commissioners followed those first sent, and these were strangers to the neighbourhood, in order that they should find fault with their report and charge them before the king. And the land was troubled by many calamities arising from the collection of money for the king.

So exhaustive was the Domesday Survey that William did not live to see its completion (he died in Normandy on 2 November 1087). The basic theme was 'who held what in the time of King Edward, and who holds it now'. This makes the Survey of paramount importance as a 'Who's Who' of the eleventh century. Here is an example – a report of the lands of the king in

Normancross hundred in Huntingdonshire, typically packed with exhaustive detail on the land and its value in cash:

> A manor. In Bottlebridge King Edward had 5 hides assessed to the geld. There is land for 8 ploughs. The king has 1 plough now on the demesne; and 15 villeins have 5 ploughs. There is a priest and a church; 60 acres of meadow and 12 acres of woodland for pannage in Northamptonshire. In the time of King Edward it was worth 100 shillings; now 8 pounds. Rannulf keeps it.
>
> In this manor belonging to the king, and in other manors, the enclosure of the abbot of Thorney is doing harm to 300 acres of meadow.
>
> In Stilton the king's sokemen of Normancross have 3 virgates of land assessed to the geld. There is land for 2 ploughs, and there are 5 ploughing oxen.
>
> In Orton the king has soke over $3\frac{1}{2}$ hides of land in the land of the abbot of Peterborough which was Godwine's.*

Clattering like a computer print-out, Domesday Book was an amazing feat when it was completed. Ninety years later, it was regarded by the officials of the royal exchequer as an indispensable document, although its money-raising purpose was glossed over. When William died, however, the fact that the Survey had been made at all was the most emphatic proof that the old freedom was gone for ever. The English and the new Norman ruling class hated it with an equal intensity.

Additional hardship was forced on the people by William's insistence on his rights to what was his by the new forest laws. There had always been royal hunting preserves in England, and before the Conquest Edward the Confessor himself had been a classic royal huntsman. But William's enlargement of the royal forest and the creation of new preserves – particularly the New Forest – bore down heavily on the local peasantry, especially when times were naturally hard. The *Chronicle*'s famous poem condemns the Conqueror for this, as for the avarice behind the making of Domesday Book:

> Into avarice did he fall
> And loved greediness above all.

---

* *Pannage* was grazing for pigs, *sokemen* were men under a lord's jurisdiction, and a *virgate* was equal to a quarter of a hide.

He made great protection for the game
And imposed laws for the same,
That who so slew hart or hind
Should be made blind.

He preserved the harts and boars
And loved the stags as much
As if he were their father.
Moreover, for the hare did he decree that they should
    go free.
Powerful men complained of it and poor men lamented it,
But so fierce was he that he cared not for the rancour of
    them all,
But they had to follow out the king's will entirely
If they wished to live or hold their land,
Property or estate, or his favour great.

Another major institution of Saxon England to suffer profound change by the Norman Conquest was the Church. While preparing for the invasion of England, William had presented his case to the pope as a minor crusade, an important by-product of which would be the long-overdue reform of the corrupt English Church. It was easy to cry up Stigand, archbishop of Canterbury, as an example of deep-rooted degeneracy. On the Continent, an energetic movement towards general Church reform was already afoot – but there is no reason to suppose that the English Church would have rejected it. In its long history it had always been profoundly receptive to events and trends across the Channel. Certainly there were abuses that needed reforming. Stigand had to go; the bishop's court had to be separated from that of the hundred-court; and the individual bishops had to be brought under the tighter control of the primate of England. Also important was the fact that strict clerical celibacy had lapsed in England and needed restoring. Through the exceptional man whom he picked as the new archbishop of Canterbury, Lanfranc, William's reforms of the status of the Church in English society and government were profound. But William's passion for defining rights and powers created a situation which grew steadily worse after his death, and resulted in the head-on clashes between king and archbishop in the reigns of William II (Archbishop Anselm) and Henry II (Archbishop

Becket). And in the field of Church appointment it was the same story. No Englishmen were appointed bishops under William.

What, then, remained, if anything, of the old order? The most obvious survivor was the English language, which Alfred had once hoped to use as the key to the fuller education of his people. By 1066 it was not the English that Alfred knew: in the Danelaw shires it had taken on a Scandinavian tinge. After the Conquest of 1066, the English language was regarded contemptuously as the tongue of the conquered, uncultured churl. It naturally survived to absorb French influence as it had already absorbed Latin and Danish, to receive its official resurrection in Chaucer's time.

Although the new order of William the Conqueror rejected the language of the conquered English, the new rulers of the shires did not reject their regional organization. The shire survived, and the hundred, and the wapentake – it was more convenient to use them than to do away with them.

What of the law? As we have seen, William's technique was the literal interpretation and enforcement of largely redundant provisions which had been made before his time. William himself does not seem to have issued a code of his own but we do have a compilation known as the *Laws of William the Conqueror* dating from the twelfth century. This contains some of the innovations mentioned above, such as the replacement of the death penalty by blinding and castration, and the differentiation between Frenchmen who had come to England before the Conquest and those who had come after:

I will, moreover, that all the men whom I have brought with me, or who have come after me, shall be protected by my peace and shall dwell in quiet. And if any one of them shall be slain, let the lord of his murderer seize him within five days, if he can; but if he cannot, let him begin to pay me 46 marks of silver so long as substance avails. And when his substance is exhausted, let the whole hundred in which the murder took place pay what remains in common.

Another privilege the Frenchmen had was the choice of the newfangled, Continental ordeal by battle instead of the hot iron, if they wished. To prevent the dice being loaded too heavily in favour of the Frenchman, the Englishman could appoint a proxy to fight for him if he wished. 'If an Englishman shall charge a

Frenchman and be unwilling to prove his accusation either by ordeal or by wager of battle, I will, nevertheless, that the Frenchman shall acquit himself by a valid oath.'

The state of the freeman was made conditional by William. A freeman had to swear a public oath of allegiance to the king, and he had to have official sureties who 'shall hold him and hand him over to justice if he shall offend in any way'. In other words, you could be a freeman, but you were bound to arrange for compulsory bail for yourself in *anticipation* of any crime you felt like committing.

Above all, the language, the memory of great days, the bitter awareness of the harshness of the new order, were all preserved in that great work without which the history of Saxon England could never be studied at all – the *Anglo-Saxon Chronicle*. It was continued at Peterborough Abbey, once revered as the 'Golden City' before Hereward and his Danish allies looted it bare. With an acute sense of misery and loss, the *Chronicle* continued the story of the England which William the Conqueror left behind him – through the days of the civil wars between the Conqueror's sons, and the appalling wars of the 'Anarchy' between his son-in-law Stephen and his granddaughter Matilda, years when men said openly that Christ and his saints slept.

But the *Chronicle* ends on a note of hope: in 1154, when Henry, count of Anjou, succeeded to the kingdom of England. The unknown chronicler notes a phenomenon which had not been seen for decades: 'When the king was dead, the count was overseas, and nobody dared do anything but good to another because they were in such great awe of him.' On this note of praise for the coming of Henry Plantagenet to rule the land of the English, the chronicler turns to the election of the new abbot of Peterborough in the same year:

> . . . and he went shortly to Lincoln and was there consecrated abbot before he came home, and was then received with great ceremony at Peterborough with a great procession. And so he was also at Ramsey and Thorney and Crowland and Spalding and St Albans and . . . now is abbot, and has made a fine beginning. Christ grant him to end thus.

And that is all – the optimistic, mutilated tailpiece to the chronicle of the Anglo-Saxons, the story of their rise to power and their humiliating fall.

# Bibliography

An essential one-volume handbook to Saxon England and the Norman Conquest is provided by Sir Frank Stenton's *Anglo-Saxon England* (Oxford University Press). Next come the first two volumes in the superb Eyre & Spottiswoode *English Historical Documents*. The first, edited by Dorothy Whitelock, covers the period *c.* 500–1042; the second, edited by David C. Douglas, takes up the story with the accession of Edward the Confessor and carries it right through the Norman/Angevin period to the death of Henry II in 1189. Despite their somewhat off-putting title, they make for fascinating and entertaining reading. To these should be added Dorothy Whitelock's *The Beginnings of English Society* (Penguin).

Contemporary histories are included in both volumes of the *Documents* but *Bede* has appeared in Penguin Classics. Another version is the Loeb edition, translated in beautiful Elizabethan English with the Latin text alongside.

On the Vikings and their world two books stand out: *The Viking Achievement* by P. G. Foote and D. M. Wilson (Sidgwick & Jackson); and *The Viking*, edited by Professor Bertil Almgren (C. A. Watts).

For the eleventh-century period Professor Frank Barlow's *Edward the Confessor* (Eyre & Spottiswoode) is particularly valuable; and Henry Loyn's *The Norman Conquest* (Hutchinson University Library) is a masterpiece of economical coverage.

For the eleventh-century period Professor Frank Barlow's novels: Anya Seaton's *Avalon* (Hodder Paperbacks) and Alfred Duggan's *The Cunning of the Dove* (New English Library). Both are based on detailed research and put some intriguing flesh on the bones.

The Saxon kingdoms and the first viking raids

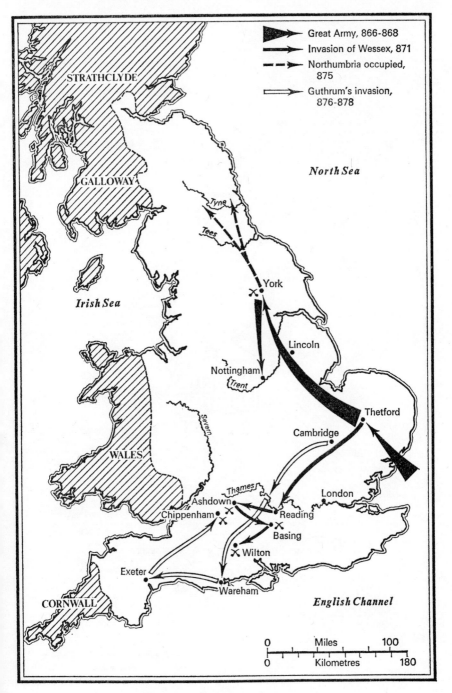

| | |
|---|---|
| Great Army, 866-868 | |
| Invasion of Wessex, 871 | |
| Northumbria occupied, 875 | |
| Guthrum's invasion, 876-878 | |

STRATHCLYDE

GALLOWAY

*North Sea*

*Irish Sea*

*Tyne*

*Tees*

✕ York

Lincoln

Nottingham

*Trent*

Thetford

Cambridge

*Severn*

WALES

*Thames*

Ashdown
Chippenham ✕✕
✕

London

Reading

✕ Basing

Wilton ✕

Exeter

Wareham

CORNWALL

*English Channel*

| 0 | Miles | 100 |
|---|---|---|
| 0 | Kilometres | 180 |

Line of march of the Great Army

Alfred's frontier and the reconquest of the Danelaw

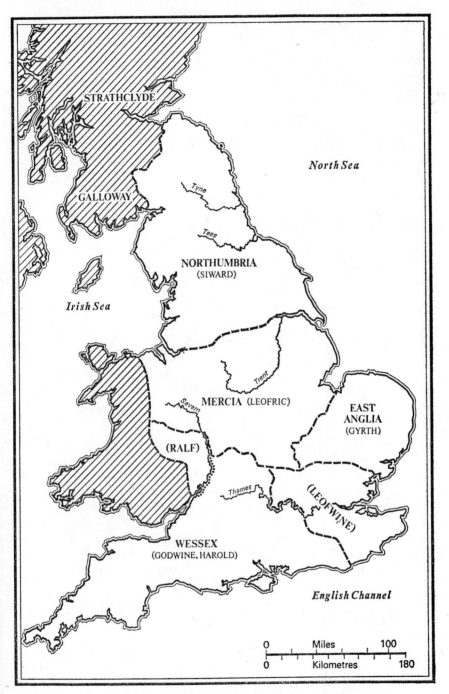

The great earldoms under Edward the Confessor

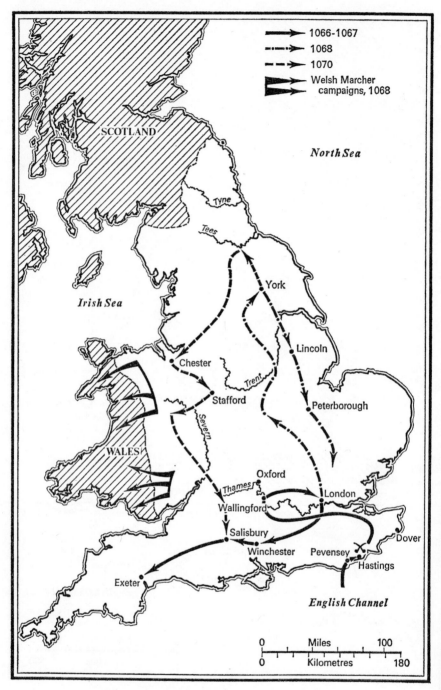

**Legend:**
- → 1066-1067
- ⟶ 1068
- ⇢ 1070
- ► Welsh Marcher campaigns, 1068

SCOTLAND

*North Sea*

*Irish Sea*

Tyne

Tees

York

Lincoln

Chester

Stafford

Trent

Peterborough

Severn

WALES

Oxford

*Thames*

London

Wallingford

Salisbury

Winchester

Pevensey

Dover

Hastings

Exeter

*English Channel*

| 0 | Miles | 100 |
| 0 | Kilometres | 180 |

William of Normandy's main campaigns

# Index